INDIA
PAST AND PRESENT

INDIA
PAST AND PRESENT

BY

C. H. FORBES-LINDSAY

ILLUSTRATED

IN TWO VOLUMES

VOL. II

GYAN

Published by

Gyan Publishing House
5, Ansari Road
Daryaganj, New Delhi-110002
Phone: 011-47034999, 9811692060
E-mail: books@gyanbooks.com

Distribution Network
gyanbooks.com
India, USA, Canada, UK, Australia, France

ISBN : 978-81-212-3593-8 (Set)
ISBN : 978-81-212-4882-2 (PB)
First Published, 1903

2nd Impression 2020

Printed at: Gyan Press, Delhi.

India Past and Present Vol. II
Author: C. H. Forbes-Lindsay

INDIA

PAST AND PRESENT

BY

C. H. FORBES-LINDSAY

ILLUSTRATED

IN TWO VOLUMES

VOL. II

PHILADELPHIA
THE JOHN C. WINSTON CO.
1903

CONTENTS.

Vol. II.

LIST OF ILLUSTRATIONS.

Vol. II.

INDIA.

CHAPTER I.

ATTOCK, PESHÁWAR, KHYBER PASS.

WHEN Alexander, crossing the Indus by way of Attock, came into what is now the district of Ráwal Pindi, he found Taxila, or Takshá-sila, as the natives called it, "a rich and populous city, the largest between the Indus and the Hydaspes." Its site is marked by the extensive ruins which lie to the north of the Margala Pass.

Impressed by the fate of the border tribes that opposed the Macedonian's advance, or actuated, perhaps, by the knowledge that, after the passage of his kingdom, Alexander would enter the territory of his enemy Porus, King Taxilus offered no impediment to the onward march of the Greeks, and so, in all probability, saved himself from the fate of Astes of Peukelos. At any rate, the Taxilæ seem to have passed scathless through the period of storm and stress which marks the great Alexander's expedition to India.

After many centuries of obscurity, the country reappears in history as the territory of a savage, but powerful, non-Aryan race named the Gakkurs, who were addicted to polyandry, infanticide and many other gross and superstitious practices.

When Mahmúd of Ghazní so nearly met defeat on the plains of Chach, the force opposed to him under Prithvi Rájá found its main element of strength in a body of thirty thousand Gakkurs. Shaháb-ud-dín of Ghor, during an incursion to India, slew pitilessly as he swept over this district, "so that there remained not an inhabitant to light a fire." But the Gakkurs were quickly avenged. On the way back to his western capital, Shaháb-ud-dín encamped on the borders of the country he had recently devastated. During the night a band of twenty Gakkurs swam the Indus, and, stealthily threading their way through the camp, rushed the tent of the Sultán, and stabbed him to death with forty wounds.

Bábar devotes considerable space in his autobiography to an account of his campaign against the same people. Pharwála, their capital, which occupied a strong position in the hills, withstood his guns and defied assault until the garrison was starved out. When at length the country was subdued, the Gakkurs became firm allies of the Mughal power, and in its later conflicts with the Afgháns proved to be very valuable confederates.

On the decline of the Delhi Empire, the Sikhs

attacked the Ráwal Pindi District and annexed it without much difficulty to the kingdom of Lahore, and when the Sikh dominions passed to the British in 1849, Ráwal Pindi went with them. The next year the site of the present cantonment was selected, and the first barracks built in what is now the largest military station in India.

Being the principal health resort of the Punjab, and the starting point for the journey into Kashmir, Ráwal Pindi has a large floating population in the summer months, and is, next to Simla, probably the gayest station in the hills.

The town has a modern and martial appearance. The trim cottages, with lawns and gardens, not unlike what may be seen in England, are scattered along a ridge about eight thousand feet above the level of the sea. Soldiers in khaki—foot, horse and gunners—are to be seen everywhere. Their "huts," as the summer quarters are termed, stretch along the spur running to the north. The station is encircled by a ring of small forts, and in case of need would be a safe depôt for non-combatants, and an easy place to defend.

In the deep shelter of the valleys nestle prosperous villages, surrounded by fields of grain, and back of all rise the snow-clad peaks of Kashmir.

A little farther, the railroad, on its way to the frontier, passes Margala, where, upon an elevated spot, is the splendid monument "erected by friends, British and native, to the memory of Brig. Gen. John Nicholson, C. B., who, after taking a hero's part in four great wars, fell mortally wounded, in leading to victory the main column of assault at the great siege of Delhi, and died 22nd September, 1857, aged 34." There are natives who believe—and who shall contradict them?—that "Ján Nikulsyne's" spirit haunts the border. He is worshiped in these hills, and now and again some tottering, blear-eyed ancient, who fought with him upon the frontier, makes a pilgrimage to this monument, with as much reverence as he might to the shrine of a saint.

Take an ordnance map of the Ráwal Pindi District, and at its western extremity, lying along the bank of the Indus, you will see a mass of caterpillar-like contour lines. These are the Attock Hills, within whose shadow debouched every army that has entered India through the defiles of the historic Khyber Pass.

Ever since the dawn of history this duct has poured a perpetual stream of predatory humanity upon the enticing plains of India. The stream has ebbed and flowed, sometimes swelling to a torrent, at others sinking to a trickle, but never ceasing. Every invader from the north has come this way, almost always to be challenged at the Indus, so that the Attock Hills have looked on many a fierce struggle since the long procession commenced, three thousand years before the birth of Christ, when the Aryan nomads, wandering from their Central Asian home, leisurely drove their flocks across the ford.

In the dim and distant past, Semiramis attempts the passage in the face of Stabrobate's millions, and, though defeated, finds an exalted place in the Hindu Pantheon. Nonnus, the Egyptian, carries the hero of the Dionysiacs through the Hindu Kúsh and to the plains beyond. Some time came Oghuz Khán, opening the way to future Scythic hordes, who domiciled their snake-gods in the Deccan.

Following a train of shadowy predecessors, the great Macedonian looms up unquestionable flesh and blood. Kásim, the redoubtable, who lost his life for a woman's lie, completes the tail of Arab chiefs who came through the Khyber Pass to prey upon the Punjab.

Subuktigín, the Túrkí, is followed by his dread son Mahmud. Timúrlung leads his Mughal swarms past Attock to the heart of Hindustán, and returns with plunder "infinite" in its variety, and of value "great beyond imagination."

And so with march and counter-march, Pathán follows Persian, and Turk gives way to Mongol.

That the present rulers of India do not believe the stream of invasion to have run dry may be inferred from the indications of armed preparedness and the evidences of eternal vigilance which one perceives on every side from Ráwal Pindi to Peshâwar. At the "Gateway of India" all men talk with conviction of *the* future invasion. They will not pretend to predict the time, but each is convinced that some day the Muscovite will come tramping over the road his ancestors trod ages ago, with Changiz Khán at their head. They say that with the border people ever ripe for mischief, and the insidious nose of the Russian Bear perpetually protruding from the none-too-distant plateau of the Pamír, it behooves them to keep a sleepless watch upon this frontier, and they may be right.

The railroad skirts the hills upon the south before it crosses the river by a composite road-and-rail girder bridge, at each end of which is a fortified gateway.

Just below the point where the Kábul River adds its volume to the Indus, stands the Fort upon a commanding height, overhanging the river with jealous care. It stands where Akbar placed it, upon the crown of an isolated rock, rising eight hundred feet from its base. The buildings of the town used to rest within the shelter of the Fort walls, but now they lie upon a lower site, beneath its protecting guns. Akbar established a ferry, which still performs its old-time services, between the village of Múlah Tolah and Kharábád.

This is the Atak Benares of the Muhammadans—the extremity of the empire—just as Katak Benares, in Orissa, is the other extremity.

After leaving Attock, the railroad runs along the

bank of the Kábul River, and passing through a line of camps—Nawshera, with its old Sikh fort, and Mardan, the depôt of the famous "Guides"—finds its terminus at Pesháwar, for the present.

The Valley of Pesháwar is an irregular amphitheatre, resting upon the Indus, and enclosed on every other side by hills. This side was once shut in, too, and then the entire basin-like valley was a great lake, with an outlet here which has gradually worn down the hills that shut it off from the river. Now the hollow is filled up with alluvial deposits of silt and gravel, over which are scattered water-worn boulders. The Kábul, which in ancient days plenished the deep mountain lake, now flows through level marshland to its débouchure, near Fort Attock. The scenery of the western portion of the valley is beautifully wild; it abounds in craggy passes, crowned by ancient towers, and commanding prospects over fields of luxuriant vegetation, intersected by numerous canals, with a background of snowy peaks rising beyond the border.

In the earliest days of Indian history, when the Aryan settlers were divided into the two great Solar and Lunar families, the valley was occupied by the Children of the Moon. According to Arrian, its capital, Peukelos, was a large and populous city when Alexander's general, Hephaiston, took it. Its remains are to be found in the vast ruins of ancient edifices lying upon the left bank of the Swát.

Toward the close of the seventh century the Patháns made their appearance upon the scene, and from that time the Pesháwar Valley was a bone of contention between the ruling powers of Hindustán and Afghánistán. Being at the very entrance to India, each newcomer has naturally taken possession of it; so that for centuries it was constantly changing hands, and a list of the successive occupants of Pesháwar would be but a list of the invaders of India. For ages the husbandmen of the valley plowed their fields with matchlocks slung over their shoulders, and even in recent times it has been necessary for them to go armed against the depredations of the Pathán hill tribes, which lie on every side.

The city is encircled by an old mud wall, and, as might be expected, is completely surrounded by burying grounds. The streets are narrow and crooked, without order or design. Excepting the street in which the Kábul and Bokhára wares are displayed, they are little better than tortuous alleys, with mean houses built of sun-dried brick or mud, with wooden framework and wooden galleries and verandas.

But what the city lacks in attractiveness is more than compensated for by the picturesque appearance of its mixed population. One might almost imagine it to be still, what once it was, an Afghán city, so greatly does the Central Asian type of mankind predominate. At every turn the superb figure of the

Afghán holds the eye, his six feet and more of stature topped by a towering turban wrapped over a sheep-skin cap. Fierce of aspect, with piercing black eyes, and bearded face of Semitic cast, he is the essence of dignified gravity. Slow of speech and deliberate in action, he conveys the impression of latent energy as he paces leisurely by in his long caftan, quietly but forcefully making a way through the crowd. The absence of the familiar sheaf of knives gives an air of incompleteness to his ensemble, but a cautious government decrees that he shall give up his arms at the border, and resume them only when he re-enters the pass homeward bound. He may have a string of horses, which he will take hundreds of miles into the interior, returning in a year, or perhaps two. On the other hand, he may be simply bent on sombre pleasure, or he may be the C15 or R24, of the Secret Service Reports.

The bazaars are ever alive with trafficking humanity. There is an incessant flow of incoming and outgoing wares, and constant lines of laden camels passing through the streets and across the outlying plain. The principal trade is with Kábul and Bokhára, whence come richly-clad traveling merchants, with their caravans containing silk—raw and manufactured; gold bullion and gold thread; wool and woolen goods; dyes and drugs. Persia sends fruits and furs, pottery and metals, and from Samarkhand come bales of silk innumerable.

In the winter the great square of the serai is packed to suffocation. Traders from every part of Central Asia and Northern India, with their followers, are jostling their ways through the mass of merchandise and fodder scattered about. Camels, horses, ponies help to increase the confusion and add to the deafening noise of shouting, screaming men and boys. The cell-like apartments opening off the gallery surrounding the square are full to overflowing. An incessant stream of men and beasts flows through the great gateway, and even nightfall fails to bring peace and quiet to the place.

It was from here that "the man who would be king," and his faithful lieutenant, "Peachey," started upon their memorable journey into Kafirístán in the guise of crazy priests. The character is not an uncommon one in Pesháwar. The city is a favorite resort of the pestiferous fanatics, who are incessantly stirring up mischief, and often committing crime. The jail is never without five or six of them among its inmates; but, since imprisonment is a luxury to such vagabonds, and stripes affect them not, it is difficult to meet the case with good results.

In the days before the railroad, the caravans would continue on through the plains, penetrating to the other end of the country, but now the povindah ships his bundles in freight cars, and takes rail to Delhi, Agra, or Calcutta.

Pesháwar has a long-established reputation for the

manufacture of a particular kind of many-colored gaudy scarf, and there was a time when it met a large demand for cutlery of the lethal varieties.

Tuesdays and Fridays are busy days in city and cantonment, for then the pass is open for caravans. On those days, and those alone, the British authorities guarantee the safety of the caravans as far as the Afghán frontier. The Khyber Rifles furnish escorts, and line the hills on either side, sentries being posted at every hundred yards.

The Khyber Mountains form the terminal spur of the Safed Koh, as that great range gradually declines to the level of the valley of the Kábul River. The Khyber Pass is the great northern trade and military route between Afghánistán and Hindustán. The famous Bolan Pass, reaching an elevation of nearly six thousand feet, is the great southern route between the same countries. Three or four other passes, less known and more difficult, lie between these two.

The Khyber Pass officially commences at Jamrúd, to the west of Peshâwar, and twists through fort-crowned hills in an ever-varying northwesterly course for thirty-three miles, until it comes upon the plains of Jalálábád at Dákha.

This strip of no-man's-land between the territory of the Afghán and the British, whose elusive frontiers are ever shifting, never definable, is occupied by hill tribes, who have never owned submission to either power, and probably never will. They have always been on the alert to advantage by the quarrels of their more powerful neighbors, and have harried every army that ever went through the pass, slaughtering the stragglers and plundering the baggage. They have always levied heavy toll upon caravans, only restrained from seizing everything that came their way by fear of cutting off the profitable traffic entirely.

The Afridís, the nearest of these lawless mountaineers to the British, are the most turbulent and irrepressible of them all. Their enterprise extended from the pass to the valley, where they were accustomed to swoop down upon the villages, and carry off whatever was worth the taking, often adding, in sheer wantonness, death and destruction to pillage. When the British came to Peshâwar these Patháu pirates included the cantonments in their field of operations, and rejoiced in the inexhaustible supply of superior firearms brought to their very doors. Almost incredible stories of their daring and agility are told. The very guard-room has been cleared of arms, and the rifle taken from the sentry himself. Barrack-rooms have been denuded of their weapons in a night, and cook-houses stripped of copper utensils.

Utterly failing to suppress these savages, the British had recourse to bribes, or "subsidies," as a means of securing their good behavior, but with not altogether satisfactory results. In the last Afghán war they were paid to guard the British baggage and commis-

Afrídis of the Afghán Frontier

sariat trains; but it is a well-established fact that, while staving off the depredations of others, they did not refrain from looting the property they were set to protect. The British have found that, since it would require a large army to effectually guard the passes, the only feasible plan is to leave the Khyber and Michni in the hands of the local tribes, who receive a regular bounty for the service. They are pledged to keep the pass open for British troops and trade, but closed to all other troops. The arrangement is not as efficient as could be desired, but it appears to be the best that can be contrived. There is more than a suspicion that the guardians of the pass still carry on their nefarious business on the sly; indeed, it is believed by many that the Khyber Rifles, a body recruited from these tribes, and drilled and "disciplined," are no better than composite soldier-highwaymen, who alternate their military duties with the "life of the road."

Before dawn of the "open" days a confused mass of nervous pack-animals and excited men congregate beneath the thrice-walled fort of Jamrúd, impatiently awaiting the firing of the morning gun, which announces the pass open. The actual entrance to the pass is at Kadam, three miles farther on; but the low, round, bare knobs which lie about Jamrúd, and command the road, make it defensible ground.

The European traveler must here present his permit, which will probably allow him to go as far as Alí

Masjid, and certainly not beyond Landí Kotál. A soldier of the Khyber Rifles will be detailed to escort him to and fro. The journey is most conveniently made in a light cart. Horseback riding is not always pleasant in the crush of animals that occurs in the narrow portions of the defile. Each caravan has its guard of riflemen, and as soon as the way is open strings of camels, oxen and asses, laden with Manchester piece goods, Birmingham tinware and Sheffield cutlery, in bales and cases, begin the passage with all possible haste. The loads are adjusted more by balance than anything else, and it is consequently not a difficult matter to displace them. Where the road becomes narrow, the pack beasts jostle one another, with the inevitable result of upsetting their burdens, and creating delay and confusion.

The concourse includes elephants, horses and carriages. Porters, male and female, guards, caravan men, women, children, and wayfarers of every description, make up the throng on foot.

On either side rises the barrier of hills, and eagles circle overhead. As they penetrate into the depths of the pass something of the solemnity of the surroundings must impress the multitude, for the gesticulating and shouting subside, and all settle down to the steady march of thirty miles. But it is a journey full of incident. Horses bolt and camels shed their burdens; contests occur for right of way, and quarrels arise from one cause and another.

The pass lies up the bed of a torrent, and is subject to dangerous floods at certain times of the year. At Kadam is a colony of the fanatic múllahs, who keep the hill tribes in a state of mental ferment, and incite them to deeds of lawlessness and barbarity. These so-called "saints," successors in the matter of their habitations to Buddhist hermits of early days, occupy the many caves with which the hills about the village are pitted. They are a dirty, unbalanced breed, whose insane vaporings are accepted by the unsophisticated hillmen as the utterances of inspired prophets, and this despite the fact that events have time and again belied their predictions.

At Kadam the hills begin to close in, and about a mile beyond they form precipitous walls on either side, not more than three hundred and seventy feet apart. Between Kadam and Alí Masjid the road fluctuates from a breadth of two or three hundred feet to a comfortable carriageway. The hills on either side are about thirteen hundred feet in height, and vary from sheer ascents to gradients practicable for artillery.

In a sort of recess of the mountain wall stands the little white mosque, which gives the name of Alí Masjid to that place. Numbers drop out of the line of march to breathe a hurried prayer at the shrine of the ferocious soldier-saint who died in the pass, while bent on the errand of converting Hindustán to Islám by the approved method of fire and sword.

Upon the height above the mausoleum rests the "impregnable" fort, which has been carried by assault more than once, and was burned by the British after its last capture. No one of the many rock forts of India can boast a record of siege and storm equal to that of Alí Masjid.

At this point the pass has closed to a mere lane of forty feet, between perpendicular walls of bare black rock. At the Lálábeg Valley the way widens out to a breadth of over a mile and a half, but only a mile further on it has closed in to ten feet or less, a narrow slit between the summits of enclosing hills, showing a ribbon of sky above. At Landí Kotál the pass is narrow, rugged, steep, and in general the most difficult part of the road. The camel, and even the pony, find it hard to surmount; people in carts must dismount and walk; artillery can only be taken over by men with drag ropes.

At Jamrúd one is less than seventeen hundred feet above sea level; at Alí Masjid twenty-four hundred; at Landí Kotál about thirty-four hundred, and at Dháka, where the pass debouches upon the plains of Afghánistán, the elevation is only fourteen hundred feet above the sea.

CHAPTER II.

AMRITSAR.

SURPASSING Delhi and Lahore in the matter of wealth, and rivaling them in size and population, Amritsar has the further distinction of being the holy city of the Sikhs. Rám Dáo, the Guru, laid its foundation on a site granted by the tolerant Akbar. He also excavated the sacred tank, Amrita Saras—Pool of Immortality—from which the place derives its name, and in its centre he commenced the construction of a temple, which was to become the future centre of Sikh devotion. His son Arjan completed the edifice, and lived to see a flourishing town grow up around it. Then set in troublous times for the Sikhs and their Gurus. Arjan died a prisoner, and his son an exile, and the supporters of the Hindu Reformation, almost too weak for defence, were harried on every hand. Mának Sháh had sown the religious seed deep and well, but it remained for Govind Singh, the tenth and last in apostolic descent from the founder, to organize the Sikhs into a military commonwealth, in which all men were equal, all were of one religion, and all were soldiers. The system, which was a protest against caste and idolatry, developed a nation of hardy fanatics, in many respects resembling Cromwell's Ironsides.

Henceforth the character of the Sikh resistance changed; aggression took the place of defence. Amritsar became a storm centre, the scene of constant struggle. Time after time the Musalmán succeeded in capturing the Sikh capital, and each time the fanatic fervor of the young nation enabled them to regain their lost possession.

In the decade following 1710 the whole power of the Mughal Empire was exerted to crush the Sikhs, and they were well nigh exterminated. Banda, the last of the Gurus, who had preached a religious war against the Muhammadans, was captured, together with his son, and carried to Delhi. Tricked out in scarlet robes and cloth of gold, he was mockingly paraded through the city in an iron cage, to afford sport to the jeering populace. His son's heart was torn out of the living body before his eyes, and thrown into his face. Then, with red-hot pincers, his flesh was torn away in pieces, until he expired in agony.

The Sikhs have never forgotten that demoniac cruelty, and the recollection of it was sufficient, if no other inducement had existed, to throw them upon the side of the British in the Mutiny. When the storming columns entered Delhi, the watchword "Remember Cawnpur!" was passed along the English lines, but when it reached the Sikhs it was changed to "Remember Banda!"

The last great disaster to Amritsar befell when the Afghán Ahmad Sháh Duráni utterly routed the Sikhs, and drove them across the Sutlej. He sacked the city, and reduced it to ruins. He blew up the temple, filled in the sacred tank with refuse, and defiled the holy place by the slaughter of cows. But these barbarities, far from subduing the iron spirit of the Sikhs, only aroused in them a determination to be avenged, and stirred them to a fresh and final struggle, which resulted in their entire independence. Amritsar again became the capital, and was restored to more than its former prosperity and grandeur. There is nothing in the history of the world, unless it be the story of the Swiss, to equal the narrative of hardy endurance and indomitabie energy displayed by these Hindu reformers in their evolution from a petty sect to a powerful nation.

In the eighteenth century the Sikhs were composed of a number of clans under independent chiefs, but with close religious and political affiliations. Ranjít Singh, who secured possession of Lahore in 1799, gradually brought the whole confederacy and the entire country occupied by the Sikhs under his sway.

The Játs comprise a large portion of the population, especially among the agricultural people, of whom they are more than half. They are divided between the Muhammadan and Sikh religions. The Ját-

Sikhs formed the flower of the armies which contested the fields of Múdki, Ferozsháh and Sabraon with the British, and cheerfully returned to the aggressive after each severe defeat. "They are a peasantry of which any country in the world might well be proud; admirable as soldiers in war, and equally admirable in peace for their skill and perseverance as agriculturists."

The Kashmirís, of whom there are at least thirty thousand, live in the city, and, for the most part, engage in the manufacture of shawls. They have deteriorated from the original stock, are of poor physique and uncleanly in their habits. They are generally Muhammadans, of bad reputation, and may be responsible for the unenviable character earlier writers attribute to the natives of the "Happy Valley."

As a trade centre, Amritsar is probably second to no city in the Punjab. Lying in the direct caravan routes, it receives the produce of Kashmir, Kábul, Bokhára and Rájputána. It is the great distributing point for the produce of the Punjab, and for the imports through Calcutta and Bombay.

Each winter brings an influx of pilgrims from the north, bound for Mecca. They come down with the caravans, and go by rail from Amritsar to Bombay, and thence by the excursion steamers, in which the accommodation is a little worse than that of cattle, but still quite up to the standard of living of these people, who are tattered mendicants, traveling with no more baggage than can be tied in a small bundle.

Afghán and Baluchí horse traders come in for the fairs that are held at the times of the great religious festivals. The bazaars and the caravanserai present a conglomeration of humanity as picturesque and varied as any to be found in India. Of course the Sikh fills the centre of the stage with his stalwart form and swaggering gait. Like the Nazarene, he may not cut his hair, and his beard he parts in the middle and twists up under the turban. Although a Hindu by descent, he has departed far from the parent type in physical and mental characteristics, as well as in religion. While the Bengalí bends under the weight of centuries of serfdom and caste oppression, the Sikh is animated by the blood of freemen and sustained by the spirit of equality. The successful struggle of his forefathers against fearful odds has begotten in him a hardy confidence and stamina, which may wane with the soft era of peaceful civilization, but which makes him at present superior to other native races. It would be difficult to say whether his contempt for the Hindu, or his hatred of the Muhammadan, is the greater. Both feelings are deep-rooted, and displayed at every turn in this "Rome of the Punjab."

When Ranjít Singh seized Amritsar he spent large sums in beautifying the shrine, and covered it with sheets of copper-gilt, whence it is called the "Golden

Temple." Thereby he secured the love of the people, and made fast the tenure of his chieftainship. He also constructed the fastness of Govindgarh, after the designs of French officers, nominally for the protection of pilgrims, but actually as a safeguard against any attempt at a *coup* on the occasions of unusually large gatherings. It commands the city from the northwest, and is now garrisoned by British artillery and infantry. Part of the massive wall with which the "Lion of the Punjab" surrounded Amritsar remains, but the greater part has been demolished since British occupation.

When Ahmad Sháh Duráni so completely wiped out old Amritsar, he did a service to the posterity of his victims by affording the opportunity for building the present handsome modern city, the oldest portions of which date back no farther than 1762, while the greater part is of very recent erection.

Near the centre lies the sacred tank, from the middle of which rises the Darbár Sáhib, or great temple of the Sikh faith, and the focus of the believer's aspirations. From the Clock Tower, at the approach to the temple, one gets a splendid view of the city, its spires and domes and towers, and close-packed, square-built houses, relieved by the massy dark-green foliage of parks and gardens. On every one of its sides, nearly five hundred feet in length, the holy lake is enclosed by the bungahs, or palaces, of the great Sikh chiefs, who come here to worship. They stand in shady enclosures, and present a great variety of form and color, from the sombre brick building of Diyan Singh to the gorgeous pile of Sher Singh. In front of them marble terraces and balustraded walks lead to the edge of the tank, which is surrounded by a broad pavement of tesselated marble, along which sit hawkers, vending flowers and beads, and the miniature tulwar, without which, or a spear-head, a Sikh's turban is not complete.

At the Clock Tower the visitor must remove his shoes, and is given a pair of felt slippers to replace them. He is then taken in hand by a policeman, who will remain with him until he quits the sacred precincts. This is a wise precaution of the Government to check the exuberance of the indiscriminate tourist, who is very apt to make himself offensive to a proudly sensitive people like the Sikhs.

The temple is reached over a white marble causeway, with flanking balustrades and columns, supporting golden lamps. The gilded walls and dome of the shrine, rising from a base of inlaid white marble, with its graceful cupolas, backed by dark foliage and reflecting waters, makes a beautiful picture. The building, square and simple in its outlines, rests upon a platform sixty-five feet square, with an entrance on every side. The doors are of finely-wrought silver, and the copper-gilt walls are engraved with verses from the Granth in the Punjabí text.

One enters upon a hall whose walls are tastefully

treated in gilt and painted floral designs. On one side sits the priest before a gorgeous, jeweled copy of the Granth, or holy scriptures of the Sikhs, which is their only material object of adoration. Over this attendants keep up a constant fanning with chauris. A sheet is spread beneath a silken awning for the offerings of worshipers, and on it accumulate large piles of various coins, flowers, rice and sweetmeats. Meanwhile the priest reads from the holy book, and the pilgrims chant responses to the accompaniment of tom-toms and stringed instruments. Then one goes up to the roof, where is a beautiful little Shísh Mahál, even more highly decorated than the hall below. It has some very sacred associations, and is reverently dusted with brushes made of peacock feathers.

Many of the inlaid decorations used in the temple were looted from the tomb of Jahángír and other Muhammadan monuments, and their use here indicates the impartial liberality of the Sikh in matters of religion.

Returning to the gateway tower, with its massive silver doors, the visitor is led up a stairway to the Treasury, the roof of which is supported by about forty silver pillars. Among other treasures which are carefully guarded here, and used only when the Granth is carried in procession, on the occasion of a religious festival, are a magnificent canopy of solid gold, weighing ten pounds, and set with diamonds, rubies and emeralds, and a diadem of large diamonds, with splendid pearl pendants.

On one side of the square, facing the gateway, stands a small temple, which was built during the incumbency of the Guru Arjan. In an upper story is a gilt ark, containing the sword of Guru Govind, and a number of other sacred relics, besides the vessels used in the Pahál, which is the initiatory ceremony of admission to the Sikh brotherhood. There is the Charán Pahál, from which the novice drinks the water that has cleansed the feet of the Guru, and the Shamshír Pahál, from which water is poured upon a sword, and sprinkled over the head of the candidate.

In the Darbár Gardens, covering thirty acres of fruit and flowering trees, is the Bába Atal. The basement hall, thirty feet in diameter, is richly painted, and from it a stairway ascends through its eight-galleried tiers to the summit, at the height of one hundred and thirty feet from the ground. The edifice was erected in memory of Atal Rái, the youngest son of Hur Govind.

In the exercise of the supernatural powers with which he was gifted, the young man had raised to life the son of a widow. The act met with the disapprobation of the Guru, who satisfied his son that it was sinful, rather than meritorious. Thereupon Atal Rái determined to relinquish his own life for that which he had wrongly restored, and accordingly lay down and died, and was buried on this spot.

The streets of Amritsar, like those of Pesháwar, are thronged with the natives of many countries, whose contrasting features and costumes give variety and interest to the scene. In the serai or the bazaars, one sees Afghán and Baluchí horse dealers, Nepálí and Tibetan caravan men, Persian and Yarkand merchants, and in fact representatives of all the races of Northern India and Central Asia.

The specialty of the city is shawls. It is the chief mart for the genuine Kashmir article, but has an even larger trade in the produce of local Kashmirís, who sit in the dingy little shawl-shops, patiently working the intricate patterns in silk and gold thread. At one time thousands of these people were engaged in weaving the shawls from the soft hair of the Tibetan goat, but since the carpet-making industry has been introduced, most of them are employed in producing the article for which there is a greater demand.

Rampur cloth, flowered silk and leather goods, are also made in large quantities.

From over the border come the wool, raw silk, ivory, turquoise, jade and other raw materials, which the Amritsar artisans work up into various forms. But the caravans also bring the finished products of the Central Asian countries, and from Amritsar they are shipped to every part of India.

The carpet factory, which is the largest in India, presents a strange mixture of modern and primitive methods, and illustrates the determination of the natives of India to do things their own way, which is, perhaps, the best way, all things considered. There are about a hundred looms, operated by Kashmirí boys, handsome little fellows, with beautiful eyes, creamy complexions, and regular, but rather effeminate features. Each group of five or six boys works under the guidance of a man, who reads off the directions for the pattern from a greasy roll, inscribed with characters in the Kashmir language, looking as though it had done duty for a century or two, which, indeed, may be the case; for the designs are mostly of a conventional kind that have come unchanged through ages to the weavers of to-day. The overseer calls off the number of threads and the color, and the boys repeat the direction in a monotonous sing-song, suggestive of the class recitation in the primary grade of a public school. The youngsters seem to work almost mechanically, and seldom make a mistake. The process is necessarily slow—it will take from two to three months to complete an ordinary rug—but the labor is cheap, and the men, who work on contract, are satisfied with a small profit. Thus a rug, which has engaged five or six hands for ten or twelve weeks in Amritsar, may be purchased in New York, where large quantities of them go, for fifty dollars or less. The quality is determined by the number of threads and the material; the carpets which are made from the shawl wool being much more expensive than the ordinary sort.

Leaving the city on the southeast by the Chativind, one of its twelve gates, a drive by a very bad road crossing the Hasli Canal will bring one to Tarn Tarán, a place held holy by the Sikhs as the ancient dwelling of the Guru Arjan. It was an old-time stronghold of the brotherhood, and the headquarters of its army. There is a colony of lepers in the vicinity, who should be able to avail themselves of the qualities of a near-by tank, to which is attributed the property of curing the disease in all those who swim across it. The Guru himself is said to have been a leper, and the retreat is believed to date at least from his occupancy of the place.

A temple and tower stand a few hundred yards to the east of the village, upon the margin of a fine tank, which draws an inexhaustible supply of water from the Bari Doab Canal. The temple and the tank both owe their existence to Ranjít Singh. The main hall of the temple is encircled by a corridor, on one side of which is the Granth, enwrapped in silken casings and fanned by an attendant. The walls are painted in representation of trees, and are in a good state of preservation. The outside of the temple lacks the texts usually to be found on similar Sikh edifices, and is embellished with pictures of male and female deities, which appear to be strangely out of place.

CHAPTER III.

LAHORE.

LYING on the highroad from Afghánistán, Lahore has occupied an unfortunate position, immediately in the path of every invader from the West. It early became the focus of attack and defence; the rallying point of confederated Hindu forces in their endeavor to stem the ever increasing tide of Muhammadan invasion, and the objective of every foreign army bent on the subjugation of Hindustán. It has passed through periods of extremely fluctuating fortunes, through splendor as the capital of the Ghazní dynasty and the metropolis of the Mughals; through decay and depopulation in the time of the devastating Duráni, to the condition—to quote the Imperial Gazetteer—of "a municipal city, capital of the Punjab, headquarters of the Lieutenant-Governor and the Punjab Government, the seat of an Episcopal See, and headquarters of a district of the same name."

Tradition ascribes the founding of Lahore to the son of Rámá, the semi-mythical national hero. As it is not mentioned by any of the writers who recorded the details of Alexander's expedition, the presumption is that it was not a place of much importance at that time, and that it offered no resistance to the Macedonian march.

Lahore is mentioned in the "Itinerary" of Hiouen Thsang, the Chinese Buddhist pilgrim, as a Bráhmanical city of importance; and that is its first definite appearance in history.

When the Muhammadans first invaded the country, Lahore was in the hands of a Chohan chief of the Ajmír family. For the next hundred years its native rulers contrived to hold the place against the attacks of the Musalmáns; but towards the end of the tenth century Subuktigín took the city, and Jai Pál, its defeated ruler, committed johur. Later the sons of these two fought, with a similar result, and Lahore remained in the hands of one or another representative of a Muhammadan dynasty until the rise of the Sikhs. When, at the beginning of the twelfth century, the Seljuks expelled the Ghazní Sultán from their country, he settled in his Indian dominions, and made Lahore the capital of his line, and so it remained until Muhammad Ghorí transferred the metropolis to Delhi in 1160.

When Timúr swept through the Punjab, Lahore fell to one of his generals. It was sacked by Bábar; but he and his successors made it a royal residence, and many are the works of its Mughal masters that survive to proclaim their love of architectural display.

Those were the days of Lahore's glory; but they were followed by a terrible transformation when

Ahmad Sháh Duráni and his Afghán successors began their inroads. Lahore was pillaged and reduced to ruins. Its population fled, and it became as a city of the desert, until Ranjít Singh revived its fallen fortunes.

Modern Lahore stands within a level plain, but upon a considerable mound created by the débris of ages. It partially covers the site of the old city, whose remains lie scattered around its walls. In 1849, when the British assumed possession of the place, its environs still remained a mere expanse of crumbling ruins, and the houses of the first European residents clustered round the old cantonment to the south of the town. Gradually, however, the station spread eastward, and now the new town covers a large part of the area formerly given over to ruins and jungle.

The present city covers six hundred and forty acres, surrounded by a brick wall which originally rose to thirty feet, but has been lowered to a uniform height of sixteen feet. The moat has been filled in and converted into flower-beds, running round all but the north side.

From the Delhi Gate, one of the thirteen entrances to the city, the Mayo Road runs out to Mían Mír cantonment, which has the unenviable distinction of being one of the "graveyards" of India. The place takes its name from a saint whose shrine bears the date 1635 in Persian characters. In his rough-and-ready fashion, Ranjít robbed the tomb of as much of the marble as he needed for his barádari—the only one of his additions to Lahore which has any pretensions to beauty—but made some amends by decorating the interior.

On the road to the city, which is more than five miles from the cantonment—the distances at Lahore are wearisome—is a village containing a number of more or less ruined tombs, in a grove of very old trees. By the Muhammadans this is deemed the most sacred spot in the district. It is the burial place of the "Chaste Ladies," who lie under whitewashed brick, in different enclosures.

They were sisters, and step-nieces of the Prophet—daughters of a younger brother. The eldest, Rakujah Khanum, who died in Lahore at the age of ninety, appears to have been the only one canonized. After the massacre at Karbelá they fled to Baghdad, and eventually made their way to India. As the resting place of immediate members of the family of Muhammad, the place is held in the greatest reverence by the Moslem population, and all who enter the precincts are required to remove their shoes.

The tomb of a less saintly, but more celebrated, lady is one of the principal show-places of Lahore, and gives its name to the suburb in which it lies to the south of the city. Anar Kali, the "Pomegranate Blossom," was a Persian beauty and one of the chief ornaments of the harem which Akbar recruited from every available nationality. As the story goes, she excited the jealousy of the Great Mughal by smiling upon the young Prince Salím — whose amours occasioned trouble with his father on more than one occasion— and paid the penalty of her indiscretion by being buried alive. Part of the story at least seems to be borne out by an inscription upon the cenotaph, which reads, "The profoundly enamored Salím, son of Akbar." The dates are a little perplexing. One of them corresponds to 1599 of our era, which would be six years before the death of Akbar; there is another corresponding to 1615 A.D. This leaves us the choice of two equally pretty hypotheses. Either the tomb is an evidence of the remorse of Akbar, or it was erected by Jahángír in remembrance of his love of twenty years before.

The little mausoleum, graceful in its lines, but rather commonplace in its plaster casing, was at one time used as the station church, and is now occupied by offices. The exquisitely lovely cenotaph has been removed from its central position to the wall, in order to make room for prosaic furniture. It is of flawless white marble—a perfect gem of carving and ornamentation. Upon it, in relief, are inscribed ninety-nine versions of the name of Allah, the reference to Salím already mentioned, and some verses in Persian.

Lahore Museum will always be associated with the name of John Lockwood Kipling [the genial curator who exchanged spectacles for pen-case with Kim's lama], to whom it owes its position in the forefront of provincial museums. Ajaib Garb, the "Wonder House," is the expressive name the natives have for it. Much time and labor must have been expended in the collection and orderly arrangement of the extensive specimens of the manufactures, arts and products of the Punjab. The catalogue is a perfect inventory of the assets of the "pauper province." But it is in the archæological department that one is most tempted to linger. Its greatest treasures are the sculptures, which aroused the lama to ecstacy; the heroic Buddhas which, together with other ancient relics, General Cunningham brought from the site of Taxila and other points in the northwest. There is a stone with an inscription connecting it with King Gondophares, under whom St. Thomas is supposed to have been martyred. There are pillars and fragments of a thousand and more years ago, and brass cannon which must have been among the earliest cast in India.

The mineral section contains a model of the Koh-i-Núr, whose story is such a strange mixture of romance and myth. The Hindus maintain that it belonged to Karna, King of Anga, while the Persians claim that it, as well as the Darya-i-Núr, the "Sea of Light," as the other is the "Mountain of Light," adorned the head-dress of Afrasiyab. Yet another version, and the most likely one, gives its origin as Golconda, in Haidarábád. It is certain that the great stone found its way to the Persian capital with Nadír Sháh, after the sack of Delhi, and that subsequently it fell into the hands of Ahmad Sháh Duráni, from whose grandson Ranjít Singh took it.

At the entrance to the Museum stands the old bronze cannon, Zam-Zammeh, the "Roaring Lion." Kipling says: "Who hold Zam-Zammeh, that 'fire-breathing dragon,' hold the Punjab; for the great green-bronze piece is always first of the conqueror's loot." The old gun saw service at Pánípat, in the cause of Ahmad Sháh Duráni, and was used by Ranjít at the siege of Múltán.

Because the spontaneous love of color is stronger than the cultivated taste for form, the streets and bazaars of an Indian city will always exercise a greater attraction for the traveler than its architectural features; but they defy description. The streets of the old town of Lahore are extremely picturesque, with their flat-roofed, irregular houses, whose square turrets and projecting balconies have not the slightest semblance of order or design, but look like so many packing-cases in haphazard heaps. The fronts present the greatest variety; many are carved and latticed, and some painted in floral designs.

The crowd upon the narrow streets is a mixed one, made up of many races, mostly big and bearded men, wearing various costumes, and displaying a mass of variegated color. The significant green of the Muhammadan, the blue of the Sikh and the saffron of the Hindu are but definite points in a mixture of all the shades imaginable. Men, women and children—all are clad in gay raiment, and there is an appearance of perfect harmony in the restless, kaleidoscopic throng.

The hand of the vengeful Sikh and the cold-blooded British official have left their disfiguring marks on the beautiful "Sleeping Palace" of Jahángír. The handsome, lofty pavilion in the Mughal style overlooking the Rávi, with its flanking chambers and finely-decorated verandas of Hindu architecture, is now used as a mess-room. Beneath this pavilion were the underground chambers to which the household retreated to avoid the mid-day heat. The large quadrangle once contained a garden, and was surrounded on three sides by a colonnade of red sandstone pillars, carved with figures of peacocks, elephants and griffins; but, with the aid of bricks and plaster, it has been converted into officers' quarters.

The Diwan-i-Ám, "Hall of Public Audience," has had its arches bricked in, and the whole has been whitewashed, the better to adapt it to its present use as a barrack. The beautiful white marble Diwan-i-Khás, "Hall of Private Audience," has fared better, perhaps, in that it has been turned into a church.

One of the most beautiful and best preserved buildings in the city is the Mosque of Vazir Khán, standing in a square enclosure reached by a narrow lane. About the entrance congregate hawkers of every description, beggars, barbers, public scribes and the great army of nondescripts who make up so large a proportion of the population of an Indian city.

Over the entrance to the mosque is the distich in Persian: "Remove thy heart from the world, and learn that the house of prayer is the fitting abode of man." On the front of the building is the Moslem creed, flanked by verses from the Kurán. The walls are covered with a peculiar mosaic of glazed tiles, into which the colors have been burnt by a process learned from the Persians, by whom it is called Nakkashi work. The effect is softer and more pleasing than that of the stone mosaic with surface coloring.

Thence for half a mile, along, perhaps, the most picturesque and crowded thoroughfare in Lahore, bounded by quaint houses, with curiously carved balconies, to the junction of two streets, in which favorable position stands the Sonai Masjid, with its three gilt domes. It was erected by Bikhwári Khán, whose *affaire de cœur* with the widowed ruler of Lahore ended in his being slippered to death by her women.

At the northern extremity of the city, near the Fort, cluster a number of fine buildings in comparatively open ground. A pretty garden, on the east side of which runs the wall of the Fort, with Akbar's Gateway, forms an attractive approach to Aurangzeb's Mosque.

Built with blood-money by a fratricide, although the jamá, or chief, masjid of the city, it is not the most popular. The building is imposing in appearance, but lacking in grace and the wealth of detail usually associated with Mughal architecture. It rises from a high platform, supported upon arches, and a grand flight of steps leads up to the entrance. Within are zealously guarded a number of sacred relics. There is a red hair from the Prophet's beard, the sole survivor of twelve, which, unlike the similar treasures of a celebrated shrine in the Deccan, evidently lacked the desirable property of multiplying. There are the green turbans of Alí and his sons Husain and Hasan, and the prayer-carpet of his daughter Fatima. A decayed tooth and some earth from Karbelá are amongst several other highly cherished articles with sacred associations. The mosque has been allowed to fall into decay—perhaps on account of its unpopularity—and each of the four minarets is a ruin. The earthquake which damaged Kutab's Tower of Victory at Delhi so injured the cupolas of this structure that it became necessary to remove them.

In the centre of the garden is Ranjít's Barádari, built from the white marble of which the tombs of Jahángír and Núr Mahál were despoiled. It is the only one of his buildings that does not violate the canons of artistic taste.

In striking contrast with the stiff and gloomy mosque, almost within whose shadow it stands, is the square, white stucco Samadh of the "Lion of the Punjab," resting upon a marble platform. Beneath ceiling decorations of mirrors and stucco traceries, and surrounded by shiny, chunam-covered arches, is a raised marble platform, on which are carved in relief twelve lotuses, the central flower being larger than those surrounding. Beneath lie the ashes of the great Sikh chieftain Ranjít Singh, and those of the four wives and seven concubines who committed satí on his funeral pyre.

The Adi Granth is read daily in this Samadh, scarce a stone's throw from the humble shrine of its composer, the Guru Arjan, who died in prison at Lahore during the reign of Jahángír.

Within the limits of the citadel are some of the oldest buildings in Lahore. Akbar's Palace, to which Jahángír, Aurangzeb and the Sikhs made additions, is striking chiefly for the grotesque figures of men and animals, worked in mosaic, with which the facade is inlaid. Cherubs, precisely similar to those commonly represented in Christian churches, adorn the portion of the palace attributed to Jahángír, who was suspected of having a leaning toward Christianity, and is known to have worn a crucifix and rosary.

Sentries stand at the entrance, and pace the court and corridor of the Moti Masjid. This because it is the local treasury of the British, as it was of Ranjít Singh before them. Before recent alterations were made, a court used to give access to the Shish Mahál, or Palace of Mirrors, in which Ranjít held receptions, and from the windows of which he could look over the plain where his troops were wont to assemble for review.

It was here that the sovereignty of the Punjab was formally ceded to the British. Dhulíp Singh was only fourteen years of age then, and in no way responsible for the *denouement* brought about by the ten years of anarchy under the regency of his uncles. The Government assigned a liberal pension to the boy, and undertook his education. Dr. John Logan, of the Medical Service, was appointed guardian, and Mr. Guise, of the Civil Service, tutor to the little prince. At eighteen years of age he foreswore the religion of his ancestors and became the first Christian of royal blood in India. Shortly afterwards he went to England, where he settled down and died. His son, Prince Victor Albert Jay Dhulíp Singh is a thorough Englishman, and a keen sportsman. Educated at Eton and Cambridge, he holds a commission in the Royal Dragoons, and is married to a daughter of the Earl of Coventry. The wheel of Fate surely makes few stranger turns than this.

Near the Shish Mahál is the exquisite pavilion called the Naulakha, a name which Kipling has borrowed for one of his best known novels. The word is a compound, signifying nine (nau) lakhs (lakha), and has reference to the cost of the building, which was nine hundred thousand rupees. Its walls are beautifully inlaid with flowers wrought in precious stones. On one side the pillars of the quadrangle have been connected by walls so as to form an armory. Among many curiosities this apartment contains the battle-axe and rhinoceros-hide shield of Guru Govind; some specimens of the chakra, or quoit-like steel ring, used as a weapon from time immemorial in India, and sometimes worn in miniature by the Sikhs in their turbans; curious cannon with revolving barrels, camel guns, coats of mail, cuirasses, and swords of various kinds.

About six miles to the east of the city, approached by a road which passes Sultán Beg's "Rose Garden," with its wondrous gateway, are the Shalimar Gardens, laid out in 1637 by Sháh Jahán. The gardens cover an area of about eighty acres, surrounded by a wall, with a large gateway and pavilions at each corner. They are traversed by artificial streams, and contain hundreds of fountains. The flower-beds are laid out with a geometrical precision that betrays a modern hand, and the general appearance suggests deterioration, but it must have been an extremely lovely spot at the time when the Great Mughal and his court sought the summer evening breezes beneath its mango trees. In the neighborhood are several other gardens, more or less neglected, and the mausoleum of the famous engineer Alí Mardan Khán, who designed the Shalimar Gardens.

A notable trio are buried out at Sháhdra, beyond the Rávi. Jahángír's mausoleum is one of the best-preserved buildings of Lahore, but even it has suffered considerably at the hands of successive depredators. Aurangzeb removed the marble dome which once surmounted it. The neighboring tomb of Núr Mahál is in ruins, and that of Asof Khán, the brother-in-law of Jahángír and the father-in-law of Sháh Jahán, was stripped of its marble facings and colored enamels by the Sikhs. The real wonder is that they allowed the Mughal tombs to stand.

A white marble archway, fifty feet in height, opens upon the garden-court of Jahángír's mausoleum, which is approached over a pavement of finely-veined Jaipur marble. On the right of the entrance is a stairway leading to the roof, whose flat surface is covered with a tesselated pavement. The square roof was surrounded by a marble parapet, but Ranjít removed it for use elsewhere. At each corner a four-storied minaret, constructed of enormous blocks of stone, rises to an altitude of ninety-five feet. The cenotaph is of white marble, inlaid with what is one of the best specimens of pietra dura work to be found in India. The ninety-nine names of Allah are carved in beautiful black marble script, and the south side bears the inscription, "The Glorious Tomb of His High Majesty, Asylum of Protectors, Nuru-dín Muhammad, the Emperor Jahángír."

CHAPTER IV.

ANCIENT DELHI.

If we trace the history of Delhi towards its beginnings, we are carried into the remote and hazy past—at least fifteen hundred years before the Christian era, when the Aryan pioneers had wrested from the primeval jungle scarce more than a scanty clearing here and there. One of these was Hastinápur, whence the Pandávas led their followers to take possession of the forest land newly assigned to them. The Hindu Iliad tells how they cleared the country, and built the city of Indraprástha, the site of which is identified with ruins lying to the south of Delhi.

From that time great capitals have succeeded one another here in continuous course of rise and decay, so that the whole country for ten or more miles around the modern Delhi is covered with the débris of ruined cities, closely lying over well nigh fifty square miles.

Under Yudishthira, the eldest of the Pandu brothers, Indraprástha grew into the metropolis of a kingdom powerful enough to enable the Pandávas to turn their arms against the Kauravas, with whom they had a heavy score of long standing to settle. Them they overthrew, and so became masters of all the settled country to the east.

The memorable conflict, the first decisive battle in Indian history, was probably fought on the flat, featureless plain in the neighborhood of Delhi, which has been the scene of many a fierce encounter. It was on the famous field of Pánípat that Akbar, then but a boy, gave battle to the Pathán army, despite the counsels of his omráhs, who would have retired. It was on the plain of Pánípat that the Afghán and Maráthá hosts contested for the supremacy of India. Prodigies of valor were performed in that, perhaps, the bloodiest hour in the history of the world.

Yudishthira was succeeded on the throne of Indraprástha by thirty direct descendants, until the line was overthrown by Visarwa, Minister of the last Pandávit sovereign. This dynasty held the throne for five hundred years, and was followed, "with the usual symmetry of Indian mythical lore," by a dynasty of fifteen Gautamas.

And so through tradition we arrive at the first century before Christ, when the word Dillipur appears in authentic history as the name of a city situated about five miles below the present Delhi. Ferishta attributes the foundation of this original Delhi to Rájá Dilhu, the last ruler of the Mayura dynasty. The earliest recorded information on the subject is derived from the celebrated iron pillar set up by Rájá

Dháva, some time in the third or fourth century of the present era.

Tradition, which is, however, refuted by the unimpeachable authority of the inscription, refers the pillar to Anang Pál, and a fanciful story, which pretends to account for the origin of the name of the city, is told in connection with its erection. According to this legend, a Bráhman saint assured the rájá that the pillar had been driven so far into the earth as to become immovable, fixed in the head of Vasuki, the serpent king, who supports the world, and that so long as the pillar stood, the dynasty of its founder would survive. In a skeptical mood, Anang ordered the monument to be dug up, when clots of blood and hair upon its base proved the truth of the Bráhman's assertion. But when an attempt was made to return the shaft to its place as before, it was found impossible to fix it, and so the pillar remained *dhila*, that is, loose in the ground—hence the name Delhi!

"In Sambat 1109 (1052 A.D.), Anang Pál peopled Dilli," rebuilt the city, and constructed extensive fortifications, whose remains form a great circle of massive masonry lying around the Kutab Minár.

The renowned Prithvi Rájá, last of the champions of Hindu independence, who was cold-bloodedly put to death by the cowardly Sháhab-ud-dín, erected a great wall, the remains of which may still be traced, about the entire extent of the city.

When the Túrkí Tughlak, profiting by the Hindu

revolt which followed the death of Alá-ud-dín, seized the Imperial City and the throne, Ghiyás-ud-dín, the first of his line, decided to remove the seat of government from Delhi, which was then a hotbed of Hindu intrigue and insurrection. He laid out a new capital at Tughlakábád, on a rocky eminence about four miles to the east of the modern Delhi. The remains of a massive citadel, and deserted streets and lanes, still mark the spot; but save for a few goat-herds, no human being inhabits these vast and desolate ruins.

Firoz Sháh Tughlak removed the metropolis to Firozábád. The city has disappeared, like its forerunners, but traces of it may be found along the ground extending from Humáyun's tomb to the ridge. The same Firoz brought from Khizrábád, and set up here, the pink sandstone pillar of Asoka, which the natives called "Firoz Sháh's Club."

The present city owes its being to Sháh Jahán, the greatest builder of them all. Under his direction rose the fort on the right bank of the Jumna, with its five mile circuit of lofty wall. He called the city Sháhjahánábád, but the name Delhi was too dear to the Hindu to die.

The roads running south from the Delhi and Ajmír Gates form sides of a triangle, with Tughlakábád and the Kutab Minár at either end of the base. The section thus enclosed is closely packed with ruins of ancient cities and monuments, tombs of royal person-

THE ENVIRONS OF DELHI.
Old Cantonments
East Jumna Canal
East India Railway
DELHI
SHAHJAHANABAD
Palace
Delhi Gate
Jay Singh's Observatory
Ferozabad
Feroz Shah Kotila
Jumna River
Indraprastha
Lal Darwaza
Indrapat or Poorana Kila
Khairpur
Humayun's Tomb
Safdar Jang's Tomb
Tomb of Nizamuddin
Bara Pool
Mobarikpur
Ferozpur
Howz Khas
Tomb of Feroz Shah
Siri
Jahanpana
Begumpur
Chiragh Delhi
Keerkee
Rai Pithora
Lalkot
Kutb Minar
Maharoli
Toghlukabad
Toghlak's Tomb
Budderpore

ages and of saints, mosques, memorial pillars, a vast conglomeration of remains in various stages of decay. The history of Hindustán for the past two thousand years might almost be educed from the clues this district affords.

In the apex of the triangle are the vestiges of the city which the Tughlak Emperor, Firoz Sháh, built in the fourteenth century. It extended northward over the ground later covered by Sháhjahánábád. All that remains of it is a memory suggested by a heap of rubbish. But there is more to perpetuate the name of its founder. The three-storied Kotila near the Jumna still supports the Asoka pillar which Firoz brought from the Siwalik Hills. William Finch, who visited the place in 1611, describes the pillar as passing from the ground up through the three stories of the building and rising twenty-four feet above the roof, and having on the top a globe with a crescent. It is now something short of forty-three feet in total height, and terminates in a splintered top, a considerable portion having been broken off. There are a number of inscriptions on the shaft, which have been engraved at different times, but its glory lies in the Asoka Buddhistic edict set forth in Páli script, the oldest characters known to India.

The crumbling walls of the ancient fort of Indrapat mark the site of Indraprástha. Near by is a fine red sandstone mosque, built by the Pathán Shir Sháh in 1541. Its walls are inlaid with marble and covered

Hall of the Sixty-four Pillars, Delhi

with texts from the Kurán in Kufik characters. The neighboring building witnessed the death of the Emperor Humáyun, who fell down its stairway whilst engaged in astronomical observations.

About two miles out upon the road that starts from the Ajmír Gate is the Jantr Mantr, a collection of buildings which Jai Singh erected for astronomical purposes. His enormous "Prince of Dials," which has its counterpart at Jaipur, has a gnomon whose hypothenuse is over one hundred and eighteen feet.

A cluster of tombs surround the spot which is held sacred as the burial place of Nizám-ud-dín. He is variously said to have been a saint, a sorceror, a secret assassin and the founder of thagí. In order to reach the dargah of this worthy, from the road, one has to pick his way over a few hundred yards of ground thickly strewn with ruins, and pass through the intervening buildings. The first of these is the white marble "Hall of Sixty-four Pillars," which contains the cenotaph of the foster-brother of Akbar. Entering an enclosure to the west, one comes upon the tomb of Abúl Hasan, the poet, who was popularly known by the somewhat ambiguous *sobriquet*, "The Parrot of Hind." He was the grandson of a Turk who immigrated to India in the time of Changiz Khán. Abúl Hasan, by talent or diplomacy, gained the favor of one of the Tughlaks, and contrived to maintain his footing at the courts of seven successive emperors. His fame spread throughout Central Asia, and Sadi, the celebrated Persian poet, paid him a visit. He was the author of ninety-eight works, but like many another poet, he lives in his ballads, which are sung in the streets of Delhi to this day. Near by are the tombs of a son of Akbar II, of the Muhammad who lost his treasure to Nadír the Persian, and of Jahángara, the favorite daughter of Sháh Jahán. The headstone of her tomb bears the text, "God is the life and the resurrection," and below the following verses, in Persian,

> "Save the green herb, place nought above my head,
> Such pall alone befits the lowly dead;
> The fleeting, poor Jahánara lies here,
> Her sire was Sháh Jahán, and Chist her Pír.
> May God the Ghazi monarch's proof make clear."

After which a prayer for the welfare of her father, and the date 1681.

The tomb of Nizám-ud-dín, who belonged to the Chisti order of saints, is in a square, white marble building, overshadowed by a tree which is said to be as old as the structure. The mausoleum is ornamented with exquisitely carved lattice-work screens of white marble.

To the north of the building is a well about forty feet deep, which was the work of the saint, who is said to have blessed it so that its waters would never drown any one. There are always a number of boys prepared to dive into the well, for a small monetary

Tomb of Humayan, Delhi

consideration, from the roof of the building, at a height of forty or fifty feet.

Humáyun's mausoleum is built upon a plan which was afterwards followed in the construction of the Táj; but the Emperor's tomb lacks the richness and delicacy of detail which distinguish the monument of Múmtáj Mahál. Humáyun died in the middle of the sixteenth century, and his widow erected this noble building of granite, inlaid with marble. Sixteen years were spent in its construction, and it cost fifteen lakhs of rupees, at a time when labor was the least item in the calculation. It stands amid acres of gardens, and terraces and fountains, enclosed in embattled walls, with towers and lofty gateways. In the centre of this enclosure is a platform, about twenty feet high and two hundred feet square, supported by cloisters, and ascended by four great flights of granite steps. From this platform arises the square, red sandstone mausoleum, with its corner octagonal towers and white marble dome. Humáyun's cenotaph stands immediately under the centre of the dome in the main octagonal hall. It is of plain white marble, without ornament or inscription. In an adjoining chamber are the sarcophagi of Alamgír II., Farakh Sír and Jahándar Sháh.

On the morning of the 20th September, 1857, a crowd of frightened fugitives took refuge in the group of buildings known as Humáyun's Tomb. They were Bahádur Sháh and a number of followers, fleeing from the avenging army which had fought its way through the streets of Delhi, and was even then battering down the walls of the palace. As soon as it became known that the royal puppet had flown, Major Hodson, the famous cavalry leader, went in pursuit. Upon a promise that his life would be spared, Bahádur Sháh surrendered, and he, his favorite wife Zenát Mahál, and their young son, were taken back to the city. The next day Hodson returned to the spot, bent upon the capture of three of the royal princes, who were understood to be still lurking there. By this time an armed mob of five or six thousand had gathered in the enclosure; but the intrepid Hodson, although accompanied by only one hundred troopers, advanced to the mausoleum, and succeeded in securing the persons of two sons and a grandson of the King. The prisoners were placed in a carriage and driven slowly towards the city. As the cortége approached Delhi, the vehicle was stopped and surrounded by an immense crowd, who would, if not immediately checked, have attacked the escort, and probably have effected a rescue, with the result of giving a fresh impetus to the mutiny. It was an extremely critical moment, and one demanding prompt and decisive action.

Hodson immediately decided upon his course. He was fully alive to the grave responsibility he incurred, but without hesitation he forced his way to the side of the carriage, and, drawing his revolver, shot the princes through the head in rapid succession. The effect of the deed upon the rabble was profound. Amazed and stunned, they permitted the troopers to proceed. Not a hand was raised; not a voice was heard as the carriage and horsemen made their way leisurely into the city.

This action of Hodson's excited at once the most severe censure and the most extravagant praise. When, a few months later, he received his death-wound at the storming of the Begam's Palace in Lucknow, the English press and people were still discussing the deed with considerable heat, and little understanding of the circumstances. Opinion is still divided upon the subject; but, at least, there is general agreement that the officer acted with conviction of the rightness of his conduct.

As for the princes, armed rebellion was the least of the crimes of which they had been guilty. Helpless women and children had been barbarously murdered by their orders and under their supervision; and at least one of the sháhzádars had himself enacted the part of butcher by cutting down a mother with a babe at her breast. Their deaths were only too merciful, and it was scant justice that their bodies should be exposed upon the spot where their victims had been subjected to the vile insults of the populace before being massacred.

On the left of the cross-road which runs from Humáyun's Tomb to that of Safdar Jang is a group of buildings of which General Cunningham writes: "The north group, consisting of two octagonal tombs and a bridge of seven arches, is attributed by the natives to the time of the Lodi family, the larger tomb, within a square, being assigned to Sikandar Lodi; and I believe that this attribution is most probably correct. But the south group, which consists of a mosque and two square tombs, belongs, in my opinion, to an earlier date."

To the south is the huge tank, covering an area of one hundred acres, which Alá-ud-dín constructed. It has long since been filled in, and now the villagers of Khaura raise rice crops upon the site. Firoz Sháh's tomb is here, and the ruins of the city he built and named after himself, scarce a mile to the northeast.

On what is probably the site of the ancient Dillipur are traces of the forts built by Anang Pál II. and Rái Pithora. Within the circuit of the mounds which mark these fortifications stand the Minár and Mosque of Kutab. The natives credit Rái Pithora with having erected the Minár, in order that his daughter might enjoy a view of the Jumna from the fort.

The Kutab Minár is two hundred and forty feet in height, and rises in five stories, with a diameter of forty-seven feet at the base, gradually diminishing to nine feet at the top. It is said that the height of this column was once three hundred and forty feet, and it

Kutab Minár and Iron Pillar—Delhi

is certain that in 1797 it stood two hundred and fifty-seven feet from the ground.

"The base of this Minár is a polygon of twenty-four sides, altogether measuring one hundred and forty-seven feet. The shaft is a circular form, and tapers regularly from the base to the summit. It is divided into five stories, round each of which runs a bold, projecting balcony, supported upon large and richly-carved brackets, having balustrades that give to the pillar a most ornamental effect. The exterior of the basement story is fluted alternately in twenty-seven angular and semi-circular faces. In the second story the flutings are only semi-circular; in the third they are all angular. The fourth story is circular and plain; the fifth again has semi-circular flutings.

"The relative height of the stories to the diameter of the base has quite scientific proportions. The first, or lowermost story, rises ninety-five feet from the ground, or just two diameters in height; the second is fifty-three feet farther up; the third forty feet higher. The fourth story is twenty-four feet above the third, and the fifth has a height of twenty-two feet. The whole column is just five diameters in height. Up to the third story the Minár is built of fine red sandstone. From the third balcony to the fifth the building is composed chiefly of white Jaipur marble. The interior is of gray rose-quartz stone.

"The ascent is by a spiral staircase of three hundred and seventy-six steps to the balcony of the fifth story, and thence are three more steps to the top of the present stonework. Inside it is roomy enough, and full of openings for the admission of light and air. The ascent is very easy; the steps are almost 'lady steps.'

"The ferruginous sandstone has been well selected to lend a rich, majestic appearance to the column. The surface of the material seems to have deepened in reddish tint by exposure for ages to the oxygen of the atmosphere. The white marble of the upper stories sits like a tasteful crown upon the red stone; and the graceful bells sculptured in the balconies are like a kummerbund around the waist of the majestic tower. The lettering on the upper portions has to be made out by using a telescope."

The origin of the Kutab has been the subject of controversy. A theory in favor of a Hindu origin has been advanced, but with little to substantiate it. No man who sees the Minár can take it for a moment for anything other than a thoroughly Muhammadan building—Muhammadan in design and Muhammadan in its intents and purposes. The object is at once apparent to the spectator—that of a mazineh for the muezzin to call the faithful to prayer.

The adjoining mosque, fully corresponding in design, proportion and execution to the tower, bears out such a view of the lofty column, and there is the recorded testimony of Shams-Í-raj and Abúlfeda to place the fact beyond a doubt.

If that were not enough, unimpeachable evidence is afforded by the declaration cut deep in its walls, "The erection of this building was commenced in the glorious time of the great Sultán, the mighty King of Kings, the Master of Mankind, the Lord of the monarchs of Túrkístán, Arabia and Persia, the Sun of the world and religion, of the faith and of the faithful, the Lord of safety and protection, the heir of the kingdoms of Suláimán-Abú Muzeffa, Altemsh Nazír Amín-ul-Momenin." From this it would seem that Altemsh was the builder of the Minár, and it has come to be associated with the name of Kutab-ud-dín, probably because he erected the mosque of which it is the complement.

In the time of Firoz Sháh, the Kutab was struck by lightning, necessitating extensive repairs. It was again injured during the reign of Sikandar Lodi, and again repaired by that liberal patron of literature and the arts. Exactly three hundred years later (1803), an earthquake caused such serious hurts to the column as to threaten its downfall. The British Government undertook its reparation, and completed the work in twenty-five years. In place of the old cupola of Firoz Sháh, which had fallen down, a plain octagonal red-stone pavilion was constructed on the summit.

There was something so incongruous and inartistic about this structure that a strong protest was raised against its continuance in position. Lord Hardinge ordered it to be taken down in 1847, and the present unpretentious, but satisfactory stone-work substituted for it. The old head piece now occupies a platform, upon a mound near the base of the tower, where it stands like the culminating ornament of an old-fashioned wedding cake.

Colonel Sleeman, writing in 1844, tells us that five years previously, "while the Emperor was on a visit to the tomb of Kutab-ud-dín, an insane man got into his apartment. The servants were ordered to turn him out. On passing the Minár he ran in, ascended to the top, stood a few moments on the verge, laughing at those who were running after him, and made a spring that enabled him to reach the bottom without touching the sides. An eye-witness told me that he kept his erect position till about half-way down, when he turned over, and continued to turn till he got to the bottom, where his fall made a report like a gun. He was, of course, dashed to pieces."

Near by is the remnant of an unfinished Minár. When it had been carried up to thirty feet, errors in the dimensions and in the slant of the shaft were discovered; so it was abandoned, and a second essay resulted in the Kutab.

Even in its present ruined condition the Mosque is a magnificent work. Batuta, who saw it about one hundred and fifty years after its erection, described it as being the most beautiful building in India at the time. Tamerlane was so impressed by the Mosque and Minár, that he had exact models of them made, and took from Delhi all the masons he could procure to reproduce the buildings at his capital of Samarkhand.

The Mosque stands upon the platform of Rái Pithora's Hindu Temple, the last vestiges of which were swept away to make room for it. According to the inscription over the archway within the east entrance, the construction was commenced by Kutab-ud-dín in 1191. Altemsh built a more extensive cloistered wall around the original enclosure. In the court thus formed stands the Kutab Minár, in the southeast corner. By prolonging the walls of Altemsh eastward, Alá-ud-dín added another court, surrounded by similar cloisters. This court is entered by the splendid Alái Dárwazá on its south side. It is a square building of richly carved red sandstone, with lofty, ornamented doorways on either flank. The inscriptions over the entrances refer to Alá-ud-dín, by his favorite title of Alexander II.

The main entrance to the Mosque is from the Court of Altemsh, through an arched gateway in the centre of the east wall of the inmost enclosure. This is a courtyard running one hundred and forty-two feet east and west, and one hundred and eight feet north and south. The surrounding cloisters are formed by Hindu, Buddhist and Jain pillars to the number of twelve hundred or more. Many of them were richly carved, but now almost all are in an advanced condition of decay, and display signs of deliberate mutilation, the work, doubtless, of fanatic Muhammadans.

An inscription over the entrance states that the materials were obtained by the demolition of twenty-seven idolatrous temples. Strangely enough, a Hindu monument—no less than the famous Iron Pillar—stands immediately in front of the chief entrance to the mosque building. The latter is now completely in ruins, but the vast screen of majestic arches, which extended across its front, and was carried one hundred and fifteen feet further on either side by Altemsh, is in a fair state of preservation. The central arch is fifty-three feet high, and thirty-one feet broad.

There is a distinct correspondence in design, proportion and execution, between such portions of the Mosque as remain and the great Minár.

From the top of the Kutab a splendid view may be had over ten miles or more of ruins and ancient remains to Delhi, with its glittering mosques and palaces, and the silvery Jumna washing its walls.

The Iron Pillar—the palladium of Hindu dominion—has probably stood in its present position for upwards of fifteen hundred years. It is a solid shaft, more than sixteen inches in diameter. Analysis shows it to be pure malleable iron. It is probably not less than sixty feet in length, of which less than thirty feet are above ground. Excavations are said to have been made to a depth of twenty-six feet, without reaching its base or loosening it in any degree. Its entire weight cannot be less than eighteen or twenty tons.

The pillar "records its own history in a deeply-cut Sanskrit inscription of six lines on its western face." This inscription refers to the pillar as "the arm of fame—Kirtibhúja—of Rájá Dhava," who is stated to have been a worshiper of Vishnu, and to have "obtained with his own arm an undivided sovereignty on the earth for a long period." The letters upon the triumphal monument are described as "the typical cuts inflicted on his enemies by his sword, writing his immortal fame."

The conclusion of patient antiquarian research is that the pillar marked the centre of the great Rájá's capital, and probably stood within a magnificent temple; and the date assigned to it is 319 A.D.

Through all the changes of the intervening centuries the Iron Pillar has stood, a melancholy monument of the departed glory of an ancient Hindu civilization, overshadowed by the Muhammadan Tower of Victory, symbolical of the eclipse of the Hindu by the Moslem. And just as the older civilization has displayed the greater endurance, so the Pillar has defied the onslaughts of Time, whose ravages are only too plainly discernible in the Minár.

Rájá Dhava's "arm of fame" is held in the greatest reverence by the Hindus, and many and curious are the traditions with which it is connected.

At the northwest corner of the mosque enclosure, but without the walls, stands the red sandstone tomb of Altemsh, who died in 1235. Fergusson says that, "in addition to the beauty of its details, it is interesting as being the oldest tomb known to exist in India."

Somewhat over four miles to the east of the Kutab Minár is Tughlakábád. Cunningham thus describes the fort: "It may be described with tolerable accuracy as a half hexagon in shape, with three faces of rather more than three-quarters of a mile in length, and a base of one and a half miles, the whole circuit being only one furlong short of four miles. It stands on a rocky height, and is built of massive blocks of stone, so large and heavy that they must have been quarried on the spot. The largest measured was fourteen feet in length by two feet two inches, and one foot thick, and weighed rather more than six tons. The short faces to the west, north and east are protected by a deep ditch, and the long face on the south by a large sheet of water (dry, except in the rainy season), which is held up by an embankment on the southeast corner. On this side the rock is scarped, and above it the main walls rise to a mean height of forty feet, with a parapet of seven feet, behind which rises another wall of fifteen feet, the whole height above the low ground being upwards of ninety feet"

The Fort contains the ruins of a number of large buildings and residences. About one-sixth of the entire area is occupied by the Citadel, in which are the remains of what must have been a grand palace.

The Tomb of Tughlak is on the south side of the Fort and without the walls. It stands in an artificial lake, and is connected with the Fort by a causeway six hundred feet long, carried over a string of twenty-seven arches.

"The sloping walls and almost Egyptian solidity of this mausoleum, combined with the bold and massive towers that surround it, form a picture of a warrior's tomb unrivaled anywhere."

The building is circumvented by a pentagonal outwork, whose walls diminish, with a slope of about one in five, from eleven and a half feet at the base to four feet at the top. The mausoleum is a massive square of red sandstone, surmounted by a white marble dome. On three of its sides are lofty entrance archways, whose doors open beneath marble lattice screens. The exterior walls are relieved by bands and scrolls of white marble, forming a striking contrast with the underlying material. Within are three cenotaphs—those of Tughlak, his wife and son. This son, who succeeded to the throne under the title of Muhammad Sháh, earned the popular pseudonym of "The Bloody

Sultán." He was a hardened and conscienceless tyrant, but his successor, Firoz Sháh, appears to have been deeply concerned about his misdeeds, for he went to the trouble of collecting acquittances from all who had been wronged by Muhammad. These were placed in the tyrant's tomb, with a view to affording him justification on the day of judgment.

CHAPTER V.

THE IMPERIAL PALACE.

THE first landmark to arrest the eye of the traveler approaching Delhi from the west is the Mutiny Memorial, standing in bold prominence upon the southerly spur of the Ridge. It is a red sandstone, Gothic spire, resting upon a triple platform. From its windows may be identified many of the points of chief interest in connection with the memorable siege of Delhi. The Kashmir Gate, associated with one of the most gallant deeds in the annals of warfare; near by the Kudsiya Gardens, and the adjoining cemetery, in which lie the bones of General Nicholson, "who led the assault of Delhi, but fell in the hour of victory." Just beyond, Ludlow Castle, the residence of the murdered Simon Fraser, and the site of the two breaching batteries. Immediately north, and barely half a mile distant, is the celebrated Hindu Ráo's House, a whitewashed bungalow, now used for convalescent soldiers. Farther north, a mile or more, is the abandoned tower, whose castellated walls sheltered the Flag-staff Battery. But every inch of ground between the Jumna and the western edge of the Ridge calls to mind some incident of "the siege."

The chief point of attraction in modern Delhi must be what was the Imperial Palace—now the Fort. It lies directly on the river, and is surrounded on three sides by an imposing wall of red sandstone, topped by small, round watch towers. It has two magnificent gateways. The Lahore Gate, directly in the centre of the western wall, leads to the Chándni Chauk, or "Silver Square," the main street of the city, which runs due west right through it, and divides it into two almost equal parts. The Delhi Gate lies in the southeast corner of the Fort.

Since the Mutiny extensive portions of the Palace have been ruthlessly demolished, and others adapted to the purpose of barracks. Although much of the old grandeur of the place remains, it has lost the uniformity and completeness which were among its conspicuous characteristics, and the most delicate of its architectural and ornamental features have been destroyed or injured.

The outline of the Palace forms an immense parallelogram, sixteen hundred feet east and west, by exactly twice that distance north and south. The entire space was occupied by a symmetrical arrangement of halls, pavilions, baths, women's quarters, garden courts, and all the offices necessary to the order and comfort of the enormous household of a Great Mughal.

From the Lahore Gate a vaulted arcade of two stories, three hundred and seventy-five feet long, runs due east to the entrance of the Palace proper. It is like the nave of some gigantic Gothic cathedral, the noblest approach to a palace ever conceived. The passage is between two rows of shops, which occupy the ground story, to the Nákar Khána, or Music Hall, beyond which is the Diwán-i-Am, the Hall of Public Audience, open on three sides, and supported by rows of red sandstone pillars, formerly adorned with gilding and stucco-work. In the wall at the back is a staircase that leads up to the throne, raised about ten feet from the ground, and covered by a canopy, supported on four pillars of white marble, the whole being curiously inlaid with mosaic-work. Behind the throne is a doorway, by which the Emperor entered from his private apartments.

The whole of the wall behind the throne is covered with paintings and mosaic, in precious stones, of the most beautiful flowers, fruits, birds and beasts of Hindustán. They were executed by Austin de Bourdeaux, who, after defrauding several of the princes of Europe by means of false gems, which he fabricated with great skill, sought refuge at the court of Sháh Jahán, where he made his fortune, and was in high favor with the Emperor.

In front of the throne, and slightly raised above the floor of the hall, is a large slab of white marble, which was formerly richly inlaid with mosaic-work, of which the traces only now remain.

The Diwán-i-Khás, Private Hall of Audience, is

about a hundred yards beyond the Public Hall of Audience, to the east, and overhanging the river. Nothing can exceed the delicacy of its inlaid work and the poetry of its design. Nowhere else in the world can be found an apartment of such elegance as this poem in stone.

It is a white marble pavilion, open on all sides, and richly ornamented with gilding and pietra dura. The front opens upon a large quadrangle, and the building once stood in a beautiful garden. It was one hundred and fifty feet long and forty feet in breadth, with a graceful cupola at each corner. Colonnades of white marble pillars supported the roof. "The polished marble has been worked into its forms with as much delicacy as though it had been wax, and its whole surface, pillars, walls, arches and roof—even the pavement—was inlaid with the richest, most profuse and exquisite designs in foliage and arabesque; the fruits and flowers being represented in sections of gems, such as amethysts, carnelian, blood-stone, garnet, topaz, lapis lazuli, green serpentine and various colored crystals. A bordering ran round the columns, similarly decorated, inlaid with inscriptions in Arabic, from the Kurán. The whole had the appearance of some rich work from the loom, in which a brilliant pattern is woven on a pure, white ground, the tracery of rare and cunning artists. Purdahs of all colors and designs hung from the crenated arches on the outside to exclude the glare and heat."

Hall of Audience—The Palace, Delhi

It is said that the roof was covered with plates of solid silver, which became part of the Maráthá loot in 1760. Round this roof runs the famous inscription, in Persian: "If there be a paradise on the face of the earth, This is it, this is it, this is it." In the centre of the hall stood the barbaric Takt Taus, the Peacock Throne of Sháh Jahán, on which he laid out $150,000,000.

This gorgeous structure was reached by an ascent of solid silver steps. It was a massive chair of pure gold, overhung by a canopy of the same metal, inlaid with jewels. Behind the throne, whose surface was thickly set with precious stones, stood two life-size peacocks, with tails outspread. These figures were so encrusted with diamonds, emeralds, sapphires and other appropriate jewels as to reproduce the natural colors of the birds. Between the peacocks stood the full-sized figure of a parrot cut from a single emerald. The design was completed by a vine, the leaves and fruit of which were formed from gems whose rays were reflected by mirrors set with pearls. This splendid chair of state was carried away in 1739 by Nadír Sháh, who further embellished it, and added several costly accessories in the form of bejeweled screens and canopies. Nadír's nephew, Adil Sháh, who succeeded him on the Persian throne, broke up the Peacock Throne, and probably disposed of some of its component parts, but a considerable portion of the valuable gems figure in the richest collection of jewels in the world—that of the Sháh of Persia, stored in the Palace of Teheran.

The place of the Peacock Throne was afterwards filled by an imitation of comparatively little value and of inferior workmanship. The crown of the Great Mughal was in keeping with the splendors of the Throne and the Audience Hall. It was made for Akbar upon the pattern of the crown worn by the Persian Sháhs. It had twelve points, each terminating in a large diamond of the purest water. In the centre was a similar point, surmounted by a single pearl of extraordinary size. A number of choice rubies were employed to give finish to the costly article, which has been valued at over ten millions of dollars. When the Koh-i-núr was placed in the front of this marvelous head-piece, the effect must have been magnificent.

The Koh-i-núr fell into the hands of the Mughals when Bábar defeated the last of the house of Lodi, on the fateful field of Pánípat. Tavernier, a jeweler and a competent judge, who saw the stone, valued it at £880,000 sterling.

One would naturally associate the lovely Diwán-i-Khás with the softer sentiments, but the truth is that the most memorable incidents connected with it are of a stern and unpleasant character. No building can vie with it as a scene of passion and perfidy, and many a time the poetic distich running over its arches must have struck the spectator with all the force of pointed irony. For instance, what a "paradise" it must have seemed to its builder when he stood beneath its roof to make enforced abdication in favor of his insolent grandson—an act which was not without consolation to Sháh Jahán, since it promised to debar his hated son from the throne. But Aurangzeb, not to be thwarted, appeared upon the very spot in the imperial robes, and from the Peacock Throne dictated the imprisonment, to be followed by poison, of his ambitious son Muhammad, and the assassination of his own brothers, Dara and Murad.

Here, in manacles, stood the chivalrous Suláimán, to receive sentence of death, and beside him the brave Sípur Shakuh, who, having shared toil and peril with his father, and witnessed his brutal murder, was more than willing to give up his own young life.

But most repellent scene of all is that of the effeminate Muhammad Sháh fraternizing with the ferocious Nadír, while yet the bodies of Delhi's thousands lay unburied in the streets, and the Persian soldiers were busily engaged in the sack of the city. But Muhammad was more concerned about his personal belongings, and the conqueror had not yet plundered the palace, so it behooved the Great Mughal to play the part of the suave courtier.

The bearer of the coffee on this momentous occasion had no enviable task to perform, but he was a gentleman of resourceful wit. The assembled courtiers fully appreciated his critical position, and doubtless each monarch was curious to see how he would acquit himself in the trying situation. If he offered the golden tray first to his master, the conqueror of India would almost certainly order his head to be taken off; whereas, if he presented the salver first to the Persian, the same fate most assuredly awaited him at the hands of the already deeply mortified Mughal Emperor.

Without hesitation, the officer walked up to Muhammad, and on bended knee proffered the beverage, saying, "Your humble servant cannot aspire to the honor of presenting the cup to your Majesty's honored guest, nor would your Majesty desire that any hand but your own should do so." The Emperor passed the cup to Nadír, who accepted it with a smile, and said, "Had all your officers known and done their duty like this man, you had never, my good cousin, seen me and my Kuzul Bashus at Delhi."

The closing days of the year 1857 witness the total eclipse of the old glory of the Great Mughals and their Diwán-i-Khás, when the aged and trembling Bahádur Sháh *sat*, in consideration of his infirmity, before the military commission which sentenced him to death—a sentence commuted to banishment for life. A few weeks later the magnificent Hall of Sháh Jahán had been despoiled of its glory, its marble walls and columns whitewashed, and its pavement covered with hospital cots. Was ever transformation more sudden and dramatic?

The whole of the area to the south of the central range of buildings, measuring one thousand feet each way, was occupied by the harem and private apartments, filling a greater space than that covered by the Escurial. It contained three garden courts and a number of smaller ones devoted to various purposes of state and pleasure. Of these not a vestige remains. All that now exist of the public portions of the Palace are the Naubát Khána, the Diwán-i-Am, the Diwán-i-Khás and the Rang Mahál—now used as a mess room—and one or two small pavilions. It is true that these are the most beautiful parts of the structure, but, without their connecting courts and corridors, much of the symmetry of the design and the effect of the architecture is lost. Fergusson says that, "being now situated in the middle of a British barrack-yard, they look like precious stones torn from their setting in some exquisite piece of Oriental jeweler's work, and set at random in a bed of the commonest plaster."

CHAPTER VI.

MODERN DELHI.

The European section of Delhi lies along the eastern and a portion of the northern side of the city. Dariáganj, the Fort, and the Public Offices, extend from the Delhi Gate to the Kashmir Gate, in a belt of comparatively open ground interspersed with public gardens. This section occupies somewhat less than half the entire area of the city. It is in striking contrast to the southwestern quarter, which is occupied by the native town, and densely packed with shops and dwellings.

The East India Railway from Calcutta crosses the Jumna by a magnificent bridge, and passing through the ruins of old Salímgarh, traverses the city and continues westward as the Rájputána State Railway, to Jaipur, and northward to Ambala and the hills.

Near the railway station are three time-worn gates, the remnants of the old magazine, left standing as eloquent memorials of the brave deed of Willoughby, and his companions.

On its south side the station faces the beautiful Queen's Gardens. They are very tastefully laid out,

The Pearl Mosque, Delhi

and without too great formality. Attention is immediately attracted by a huge stone elephant elevated upon a platform. An inscription states that it was brought from Gwalior by Sháh Jahán, and set up outside the south gate—that would be the Delhi Gate—of his palace in 1645. It is said that this is one of a pair of elephants, which originally bore the figures of Jaimal and Patta, the Rájput chiefs, whom Akbar defeated at Chitor. Akbar had the statues sculptured at Agra in commemoration of the event, and Aurangzeb mutilated them, as he did many other monuments. But how this monolithic beast got from Agra to Gwalior, and thence to Delhi, is not explained.

Chándni Chauk has a double row of ním and pípul trees running down its centre, on a raised pathway, which has taken the place of the masonry aqueduct through which water was formerly carried from the canal to the Palace.

Time and again this main thoroughfare of the city has been choked with corpses. Timúr, Nadír, Sindhia, and, lastly, the British, have fought their way through Delhi's streets, with fearful slaughter.

In the very centre of Chándni Chauk is the little Golden Mosque, with its three gilt domes. Upon its roof the implacable Nadír sat during the massacre, and turned a deaf ear to the pleadings of the veteran Nizám-ul-Mulk. Hard by is the Kotwali, where the bodies of the sháhzádas were exposed, after Hodson had brought them into the city.

The principal shops are in this street, which is at all times packed with a restless crowd of natives, making a scene extremely picturesque and full of color. Anything and everything may be bought in the bazaars, but particularly jewelry and gold and silk embroidery, which are the *specialités* of Delhi.

When the Mughals were at the height of their power, they drew to their capital the most skilled artisans, stone-cutters and jewelers in the kingdom. The descendants of these men are to-day employed in the same crafts, with no diminution in the old-time skill; only, perhaps, a change of direction in their efforts. The trade of the swordmaker has declined everywhere; but there are, perhaps, a greater number of the smiths here than in any other large city.

If one has the least touch of the artistic temperament, the bazaars of a large Indian city grow upon him, and take hold of him with an ever-increasing fascination; so that he never tires of the endless series of kaleidoscopic pictures presented to the eye. Even the unaccustomed odors and the discordant sounds cease with familiarity to jar the senses, and he finds himself reveling in the hive-like life of

> "The painted streets, alive with hum of noon;
> The traders, cross-legged, 'mid their spice and grain;
> The buyers, with their money in the cloth;
> The war of words to cheapen this or that;
> The shout to clear the road, the huge stone wheels,
> The strong, slow oxen and their rustling loads;

The singing bearers with the palanquins,
The broad-necked hamals, sweating in the sun;
The housewives, bearing water from the well,
With balanced chatties, and athwart their hips
The black-eyed babes; the fly-swarmed sweetmeat shops,
The weaver at his loom, the cotton-bow
Twanging, the millstones grinding meal, the dogs
Prowling for orts, the skillful armorer,
With tong and hammer linking shirts of mail;
The blacksmith, with a matlock and a spear
Reddening together in his coals. . . . .
The dyers, stretching waistcloths in the sun,
Wet from the vats—orange and rose and green;
The soldiers, clanking past, with swords and shields;
The camel-drivers, rocking on the humps;
The Bráhman proud, the martial Kshatriya,
The humble, toiling Súdra; here a throng
Gathered to watch some chattering snake-tamer
Wind round his wrist the living jewelry
Of asp and nág, or charm the hooded death
To angry dance with drone of beaded gourd;
There a long line of drums and horns, which went
With steeds, gay painted and silk canopies,
To bring the young bride home; and here a wife,
Stealing, with cakes and garlands, to the god,
To pray her husband's safe return from trade,
Or beg a boy next birth; hard by the booths
Where the swart potters beat the noisy brass
For lamps and lotas."

Delhi is the Mecca of the tourist. Every recurring cold season finds him present in ever increasing numbers. His patronage supports a considerable business in false gems, imitation antiques, spurious curios, cheap jewelry—in short, innumerable things that are not what they seem to be, and which are manufactured for the express purpose of being sold to him at five or six times their actual value.

At the Burra Bazaar end of Chándni Chauk is a red sandstone mosque, with two minarets over one hundred feet in height. The building, which is in good preservation, was erected by one of Sháh Jahán's wives.

The Jamá Masjid—the largest mosque in India—is faced by an open park-like garden. Five thousand workmen labored six years on the construction of this splendid pile of sandstone and marble, with its snowy domes and graceful minarets. It stands upon a terraced rock, and has an approach of forty steps on three sides. On certain days markets are held around these steps. The Muhammadan Sabbath—that is, Friday—brings twelve to fifteen thousand worshipers to the building, and upon special occasions the number is greatly increased. Women are seldom seen within the precincts; indeed, it is a question whether, according to the Muhammadan idea, they have any souls. Fergusson says of this Jamá Masjid that, "It is not unlike the Motí Masjid in the Agra Fort in plan, though built on a very much larger scale, and adorned with two noble minarets, which are wanting in the Agra example; while from the somewhat capricious admixture of red sandstone with white marble, it is far from possessing the same elegance and purity of effect. It is, however, one of the few mosques, either in India or elsewhere, that are designed to produce a pleasing effect externally. It is raised on a lofty basement, and its three gateways, combined with the four angle towers and the frontispiece and domes of the mosque itself, make up a design where all the parts are pleasingly subordinated to one another, but at the same time produce a whole of great variety and elegance. Its principal gateway cannot be compared with that at Fatehpur-Sikri, but it is a noble portal, and, from its smaller dimensions, more in harmony with the objects by which it is surrounded."

The galleries over the gateways are surmounted by marble domes, with gold-tipped spires. Rising above these are fluted, marble minarets, ending in open arched chambers, with gilded pinnacles.

Since the erection of the building the main entrance has only been opened to the chief ruler of the land, and now none but the Viceroy may pass its portal.

The massive doors, overlaid with thick, brass arabesques, give access to a quadrangle, three hundred and twenty-five feet square, open to the sky. In the centre are a marble basin and fountains for the ablutions of the faithful. On the north, south and east sides runs a red sandstone colonnade of open arches, forming a cloister. On the western side, toward Mecca, is a building of white marble, open along its front of two hundred feet. In the centre is a majestic arch of white marble, and smaller arches on either side—all covered with Arabic inscriptions. The roof is surmounted by three graceful, white marble domes, with spires of copper gilt.

The interior is paved with nine hundred immense slabs of white marble, bordered with black. In the centre of the wall at the back is the niche, or kibla, in the direction of the sacred city, toward which the worshiper faces when uttering his prayers. At each corner is a minaret one hundred and forty feet in height, of white marble and red sandstone, laid in vertical, alternating strips. From the summits of these minarets the muezzins call to prayers at certain hours of the day. At that summons the faithful follower of the Prophet must turn toward Mecca and prostrate himself, and that no matter where he may be or what he may be doing.

There are a number of more or less interesting relics treasured in this mosque. There are Kuráns penned by the Imams; a slipper of the Prophet, and a hair of his moustache, and a fragment from the canopy which surmounts his tomb.

The Kálá Masjid, or Black Mosque—black with age—was built by one of the early Afghán sovereigns. It is a sombre, uninviting building, with no attempt at adornment. Its plan is "exactly that of the original Arabian mosques—a square court, surrounded by a cloister and roofed with many small domes of the plainest and most solid construction."

The palaces of nobles, which in olden times made Delhi a city of architectural grandeur, have for the most part disappeared, marble columns and architraves, and heavy stone foundations, alone attesting to their former presence, where their sites are not completely occupied by modern buildings.

In a tortuous little street that runs out of the Faiz Bazaar, near the Native Infantry Lines, stands one of the oldest houses in the city within a rather extensive compound. It is in reality only a portion of the original building, which was of stone, and, tradition says, once occupied by the fated Shir Afghán. It is now a training school for nautch girls.

These establishments are common in all the large cities of India. The girls are taken into these gymnasia—for such they are, in fact—at young ages, and while their limbs are yet supple. They are put through a rather severe course of physical culture, taught to dance, to sing, to play musical instruments, and perhaps to act. Almost all of them learn some special feat in connection with the ordinary nautch. One of the prettiest of these is the egg dance, which is a very ancient performance, but one which never fails to delight on account of the dexterity and grace involved in it. A light, wicker-work frame, with a revolving disc, is fastened to the head of the nautchní. Falling from the disc, or wheel, are a dozen or more strings of whipcord, terminating in slip-knots. The dancer commences a whirling motion on the tips of her feet, meanwhile filling the slip-knots with eggs from a basket held in her hand. At length each cord bears an egg, the whole circling round the spinning figure with rapidity. After a space of ten or fifteen minutes the nautchní detaches the eggs one by one, and replaces them in the basket. Sure feet, a quick eye and a light hand are necessary for the successful performance of this dance; and also long and patient practice with artificial eggs.

Some of the feats depend upon bodily contortions, but they are of a pleasing and graceful character, unlike the repulsive exhibitions of the music halls of the Western hemisphere.

As a rule, the young girls who enter these training establishments are bound for a certain number of years, in consideration of a payment made to their parents or guardians. If one serves out the term of apprenticeship, so to speak, she usually follows the profession for the remainder of her life, unless, as frequently happens, she marries a man of means, or enters some rájá's household as a concubine. They are generally well treated by the trainers, and comfortably lodged. During the time that they are attached to the school, all the money they earn goes to the proprietors, but they are allowed to retain presents. The nautchní recruits are drawn mainly from Upper India, Kashmir and Kábul, and from the Muhammadan and Hindu population alike.

The nautchní is the only educated woman in India. She can read, write, quote from the poets, philosophers and dramatists; is often genuinely witty, and sometimes speaks English with fluency and correctness.

The old-time nautch is a mixture—dancing, pantomime and song. The first consists chiefly of posturing; the second is sometimes clever, but the singing is not pleasant to the Western ear, for the native women have no idea of modulating their voices. The main desideratum is to sustain a succession of notes at a high, shrill pitch as long as possible. The music is furnished by male supernumeraries, the instruments being of the stringed order, and small kettle-drums, or "tom-toms."

The dress of the nautchní is picturesque, though cumbersome by reason of its voluminous folds. The quantity of solid metal worn upon the person must be often a task upon the strength.

The dancing costume consists of close-fitting, bright silk trousers, embroidered with gold lace and strung with colored beads. Over this garment is a petticoat or skirt of ten or twelve breadths, profusely trimmed and bordered with gold fringe. The bodice fits closely and comes no lower than the breast. An immense veil of rich material is wrapped about the head and trunk in many folds. The hair is braided with bands of gold or silver thread-work, and fastened with bodkins of filigree or chased metal. The neck, arms, hands and toes are covered with jewelry, sometimes of great value. Heavy anklets are worn over the feet, and massive bangles upon the wrists. In addition to rings of the drop pattern, a jeweled ornament, something like a metal rosette, is attached to the ears.

A light circle of gold is pendent from the nose, and upon it are strung two or three gems. The genuine nautchní is disappearing, and the systematic cultivation of the art is no longer prosecuted as of old.

The casual tourist very seldom sees the nautch as it is presented to the natives. His experience is usually limited to the common street-dancer, whose performance is on a par with her morals, both being about as poor as possible. The common belief that all dancing-girls are *femmes de mauvaise vie* is an erroneous one. There is a class of nautchní who do not perform in public, nor before men, unless they be members of the families of their patronesses. The nautchní must take life as she finds it. She has no control over conditions, and conceives no evil in following the customs of a hundred generations of predecessors. If her habits are faulty, judged by the standard of latter-day civilization, her principles are sound; for it is a well-attested fact that when these girls marry, they almost invariably become chaste wives and admirable mothers.

Unfortunately the kúsbán, or street-dancer, cannot be included in the benefits of this apology. She is generally a Muhammadan or low-caste Hindu, who has taken up the calling *after* a fall from grace. In one case the immoral feature of the life is incidental —one might say accidental; in the other it is the prime purpose, followed with deliberation, and associated with the terpsichorean art for mere convenience.

Dancing Girl

The bhayádhyás are a class of dancers attached to the temples. It is not an uncommon thing for Hindu parents, as it has been in all ages for parents of every race, to consecrate children to the divine service. When the child is a female there is no capacity in which she can be attached to the establishment of a temple, save that of dancing-girl. The child is usually left with the priests at an early age, and by them is tutored in her future duties. At the age of sixteen or eighteen the formal consecration takes place, after which the *devotée* is bound for life to the service of the temple, and debarred from forming other ties.

A Hindu would never allow his wife or daughter to dance, even in the privacy of the zenana, but all classes are passionately fond of the nautch. The performances last for hours, and are commonly carried on through the entire night. Europeans may be invited to these entertainments. They are sometimes diversified with a dramatic performance in which nautchnís take parts. The women of the household see and hear all that goes on, from behind a thin purdah, which, since there is no light on their side of it, entirely excludes them from the view of the audience.

Zenana boxes are a feature of all the European theatres and places of amusement, and Hindu ladies frequently attend such places, probably more for the sake of inspecting the audience than anything else. A lightless box, with a dark mosquito curtain covering the front, affords all the privacy the highest caste demands. It is a curious fact that the seclusion of the Hindu women in the zenana is a custom copied from the Muhammadans, and in the days of early Moslem occupation was likely enough adopted as a measure of defence and protection against the unbridled license of the invaders.

CHAPTER VII.

AHMEDÁBÁD.

LEGEND says that Yama Rájá, some time in the eighth century, ruled over a great kingdom in Gujarát, and had for his capital the city of Anahelavada, which stood about sixty miles to the northeast of Ahmedábád. Anahelavada was then in its infancy, but it grew in course of time to be the greatest city in India, a marvel of magnificence and beauty and learning. Yama Rájá founded a dynasty which reigned over Gujarát for upwards of a hundred years. Then came another line of kings, whose great progenitor was the renowned Mula Rájá, whom "all kings worshiped as they worshiped the sun." It was during the reign of his son that Mahmúd of Ghazní made his memorable raid into Gujarát.

The reign of Sidh Rájá, "the ornament of Goojatland," occurred in the long interval of peace which followed Mahmúd's departure. He occupied the throne during nearly fifty years, and in his time Gujarát attained its greatest prosperity and Anahelavada reached the zenith of its glory.

Later, Gujarát fell to the Delhi Emperors, and in

time their Viceroys established an independent dynasty. The ancient capital was deserted, and its glory was transferred to Ahmedábád.

At the time when Muhammad Ghorí commenced the era of Pathán conquest in Hindustán, the great Rájput kingdoms were those of Delhi, Ajmír, Kananj and Gujarát. Mahmúd of Ghazní had been to Gujarát on his memorable iconoclastic expedition, and on his return the Rájputs of Ajmír had well-nigh cut his army to pieces. This was in 1026, and Mahmúd was a Turk. More than one hundred and fifty years later the Afghán master of Ghazní and of Ghor came to stay. The feud between Delhi and Kananj simplified the task of the invader. Muhammad disposed of one after the other, and then reduced Benares. The defeated Rájputs left their ancestral homes, never to return, and with their swords hewed new kingdoms out of the jungles and hills "in the region which to this day is called Rájputána, or Rájásthán, the land of the Rájputs or Rájás." Then the Rájputs had a breathing spell until Alá-ud-dín turned his attention to Rájputána. His first move was to reduce Gujarát. Ahmedábád fell into his hands, and the Rájput reigning family were made prisoners. Kála Devi, the wife of the Rájá, was transferred to the harem of the conqueror, but the Rájá effected his escape, and conveyed away his little daughter. The young lady, who was eight years of age, had been sought in marriage by Ram

Deo, the son of the Maráthá chief of Deogírí, but her Rájput father had refused to make what would have been considered a misalliance. As a fugitive, however, the Gujarátí prince reconsidered the proposition, and sent the child to the court of Deogírí. Alá-ud-dín was not to be easily balked, however. He sent Kafur Khán in search of the little princess. The Maráthás hid her in the Caves of Ellora, where the emissaries of the Emperor found her. She was carried off to Delhi and at once married, not very reluctantly, it is said, to the eldest son of Alá-ud-dín.

Ahmedábád rivals Delhi and Agra in architectural beauty. At one time it excelled both, and at the height of its glory this metropolis of the Gujarátí Sultáns is said to have been the most magnificent city in the world. When Sir Thomas Roe, the Ambassador of King James of England to the Court of Jahángír, visited Ahmedábád, "it was a goodly city, as large as London."

Since 1411, when Sultán Ahmad made the old Hindu town of Asaval the nucleus of a new capital, Ahmedábád has waxed and waned, time and again, in harmony with the fluctuating fortunes of its successive masters. During the first century of its existence the city expanded and grew in wealth. Then came a period of decline, coincident with the decay and fall of the dynasty of Gujarát. Ahmedábád rose again on the tide of Mughal prosperity, and sank once more with the setting power of the Delhi Empire.

Under British rule the city has revived, and is now a thriving commercial centre, with a population of about one hundred and fifty thousand. Its people must always have had a strong artistic tendency, for every house in the old town is carved from roof to threshold; and even the curious Jaina feed-bins for pigeons, standing upon posts all about the streets, are carved and painted. But "nowhere did the inhabitants of Ahmedábád show how essentially they were an architectural people as in their utilitarian works—wells and inlets to water reservoirs. It was a necessity of their nature that everything should be made ornamental;" and so we see traces of the striving after embellishment in every direction—on the walls and the wells; in the temples and the tombs; on the doors and framework of the houses, and even in the products of the place, which are mostly ornate in character.

The goldsmiths of Ahmedábád produce the finest archaic jewelry in all India. Its copper and brass workers are noted for their graceful and delicate productions, and its silversmiths for the lightness of their filigree. Then the cabinet-makers are famous for their superior carving in black-wood, and the stone-masons for their chaste chisel-work. Still other handicraftsmen exercise their hereditary skill on lacquer, leather and inlay work. Many kinds of the finer fabrics are made by hand, such as gold and silver lace, gold and silver tissue and tinsel trimmings. The brocades of Ahmedábád have not their equal in India; nor in the world, for that matter. In short, nine-tenths of the artisans of the city are engaged in the production of ornamental wares, and the rest are employed in steam factories, that turn out cheap print-goods.

The old capital of Gujarát displays ample evidence of its long occupation by the Muhammadans; but traces of its ancient Hindu rulers appear at every hand. With their unfailing vandalic propensity, the invader destroyed the Hindu temples; but the material was largely used in the construction of Muhammadan edifices, and seldom with good effect. Not infrequently they effected the conversion of a temple to a mosque, with even worse result. Not only were the styles essentially dissimilar, but the very spirit of the architecture was in one case opposed to the other. "The Hindu worked out in rock-hewn cavern and dark-pillared hall those ideas of fear and gloom with which his religion associates the divinity. The Muhammadans expressed the simple ideas of glory and praise to an all-powerful Jehovah. All the Muslim wants is a courtyard, with a tank for ablution, roofed cloisters to shelter the worshipers, a niche in the east wall to indicate the direction of Mecca, a pulpit for the Friday sermon, and a tribune or raised platform from which the Kurán is recited and prayers intoned. There must be, if possible, a minaret, from which to call the faithful to prayer; but the dome is not an essential feature."

The city covers two square miles, and is surrounded

by the crumbling remains of the old wall, with its twelve gates. Without, on every side, lie tombs and tanks, temples and mosques.

Crossing the Manik Chauk, the main street, is a fine structure of richly-carved stone, called the Tín Darwazah, or Three Gateways. This was the entrance to the "Royal Square," and in the early days of Ahmedábád was the most imposing portion of the city.

Mandelslo, the Dutchman, who visited Ahmedábád in 1638, writes of the King's Palace, which was near the Tín Darwazah, or Triple Gateway, that "over the gate there was a kind of curtain, or stage, for the music, consisting of violins, hautboys and bagpipes, which play there in the morning, at noon, in the evening and at midnight, as they do in Persia and all other places where the prince professes the Muhammadan religion. All the apartments of the house were sumptuous, gilt and adorned with painting, according to the mode of the country; but more to the satisfaction of those who are pleased with diversity of colors than of those who look for invention, and stand upon the exactness of invention."

The Palace now serves as the city jail, and the "diversity of colors" has disappeared under a uniform coat of whitewash. The inscription over the gateway—"The House of Goodness and Favor"—is hardly descriptive of the building in its present capacity.

Near by on the same street is the Jamá Masjid,

built, like the Tín Darwazah, by Sultán Ahmad in 1424. There are larger mosques in India, but few more beautiful than this. A porch gives access to the enclosure from the street. The court is surrounded by the conventional cloister, and the mosque building is in the usual place on the western side.

The material and the columns used in the gallery and arcade have been gathered, as an inscription states, from various infidel temples, and, as a consequence, display a great variety of styles. The roof of the mosque is supported by two hundred and sixty pillars, and is surmounted by fifteen cupolas, the three in front being encircled by galleries. The minarets are over forty feet high, but rose to twice their present height before an earthquake shattered them.

On a marble tablet over the Kiblah is an Arabic inscription to the following effect: "This high and far-stretching mosque was raised by the slave who trusts in the mercy of God, the compassionate, the alone-to-be-worshiped." Then follows the name and style of "the slave"—to wit, "Nasírud dunya va dín Abúl Fath Ahmad Sháh, son of Muhammad Sháh, son of Sultán Muzaffar."

In the domed building, with its eighteen pillared portico, on the east side of the courtyard, are the tombs of Ahmad Sháh, his son Muhammad Sháh and his grandson Kutab Sháh. The cenotaphs lie in a square chamber, upon a pavement of vari-colored marble, upon which the light filters through windows of perforated stonework. Across the street from the mosque are the tombs of the wives of Ahmad Sháh. The mausoleum is a splendid building, but unfortunately the neighboring houses encroach so closely upon it as to almost shut off the view of the beautiful facade, which is embellished with thirteen exquisitely carved recesses. Within, a rectangular court contains the cenotaphs. There is a central group of eight large ones, surrounded by several smaller. Directly in the middle is the sarcophagus—black marble inlaid with white—of Mughlai Bíbí, the chief of all these royal ladies. This mausoleum was originally, perhaps, the finest in Ahmedábád, but it has been much neglected, and is falling into decay.

At the southern edge of the city, near the Astoria Gate, are the tomb and mosque dedicated to Ráni Sípari, the mother of Ahmad. The tomb is a beautiful specimen of delicate and ornate carving, with "walls of lace, balconies of brocade carved in stone. Opposite this mausoleum are an open mosque, and two minarets as slim as sapling pines, wrought with arabesques as fine as carved ivory. There are lamps carved in relief on the walls, each hung by chains undercut in stone with Chinese elaboration; and this lamp is everywhere repeated—on the mosque, on the tomb and on the base of the minarets. The building, which has the faintly russet tone of old parchment, when seen in the glow of sunset takes a hue of ruby gold that is almost diaphanous, as filmy as embroidered gauze."

A few hundred yards along the street, and just beyond a mosque built by Dastúr Khán in 1486, is a mound which marks the spot where long ago stood the fort constructed by the Bhíl chieftain Asa, who gave his name to the ancient Hindu city Asaval.

Close to the jail is the temple dedicated to the goddess Bhadra Kálí Mata, in honor of whom the place was named the Bhadr. In the northeast corner of the Bhadr, and forming its wall at that point, is the Sídí Sayid Mosque. It is noted for the marvelous beauty of the lace-like stone tracery with which two of its windows are filled. "It would be difficult," says Fergusson, "to excel the skill with which the vegetable forms are conventionalized just to the extent required for the purpose. The equal spacing also of the subject by the three ordinary trees and four palms takes it out of the category of direct imitation of nature, and renders it sufficiently structural for its situation; but, perhaps, the greatest skill is shown in the even manner in which the pattern is spread over the whole surface. There are some exquisite specimens of tracery in precious marbles at Agra and Delhi, but none quite equal to this." This mosque is occupied by an official and his staff of native clerks.

Diagonally opposite to the Sídí Sayid Mosque is that of Ahmad Sháh. Its date, 1414, twenty years earlier than that of the Jamá Masjid, would indicate that it is almost, if not quite, the oldest mosque in the city. It is said to have been the Sultán's private chapel.

There are within the city limits several other mosques, all more or less notable on account of architectural features or historical associations.

The Pínjrapal is, like the feeding places for birds, an institution due to the Jains. Hundreds of sick and crippled animals are housed in the sheds contained in the enclosure, and there is a room devoted to the care and comfort of needy insects.

There was a time when all India was Jain by practice, if not by profession. The sect has been very generally believed to be an offshoot of Buddhism, but latter-day investigation contradicts the theory, and assigns to the Jains a distinct place among the seceders from Bráhmanism. "The two schisms have so much in common, especially in outward features, that for a long time it was thought that Jainism was a sub-sect of Buddhism. In their legends, in the localities in which they flourished, and in many minutiæ of observances, they are alike. Nevertheless, their differences are as great as the resemblance between them, and what Jainism at first appeared to have got of Buddhism seems now rather the common loan of each sect from Bráhmanism."[1]

The disciples of Jaina are morbidly sensitive on the subject of taking life or harming living thing. They carry the doctrine of Dharma farther than the origi-

[1] "The Religions of India," Hopkins.

nators of it. The Jain walks the street with downcast eyes and broom in hand, prepared to step over or brush aside any creature that may be in his pathway. Lest he should swallow unawares some minute insect, he wears a gauze bandage over his mouth, and for the same reason filters all the water he drinks, and refrains from eating after dark. The Jains have always been strongest in the west, and Ahmedábád is at the present time one of their chief centres.

Just outside the Delhi Gate is a magnificent modern Jain Temple, which was finished in 1648 at a cost of about one million rupees. It is surmounted by half a hundred pagoda domes. It is richly sculptured throughout; conspicuous among its carvings being representations of the twenty-four holy men, or tirthankars. The entrance to the temple is through a portico, supported by richly carved pillars. The interior consists of two chambers, the whole being paved with different colored marble slabs. The inner apartment, which is the sanctuary, contains an image of Dharmnath, in the form of a beautiful youth, whose head is encircled by a glittering tiara.

Fergusson says of this temple, "Each part increases in dignity to the sanctuary. The exterior expresses the interior more completely than even a Gothic design, and, whether looked at from the courts or from the outside, it possesses variety without confusion, and appropriateness of every part to the purpose intended."

If a circle were drawn around Ahmedábád, with a

ten mile radius, the ground so enclosed would be thickly dotted with ancient and interesting ruins.

The man who sinks a well in a thirsty land is a benefactor to his kind, but what shall we say of him who makes it a thing of beauty and a perpetual delight to the eye? This did Dada Hari, the "genial," for the people of Ahmedábád. From a platform surrounding the mouth one enters a domed portico, supported by twelve graceful pillars. Thence the descent is made to the well through three tiers of galleries running round the excavation below the surface of the ground. The stonework of these galleries is beautifully carved and embellished with incised texts in Sanskrit and Arabic. As an adjunct to this well is another adapted to the purpose of irrigation. Close by stand the tomb and mosque of Dada Hari, both presenting fine examples of decorative stonework.

About one hundred yards from Dada Hari's well is another, which evidently furnished the plan for the former. It is, however, very inferior in treatment, but much older; in fact, it is said to date from the time of Karan, when Ahmedábád was called Karanaváti.

Saraspur is a walled suburb of considerable extent, situated on the east side of the city. It contains a large Jain temple, which Aurangzeb maliciously defiled and damaged. After breaking the images, he converted it into a mosque.

Less than a mile from the Rájpur Gate is one of

Ekka or Bullock Cart

those enormous tanks which are to be found in various parts of India. This one has an area of over seventy acres. It is a regular polygon, of thirty-four sides, each one hundred and ninety feet in length. When first constructed by Sultán Kutab-ud-dín in 1451, the tank was surrounded by tiers of steps, with six approaches flanked by cupolas. In the centre was an island, with an exquisite garden and a pavilion.

A six-mile drive in a native cart, through patches of cultivation and across the river, will bring one to Sarkhej, surrounded by a dilapidated wall, in some places sixty feet high. Sarkhej was once an extremely beautiful city. Its principal buildings were designed by two brothers, Azam and Mozam, immigrants from Khorasan, who are interred here in an immense mausoleum.

Numerous royal personages repose in splendid tombs at Sarkhej, but perhaps the most magnificent mausoleum in the place, and certainly the largest in Gujarát, is that of Ganj Bakhsh, a renowned Muhammadan saint, and the spiritual adviser of the first Sultán Ahmad. The building has a huge central dome, surrounded by several smaller ones. Over the main entrance is an inscription in Persian, with the date 1473 A.D. The octagonal shrine has on every side fine brass lattice-work windows. The pavement is of many colored marbles harmoniously blended. From the centre of the richly gilt dome hangs a silver chain, which once touched the ground, but now hangs just beyond the reach of the outstretched hand of a tall man standing upon the tips of his toes.

Near by is the tomb of a saint even more venerated than Ganj Bakhsh; but he had not the advantage of an imperial patron, and so his remains are housed in an ugly little whitewashed building.

There is a tank, once highly decorated, which was constructed by one of the early rulers, and hard by the ruins of a splendid palace and harem. The tank is alive with men and women—and crocodiles; but the former bathe as unconcernedly as if the reptiles were muzzled.

A volume might be devoted to a description of the ancient remains in and about Ahmedábád—at Batwa, at Giramtha and the monastery of Pirana. Strangely enough, notwithstanding its accessibility, this extremely interesting city is generally neglected by travelers.

CHAPTER VIII.

PÁLITÁNA.

PÁLITÁNA is one of the numerous States, many of them hardly more than village communities, into which Kathíawar is divided. The Rájá has a comfortable income, and the town enjoys a considerable degree of prosperity from the constant coming and going of pilgrims, attracted by the "Holy Mountain," Satrunjaya. The road is crowded along its mile and a half of length with native carts, palanquins and pedestrians. From the foot of the hill the only practicable conveyance is the dúli—a seat hung on two poles and carried by four men—but the majority of the pilgrims must make the difficult ascent on foot. All the way along the route one passes them—men, women and children, of all castes and conditions—laboriously mounting, with the aid of staves, or resting beneath the trees which grow at intervals upon the hillside. The road—in some places a steep incline, in others a flight of steps—leads straight up to the top of the hill, past prayer shrines, little niches, two or three feet square, with marble floors, on which is cut the representation of the soles of two feet.

Towards the top stands a little temple, dedicated to Hanuman, the Monkey-god of the Hindus; and still a short way higher, the shrine of a Muhammadan saint.

The hill is composed of two flat ridges, each about three hundred and fifty yards long, with a valley between them. The temples range over all this space, and the whole is enclosed in massive walls. Each of the principal temples has its own enclosure again, with strong walls and gates, which are carefully closed at night, and every one jealously excluded. Within there is usually one large temple and a number of smaller ones.

"The grouping together of these temples into what may be called 'Cities of Temples' is a peculiarity which the Jains practiced to a greater extent than the followers of any other religion in India. The Buddhists grouped their stupas and viharas near and around sacred spots, as at Sanchi, Manikyala, or in Pesháwar, and elsewhere; but they were scattered, and each was supposed to have a special meaning, or to mark some sacred spot. The Hindus also grouped their temples, as at Bhuwaneshwar or Benares, in great numbers together; but in all cases because, so far as we know, these were the centres of a population who believed in the gods to whom the temples were dedicated, and wanted them for the purposes of their worship. Neither of these religions, however, possessed such a group of temples, for instance, as that at Satrunjaya, in Gujarát. It covered a very large space of ground, and its shrines are scattered by hundreds over the summits of two extensive hills and in the valley between them. The larger ones are situated in tuks, or separate enclosures, surrounded by high, fortified walls; the smaller ones line the silent streets. It is a city of the gods, and meant for them only, and not intended for the use of mortals.

"All the peculiarities of Jain architecture are found in a more marked degree at Pálitána than at almost any other known place, and, fortunately for the student of the style, extending through all the ages during which it flourished. Some of the temples are as old as the eleventh century, and they are spread pretty evenly over all the intervening time down to the present century." [1]

On every hand one is confronted with startling figures of monsters, or gigantic forms of elephants, horses, lions, in every conceivable phase of action. On frequent ceilings four large female heads appear in red paint. In every shrine are white images, covered with imitation gems, and each with a huge counterfeit diamond on its forehead. In striking contrast with the whiteness of the idols is the gaudy coloring of their surroundings. One hall is painted a vivid red over floor, ceiling and walls, with borders of yellow and green. A large temple contains fifty-two cells, and in each cell four images, the whole two hundred

[1] Fergusson.

and eight figures exactly alike, even to their ornaments. This endless repetition is a characteristic of Jain architecture, and here you see it in the sculptures and in the paintings, in form and subject, repeated again and again in wearying monotony.

The pilgrims, with their paltry offerings of rice or grain in little silken bags, move noiselessly between the avenues of temples, or prostrate themselves before some image, half obscured by clouds of incense, while a prayer-bell tolls with insistent regularity, or a priest chants in a nasal monotone.

As noon approaches, and the greatest heat of the day sets in, a strange stillness and silence steal over the place. The pigeons seek shady nooks in the buildings, the parrots leafy cover, while the votaries nod and doze in the temples, or in the shadows of their walls, or under trees. One almost imagines that he can hear the silvery Satrunji rippling over its bed to the south of the hill. As the shadows begin to lengthen toward the east, the descent commences, and by nightfall Satrunjaya is abandoned to the fourteen hundred and fifty-two gods of the Jain paradise, who frequent its temples when mortals are not about.

The site of the ancient city of Valabhipur is about fifteen miles from Pálitána. It was the capital of the Valabhi Rájás, who supplanted the Guptas about 300 A.D.; but Valabhipur was a great city, by another name, several hundred years before that date. The ground on which it stood is now covered by the modern town of Walat and by the jungle; but the ancient site may be traced by massive foundations of what must have been noble buildings; and coins, metal vessels, seals, images and other relics have been found upon the spot.

Old Junagadh lies in the shadow of the close-packed group of hills of which Girnar and Datar are the central points of interest, and on the border of the wild Gir, where game abounds and jungle fever is rife.

There is an ancient romance associated with Junagadh, which is thoroughly characteristic of the times. Many hundred years ago, when Ra Khengar ruled at Junagadh, there lived in the city a very beautiful maiden. Her name was Ranik Devi, and she was betrothed to Sidh Rájá of Patán. Ra Khengar was a man without principle, and he seized Ranik Devi and married her forcibly. Then Sidh Rájá brought an army against Ra Khengar, and took his fortress and slew him. But when Sidh Rájá would have married Ranik Devi, she refused, and committed satí. Now either she had learned to love Ra Khengar, or she considered it her duty in any case to follow him "through the flames." History fails to throw any light upon the mystery.

Sidh Rájá took her loss sorely to heart, and erected at Wadhwan city a beautiful temple to her memory. The temple stands to-day, much worn and weather-beaten, and near it is a satí stone bearing date 1519;

but that must commemorate another affair, for Ranik Devi's time was long before then.

Junagadh was an important fortress in the time of Asoka, and later when the Gupta kings ruled over this part of the country. The walls of the ancient citadel on the east side of the city have been raised at different times, until now they stand from sixty to seventy feet in height. In the fort is a cumbersome old ten-inch-bore cannon, which was brought from Diu, where it had been abandoned by the Turks. It bears the following inscription at the muzzle in Arabic characters: "The order to make this cannon, to be used in the service of the Almighty, was given by the Sultán of Arabia and Persia, Sultán Suláimán, son of Salím Khán. May his triumph be glorified to punish the enemies of the State and of the Faith, in the capital of Egypt, 1531."

Girnar, the sacred mountain, rears its head above the intervening peaks, and attains an altitude of over three thousand five hundred feet. It was held holy by the ancient Buddhists, and has attracted pilgrims since centuries before the Christian era.

The road which runs from the fort to Girnar passes one of the famous Asoka stones. It is a huge boulder, covered with inscriptions in Páli. These are the fourteen Buddhist edicts of the imperial convert. Temples are passed at intervals all along the way. One group upon the bank of a river is frequented by yogís as naked as on the days they were born.

The ascent to the temples is by no means easy. It may, however, be made in a dúli. For about two-thirds of the distance the way is somewhat roughly paved. There is a rest-house at each five hundred feet elevation, until a height of fifteen hundred feet above the plain has been reached. The next thousand feet is along a path which skirts the edge of the precipice, and is so narrow that the dúli bearers have hardly room to proceed. The scarped rock rises in a sheer wall two hundred or more feet above the footway. At the top of this wall, or cliff, on an extensive level, about six hundred feet from the summit of the mountain, stand sixteen temples. The largest of these is enclosed in a quadrangle about one hundred and ninety by one hundred and thirty feet, around which are ranged seventy cells, each holding a marble image. The temple is dedicated to Neminath, the Jain pontiff, and the shrine contains a large image of him in black marble, adorned with heavy gold chains and jewels.

Through a passage one gains a dark temple, with low roof supported by granite pillars. Opposite the entrance is an alcove, at the back of which a stone lion rears, surmounted by a crocodile. Passing behind the sculptured figures, one enters a small chamber, from which a descent is made into a cave containing a large white marble image. This idol is held in extreme veneration by the Jains, and the priests are not inclined to encourage infidels to visit its shrine.

A groove has been worn in the shoulder of the image by water dripping from its ear, so it is said, and hence they call the idol "Nectar-drop."

In another temple is a colossal figure of Rishabha Deva, the first of the tirthankars, or high priests. This image has been exactly duplicated at Satrunjaya. The platform upon which it is enthroned supports a large slab of stone, upon which are carved the figures of the twenty-four tirthankars.

On the summit of the mountain, which is reached by flights of steps cut in the rock, is the ancient temple of Amba Mata. It is a sort of honeymoon resort of Bráhmans. As soon as convenient after marriage the young couple, attended by their relatives of both sexes, come up to the shrine of the goddess. Here they make offerings, including the symbolic cocoanut, and go through a mystic ceremony, which is supposed to assure to them all that counts for marital bliss.

The Datar peak is considered sacred by Muhammadans as well as Hindus. Lepers repair to the hill for the sake of the curative properties which are believed to reside in the rock. Three or four miles away, in picturesque surroundings, stands the Datar Temple, and an asylum for lepers, the foundation stone of which was laid by the late Prince Albert Victor in 1890.

Verawal, on the Arabian Sea, is a very ancient seaport, and, until superseded by Surat, the most important in this part of the country. It reached its greatest prosperity under the Sultáns of Gujarát, and was for a long time the principal point of embarkation of Muhammadan pilgrims to Mecca. Verawal still commands a considerable carrying trade in connection with coasting vessels. It has a sea wall and a light, a custom house and a dock.

Much of the ancient prosperity of Verawal was doubtless derived from its relations with Patán Somnáth, which stands something less than three miles farther south upon the coast. Marco Polo, who had a critical eye for a seaport, mentions the latter place by the name of Semenat as a thriving mart of ocean trade, although an indifferent harbor. Hundreds of years before his visit—from the earliest times, indeed—ships had voyaged between Patán and the ports of the Red Sea, the Persian Gulf and the African coast. A result of that traffic is found in the neighboring Gir forest, which shelters two or three different communities of African negroes, and this is the only place in India where they exist, except as casual immigrants, or the descendants of such.

The expedition of Mahmúd of Ghazní against Patán and its celebrated temple of Somnáth marks the downfall of Hindu power in this quarter. The district is now in the hands of the Nawáb of Junagadh, and Verawal has eclipsed the city upon which, in olden times, it depended for its prosperity.

Within the walls of Patán are many ancient Hindu

and Muhammadan remains, the former merely traces of buildings which suffered the usual fate of Hindu structures at the hands of the Musalmán conquerors. There is a mosque which was erected shortly after Mahmúd's invasion. The Nawáb has assigned the revenues of three villages for its maintenance.

The Jamá Masjid, in the construction of which material from Hindu temples was used, has been abandoned these many years past, and now affords lodging to fishermen, who cure their fish where the faithful were wont to flock on Fridays when Patán was a wealthy capital.

The historic temple of Somnáth stands close to the sea, a mere neglected wreck. How much, if any, of the original structure exists it is impossible to say. Legend has it that the first temple was built by Somráj—hence the name—of gold; next of silver by Ravana; then of wood by Krishna, and lastly of stone by Bhinadwa. It was three times destroyed by the Muhammadans, and as many times rebuilt before 1706, when Aurangzeb ordered it to be torn down. This order was not carried out literally, but the place was reduced to ruins, and stripped of its marble and many of its sculptures.

When Mahmúd made his memorable invasion, with the avowed intention of overturning the god of Somnáth, the place was at the height of its glory. Its reputation was widespread, and pilgrimages were made to it from all parts of the country. Princes vied with one another in endowing it, and in this way it enjoyed the revenues of ten thousand villages. Two thousand priests were attached to the establishment, and its staff included five hundred dancing girls, three hundred musicians and as many barbers to shave the heads of pilgrims. The interior of the temple was magnificent in the extreme. Gold, silver and jewels abounded in the midst of the richest carvings. It is just possible that the wealth of Somnáth may have had as much to do as any religious motive toward actuating Mahmúd in his attack.

The temple was strongly fortified, and upon the approach of the invader the neighboring princes threw their forces into the place, and opposed the Túrkíman with a determination which he had little expected to encounter. The fighting was incessant for two days, and the slaughter immense. At length the surviving Rájputs, realizing that further resistance would be futile, took to their boats and abandoned the place.

There is a curious legend which attributes this invasion of Mahmúd to a certain woman, who was called the Mai Púri, or "Perfect Mother." She is buried in a building which stands outside the walls of Patán, upon the road to Verawal. The building, which has been converted into a mosque, was in ancient times a temple of the sun. It contains some beautiful carvings in an excellent state of preservation.

There is near the city another temple of the sun,

very ancient and much dilapidated, which was partially destroyed by Mahmúd almost a thousand years ago. Near by is a large tomb, and beneath it a subterranean temple.

The city contains a temple which was erected by the benevolent Ahalia Bai to take the place of the ancient temple of Somnáth. This building also stands over a curious underground temple, which is reached by a flight of steps, and has its roof supported by heavy stone pillars.

CHAPTER IX.

THE RÁJPUTS—MOUNT ABÚ, AJMÍR.

NINETEEN different native States, more or less independent — officially termed "protected" — with a population in excess of ten millions, go to make up Rájputána.

Harried by every Moslem invader, driven from pillar to post, often at the lowest ebb of distress, the hardy Rájput has, nevertheless, survived the wear and tear of foreign aggression better than any other race in India. He is to-day the finest representative of the Hindu people.

The Rájput has always been distinguished for chivalry, courage and honor. In the old days of strife and struggle he never failed to give a good account of himself, and either held his own or died in defence of it, like the born warrior that he is. His sole dependence was upon his own right hand and his good blade. Treachery and deceit were as foreign to his frank, generous nature as was diplomacy. Akbar knew him for a powerful friend and a fearful foe, and Jahángír learned the value of his goodwill; but Aurangzeb utterly missed the keynote to his character, and undid much of the good work of his predecessors.

A fair type of the race was that chief of Chitor who, in the Audience Hall, promptly avenged an insult by plunging his dagger into the heart of a Minister of State. Taxed with the yet more heinous offence of drawing in the presence of the Great Mughal, he answered, in almost the exact words of Roderic Dhu:

> "I right my wrongs where they are given,
> Though it were in the court of heaven."

The Rájput of to-day betrays his royal lineage and descent from a race of hardy fighters by his clear-cut features, small hands and feet, erect carriage, and fearless and self-possessed bearing. He is a lover of horses, a keen judge of their points, and has a seat like a centaur. The sporting instinct is strong in him. He is naturally a gambler, and often a great shikári. His excess of animal spirits, no longer finding the former strenuous vent for its expenditure, sometimes leads him into vices, which, however, are in general of the kind that harm none but himself.

These dull times of peace are not altogether favorable to the Rájput. His "occupation's gone," and it must be confessed that he is deteriorating. He is growing soft and indolent. He eats too much for a man every tradition of whose forebears is associated with active energy. He is not always wise in the matter of strong drink, and although he cannot probably assimilate as much of the drug as his grandfather could, he takes more opium.

Lord Elphinstone draws the following comparison between the Maráthá and the Rájput, the one a low-caste and the other a high-caste Hindu: "They (the Maráthás) are small, sturdy men, well made, though not handsome; they are all active, hardy, laborious and persevering. If they have none of the pride and dignity of the Rájputs, they have none of their indolence, or their want of worldly wisdom. A Rájput warrior, as long as he does not dishonor his race, seems almost indifferent to the result of any contest he is engaged in. A Maráthá thinks of nothing but the result, and cares little for the means, if he can attain his object. For this purpose he will strain his wits, renounce his pleasures and hazard his person; but he has not a conception of sacrificing his person, or even his interest, for a point of honor. This difference of sentiment affects the outward appearance of the two nations: there is something noble in the carriage of an ordinary Rájput, and something vulgar in that of the most distinguished Maráthá. The Rájput is the most worthy antagonist; the Maráthá the most formidable enemy; for he will not fail in boldness and enterprise when they are indispensable, and will always support them or supply their place by stratagem, activity and perseverance. All this applies chiefly to the soldiery, to whom more bad qualities might fairly be ascribed."

The reader who is inclined to learn the history of the Rájputs is recommended to read the "Annals of Rágásthán," that intensely interesting work by Colonel Tod, the first Resident of Rájputána.

In the old days the Rájputs were divided into clans, similar to those of the Scottish Highlanders. The name of the chief was borne by his followers, who were bound to him by the ties of kinship, hereditary allegiance and mutual interest. Under a sort of feudal system, each man held his land on condition of holding his sword constantly at the service of his chief. The chief's tenure of his territories was dependent upon a similar obligation to the prince. When, as not infrequently happened, a change of locality became necessary, new lands were assigned to the clans, in proportion to the number of fighting men in their ranks. They traced their ancestry

> "From times when forth from the sunlight the first of their kings came down,
> And had the earth for his footstool, and wore the stars for his crown."

For the rest they made their own fortunes, and carved out for themselves kingdoms with their swords. When the pressure of present boundaries became irksome, the chief gave a younger son a horse and lance and sent him forth to find fresh fields for occupation.

The Rájput was not the creature of the land: he took it, and made it what it became. It did not give him a name, but he gave to it his. His title of nobility was not derived from the soil, but from the blood in his veins. Every family has "its genealogical tree, describing the essential peculiarities, religious tenets, and pristine locale of the clan, and there is scarcely a chief of character for knowledge who cannot repeat the genealogy of his line. . . . The poorest Rájput of this day retains all the pride of ancestry—often his sole inheritance." His daughters were fit brides for emperors, but he did not deem all emperors fit husbands for his daughters. Indeed, the difficulty in finding suitable mates for them, and of dowering them consistently with their birth, lay at the bottom of the practice of female infanticide. It was this pride of caste that nerved the Rájput to commit johur when driven into a corner. He never gave a conqueror the satisfaction of drafting his women into a Moslem seraglio. When his flag fell, it fell into the flames. And the Rájput women were no less brave than their men; they submitted to johur or mounted the funeral pyre with stoical firmness, and even alacrity. Tod chronicles their deeds of heroism and feats of arms.

There was that princess of Kanauj, who, after defending five fortresses in succession against the Moslem invader, at last fell into his hands. He had heard of her beauty, and had proof of her bravery, and so offered her freedom and marriage. There was no alternative but to assent. The Muhammadan general was summoned to the presence of the princess. "Robed in the marriage garb presented to him by the Queen, with a necklace, an aigrette of superb jewels from the coffers of Ganore, he hastened to obey the mandate, and found that fame had not done justice to her charms. He was directed to be seated, and in conversation, full of rapture on his side, hours were as minutes while he gazed on the beauty of the Queen. But presently his countenance fell—he complained of heat; punkahs and water were brought, but they availed him not, and he began to tear the bridal garments from his frame, when the Queen thus addressed him, 'Know Khán, that your last hour has come; our wedding and our deaths shall be sealed together. The vestments which cover you are poisoned; you left me no other expedient to escape pollution.' While all were horror-struck by this declaration, she sprung from the battlements into the flood beneath. The Khán died in extreme torture, and was buried on the road to Bhopal."

When Ajit Singh of Marwar was murdered, "they placed his body in a boat and carried him to the pyre made of sandal wood and perfumes, with heaps of cotton, oil and camphor. The Nazír went to the Queen's Palace, and as he pronounced the words, 'Rao Sidaöe,'[1] the Chohaní Queen, with sixteen damsels in her suite, came forth. 'This day,' said

[1] "The King is dead."

she, 'is one of joy; my race shall be illustrated; our lives have passed together, how then can I leave him?' Of noble race was the Bhattiani Queen. She put up a prayer to the Lord who wields the discus (Krishna). 'With joy I accompany my lord; that my fealty (satí) may be accepted rests with Thee.' In like manner did Mirgaváti, the Gazelle of Derawul, and the Tuar Queen of pure blood, the Chaora Ráni and her of Shekhaváti invoke the name of Hari as they determined to join their lord. For these six queens death had no terror, but they were the affianced wives of their lords; the curtain wives of affection, to the number of fifty-eight, determined to offer themselves a sacrifice to Agni (the fire). 'Such an opportunity,' said they, 'can never occur.' While thus each spoke, Nathoo, the Nazír, thus addressed them:

"'This is no amusement; the sandal wood you now anoint with is cool; but will your resolution abide when you remove it with the flames of Agni? When this scorches your tender frames, your hearts may fail, and the desire to recede will disgrace your lord's memory. Reflect, and remain where you are. You have lived like Indrani (the Queen of Heaven), nursed in softness, amidst flowers and perfumes; the winds of heaven never offended you, far less the flames of fire.' But to all his arguments they replied, 'The world we will abandon, but never our lord.' They performed their ablutions, decked themselves in their gayest attire, and for the last time made obeisance to their lord in his car. The drum sounded; the funeral train moved on; all invoked the name of Hari.[1] The countenances of the Queens were as radiant as the sun. They mounted the pyre, and as the smoke, emitted from the house of flame, ascended to the sky, the assembled multitude shouted, 'Khaman! Khaman!' (Well done! Well done!)

"The pile flamed like a volcano; the faithful Queens laved their bodies in the flames, as do the celestials in the lake Mansurwar.[2] They sacrificed their bodies to their lord, and illustrated the race whence they sprang."

Mount Abú, "which rises with its gems of architecture like a jeweled island from the Rájputána plains," is one of those lovely and commanding sites usually chosen by the Jains for the erection of their principal temples. This solitary outpost of the Arávalli Hills, from which it is divided by a valley fifteen miles in length, rises in the form of a plateau to a height of four thousand six hundred feet above the land level. The plateau is about fourteen miles long and four in breadth. There is a civil and military station here, and it is the headquarters of the Resident of Rájputána.

Comfortable villas surround an artificial lake, in which are several little wooded islands. A pass is

[1] Hari Krishna, the mediator, who is always invoked in funeral rites.

[2] The sacred lake of Tibet.

Interior of Dilwara Temple—Mount Abu

required of all visitors to the temples. This precaution is rendered necessary by the vandalism of that class of tourists whose insatiable thirst for "souvenirs" does not stop short of any form of pillage or desecration.

The white marble buildings of the Dilwarra Temples make a lovely picture in their setting of dark green trees, surrounded by yellow fields of grain. The marble was brought from a distance, and the great blocks could only have been dragged up the mountain-side at the cost of infinite labor. The temples have been sadly ill-used. The depredations of curiosity hunters have been followed by very bad restoration, as usual in India. Nevertheless, they are very beautiful to-day and, as Fergusson says, "for minute delicacy of carving and beauty of detail stand almost unrivaled, even in the land of patient and lavish labor." Walls, roofs, columns—every foot of the surface marble is profusely carved in various reliefs, and with the greatest variety of subjects; pictured scenes from the lives of the saints, animals, flowers and conventional designs.

Sculptured rishis sit in niches along the cloister of the temple built by the brothers Tejahpule and Vastupala. Of the two buildings this is the richer in ornamentation. It was erected between 1197 and 1247 A.D., the work occupying fourteen years. The building is said to have cost eighteen millions of rupees, irrespective of five and a half millions spent on leveling the ground.

Referring to the other temple, which was erected about 1032 A.D., Fergusson says, "It is simpler and bolder, though still as elaborate as good taste would allow in any purely architectural object. Being one of the oldest as well as one of the most complete examples known of a Jain temple, its peculiarities form a convenient introduction to the style, and serve to illustrate how complete and perfect it had already become when we first meet with it in India."

The principal object here, as elsewhere, is a cell, lighted only from the door, containing a cross-legged seated figure of the saint to whom the temple is dedicated, in this instance Parawanatha. The cell terminates upwards in a sikra, or pyramidal spire-like roof, which is common to all Hindu and Jain temples of the age in the north of India. To this is attached a portico composed of forty-eight free-standing pillars, and the whole is enclosed in an oblong courtyard about one hundred and forty feet by ninety feet, surrounded by a double colonnade of smaller pillars, forming porticos to a range of fifty-five cells, which enclose it on all sides, exactly as they do in Buddhist viharas. In this case, however, each cell, instead of being the residence of a monk, is occupied by one of those cross-legged images, which belong alike to Buddhism and Jainism. Here they are, according to the Jain practice, all repetitions of the same image of

Parawanatha, and over the door of each cell, or on its jambs, are sculptured scenes from his life. The long beams, stretching from pillar to pillar, supporting the roof, are relieved by curious angular struts of white marble, springing from the middle of the pillar up to the middle of the beam.

Four or five miles beyond Dilwarra, upon higher ground, are other temples, and all around upon the mountain slopes and on the adjacent plain still others, some very beautiful and all interesting.

Ajmír is an isolated little British district entirely surrounded by the Rájput States. It was ceded to the English by Sindhia in 1818. Ajmír occupies the crest of the great Rájputána water-shed. The rain which falls upon its summit runs off in one direction to the Bay of Bengal, and in the other to the Gulf of Cutch.

The city stands in the centre of a plateau, the highest level in the plains of Hindustán, and, from the circle of hills which hem it in, the country slopes away in every direction toward the river valleys on the east, west and south, and the desert plain on the north. The city lies at the foot of the picturesque rocky fort-crowned hill of Táragarh, which rises to a height of three thousand feet above sea level.

Tradition attributes the foundation of Ajmír to the Rájá Aja, a Chohán Rájput, about the year 154 A.D. Aja at first attempted to build his city on the Nágpahár, or Serpent Hill, three miles to the west of the present site, where the traces of early operations are pointed out to-day, but some evil genius destroyed each night the work of the preceding day; and after his walls had thus been thrown down a score or two of times, the rájá came to the conclusion that the gods opposed his enterprise. When the operations were transferred to Táragarh, the building of the fort progressed without obstruction. In the valley below he laid out a city which he named Ajmír after himself.

Having done so much, and seeing everything in his territory in good order, he went up to a mountain about ten miles distant to pass the rest of his life in seclusion. A temple marks the spot on which stood his hermitage and where he died.

About five hundred years later the Chohán ruler of Ajmír involved his State, which appears to have been getting along very well in the occupation of minding its own business, in the Hindu alliance against the Arab Muhammad Kásim. This action was disastrous. The Rájá and a great many of his people were killed. The lesson seems to have been salutary; for, during several centuries, the isolated little State appears to have been at peace.

In 1024 Mahmúd took the route, by ill chance, of Ajmír on his way to Somnáth. He sacked Ajmír, destroying, as was his avowed mission, the gods and temples. The people found refuge in the fort, and, as Mahmúd had not the leisure for a siege, he had to forego the pleasure of cutting their throats, and to proceed on his way to Gujarát. He promised to attend to the Ajmírís on his return, but, fortunately for them, he lost his way in the desert.

This was the opportunity of the Rájputs of Ajmír, and they did not neglect it. They hung upon the flanks of the conqueror's army, and killed thousands, while thousands more perished of thirst. The guides, who had misled Mahmúd, exultantly confessed that they had avenged Somnáth, and gloried in their death by torture.

Akbar annexed the territory, and afterwards made annual visits to the shrine of the Ajmír Chisti. Some of these pilgrimages were made on foot, from Agra and other places. So frequently did the Emperor travel the road from Futtehpur-Sikri that he had milestones erected along its length. Many of these kos minárs are still standing.

In 1615 that "crack-brained Englishman," Tom Coryat, arrived in Ajmír, having tramped from Jerusalem, through Asiatic Turkey, Persia and Afghánistán, at a cost of a penny a day. Being taken for a madman wherever he went, none molested him. Some time later he died at Surat, from an excess of native liquor, and was buried near the city.

After months of wearisome delays, Sir Thomas Roe, the English Ambassador, was admitted to audience by Jahángír, in Ajmír, early in 1616. Roe likens the Durbar Hall to a London theatre. On a platform, corresponding to the stage, were the Padi-sháh, upon his throne, and the grandees standing before him like actors. They were railed off in three rows, according to their respective ranks. Beyond the outmost rail the common people crowded, representing the audience.

It was intimated to Roe that he must prostrate himself before the potentate; but he flatly refused to do so, and a compromise was made upon a profound bow.

Roe describes Jahángír as wearing a "swoord and buckler, set all ouer with great Diamondes and rubys, the belts of gold suteable," and a "quiuer with 30 arrowes and his bow in a Case, the same that was presented to him by the Persian Ambassador. On his head he wore a rich Turbant, with a plume of herne tops, not many but long; on one side hung a ruby unsett, as big as a Walnutt; on the other side a diamond as great; in the middle an emralld like a hart, much bigger. His shash was wreathed about with a Chayne of great Pearle, rubys, and diamondes driled. About his Neck he carried a Chaine of most excellent Pearle, three double—so great I neuer saw; at his Elbowes, Armlettes sett with diamondes; and on his wristses three rowes of seuerall sorts. His hands bare, but almost on euery finger a ring; his gloves, which were english, stuck under his Girdle; his Coate of Cloth of gould without sleeus upon a fine Semian as thin as Lawne; on his feet a payre of embrodered buskings with Pearle, the toes sharp and turning vp. Thus armed and accomodated hee went to the Coach, which attended him, with his New English seruant, who was Clothed as rich as any Player and more gaudy, and had trayned four horses, which were trapped and harnessed in gould veluetts. This was the first hee euer sate in, and was made by that sent from England, so like that I knew it not but for the Couer, which was a gould Persian velvett. Hee gott into the end; on each syde went two Eunuchs that carried small maces of gould sett all ouer with rubys, with a long bunch of white horse tayle to drive away flyes; before him went drumes, ill trumpettes, and loud musiqe, and many Canopys, quittasolls and other strange ensignes of Majestie, of Cloth of gould sett in many Places with great rubyes. Nine spare horses, the furniture some garnished with rubyes, some with Pearle and emraldes, some only with studdes enameld. The Persian Ambassador presented him a horse. Next behind came thrae Palenkees; the Carriages and feete of one Plated with gould sett at the endes with stones and couered with Crimson velvett embrodered with Pearle, and a frengg of great Pearls hanging in ropes a foote deepe, a border about sett with rubyes and emeralldes. A footman carried a foote stoole of gould sett with stones. The other two were couered and lyned only with Cloth of gould. Next followed the English Coach, newly couered and trimed rich, which hee had given the queene Normahall, who rode in yt. After them a third, of this country fashion, which me thought was out of Countenance; in that sate his younger sonns. After followed about 20 Eliphantes royall spare for his owne ascending, so rich that in stones and furniture they braved the sunne. Euery Eliphant had diuers flages of Cloth of siluer, guilt satten and taffeta. His noblemen hee suffered to walke afoot, which I did to the gate and left him. His wives on their eliphantes were carried like Parrakitoes half a mile behynde him."

Akbar and Jahángír treated the Rájputs as honorable allies rather than as defeated foes, and by a wise policy of conciliation gradually overcame their hostility. Thus, when Umra Singh, who had long withstood the Mughal, intimated his willingness to treat with him, Jahángír, as he states in his "Memoirs," "forgave the Rána, and sent a friendly firman, that he might rest assured of my protection and care, and imprinted thereon, as a solemn testimony of my sincerity, my 'five fingers.' I also wrote my son, by any means by which it could be brought about, to treat this illustrious one according to my wishes."

Having secured peace to his territory, Umra, like Rájá Aja, abdicated, and went up into the seclusion of the hills, and there remained until the time came "to have his ashes deposited with those of his fathers."

When the impolitic fanatic Aurangzeb ascended the musnud, he immediately instituted a series of persecutions, which aroused the Rájputs, with whom he was soon at war.

The successor of Aurangzeb acknowledged the virtual independence of Udaipur, Marwar and Jaipur, and Ajit Singh, the Rájá of Marwar, gave the Emperor a daughter in marriage. Ajit Singh took advantage of the disorder which followed the death of the Sayids, to seize Ajmír and throw off his allegiance to the throne of Delhi. For a time all went well with him, and "the records were always moist with inserting fresh conquests;" but Muhammad Sháh, having secured himself in his position, came down on Ajmír with a great army, and Ajit Singh was glad to come to terms with the Emperor.

Soon afterwards Ajit was slain with his own sword by his son Bukht Singh, at the instigation of his elder brother Abhe. When the mother of Bukht and Abhe ascended the funeral pyre of their father, she uttered the terrible anathema, "May the bones of his murderer be consumed out of Maroo!" and the curse bore fruit in the internecine conflict which broke out in the family on the death of Abhe Singh. His son, Rám Singh, not content with the ráj he had inherited, attempted to seize that of his uncle Bukht. Rám Singh was defeated in a fierce fight, but he secured the aid of Jai Appa Sindhia and returned to the attack. Bukht Singh encamped near Ajmír, prepared to contest the advance of the allies, but treachery was to rob him of the satisfaction of meeting his foes in open combat. The aid of a niece was secured, and Rájá Bukht was disposed of by a subtle method which appears to have been in favor with the Hindus at that time. "A poisoned robe was the medium of revenge." When he realized that the end was at hand, the rájá, "with perfect composure, ordered his chiefs to assemble in his tent; and having recommended to their protection, and received their promise of defending the rights of his son, he summoned the ministers of religion into his presence. The last gifts to the church, and these, her organs, were prepared; but, with all his firmness, the anathema of the Satís, as they ascended the funeral pyre on which his hand had stretched his father, came into his mind; and as he repeated the ejaculation, 'May your corpse be consumed in a foreign land!' he remembered he was then on the border. The images which crossed his mental vision it is vain to surmise; he expired as he uttered these words; and over his remains, which were burnt on the spot, a cenotaph was erected, and is still called Booro Dewul, the 'Shrine of Evil.'"

The chiefs of Marwar followed Bíji Singh to the plain of Mairta, where the year before his father had put Rám Singh to flight; but fickle Fortune gave her wheel a turn, and "the Lord of Marwar, who on that morning commanded the lives of one hundred thousand Rájputs, was indebted for his safety to the mean conveyance of a cart and pair of oxen." But the chiefs of Marwar rallied and maintained the struggle, contriving the death of Jai Appa, which metaphorically clipped the wings of Rám Singh. In the end the Maráthás got possession of the district of Ajmír, "which, placed in the very heart of these regions, may be called the key to Rájpootana," and they kept their footing until in 1818 they ceded the territory to the British in exchange for other lands.

Passing over Akbar's Palace and the mosque built by Altamsh, or his successor, both notable examples of Muhammadan architecture, we will briefly notice the Dargah, which is the most interesting building in Ajmír. This shrine is held in extreme veneration by Hindus and Muhammadans. It is the burial place of Khwajah Múin-ud-dín, who died in 1235 A.D. He was one of the celebrated Chisti family of courtier-saints, the members of which are buried in widely scattered parts of the country.

Having donned over-socks, one passes through a lofty gateway to a courtyard. The saint's tomb, a square, white marble building, with a dome, is entered through a silver arch. Near by are the tombs of the saint's daughter and a daughter of Sháh Jahán. A Christian is not permitted to approach within twenty yards of these sacred spots.

The Dargah is the centre of an annual pilgrimage which attracts twenty thousand or more devotees. The Deg Feast is a peculiar and ancient institution associated with this festival. The "great" and "little" degs are huge cauldrons, one twice the size of the other, which stand in the courtyard. The Deg Feast is at the expense of one or another of the pilgrims. The cost of sufficient rice, raisins, sugar, butter, spice and the rest to fill the larger kettle is one thousand dollars. The enormous pudding is cooked by means of a furnace beneath the vessel. Eight earthen pots of the decoction are set aside for the foreign pilgrims, after which the people of Indrakot exercise their hereditary privilege of scrambling for the remainder of the boiling mess. The Indrakotís, who are swaddled in bandages, tumble into the pot when it is nearly empty and scrape it clean. Burns and other injuries are numerous, but the fact that no lives are lost is attributed to the miraculous interposition of the saint.

CHAPTER X.

JODHPUR, AMBER, JAIPUR.

JODHPUR'S Fort, standing upon a bare, scarped rock full three hundred feet above the city, will hold the eye of the traveler approaching from any direction for miles before the place is reached.

The old capital of Marwar was at Mandor, three miles to the north, and there are the sombre chattris of the old rájás, marking the spots where their funeral pyres were laid. It is difficult to imagine what induced Ráo Jodha to transfer his capital to the city round the rock, for there was no water in the vicinity worth mentioning. For five hundred years, and until comparatively recently, the tanks would run dry in the hot weather, and then at sundown of each evening the women would troop out to Mandor, with chatties on their heads, to fetch the next day's supply of water. About thirty years ago an English engineer relieved the city of its plight, and now there are tanks fresh fed from the hills, and the water is piped even to the Fort.

The city lies round the foot of the rock, surrounded by a six-mile wall, but quite defenceless. The Fort, on the other hand, is the picture of strength. The summit of the rock is guarded by strong walls, and is accessible only by a zigzag road, with massive fortified gateways at intervals. A formidable place to storm, but what if the water supply were cut off from the outside?

The Palace occupies a large portion of the Fort. It stands at the edge of the rock where it drops down one hundred and twenty feet in a sheer precipice. Like most old Indian palaces, it is a collection of buildings erected at different times, as a consequence of the religious prohibition against a rájá occupying the apartments of a deceased predecessor. Each of Ráo Jodha's successors built solidly and lavishly, so that the Palace as it stands might serve as a citadel of considerable extent.

The Mahárájá's Treasury and his Stables are the two chief points of interest. The former contains one of the finest collections of jewels in India, and the stud is probably the first in the country in the point of numbers and quality. The Mahárájá affects English customs to a considerable extent. He is a sportsman, preserves his pigs and sticks them.

Marwar is one of the many native States which have thriven under the British rule. Despite the difficulties of cultivation, the country yields an ample revenue, and has a large surplus, where not many years ago it had a very much larger deficit. This result is largely due to the splendid management of the Prime Minister, Sir Pertab Singh, assisted by one or two English civil servants.

A cadet of the house of Jodhpur rules over the desert State of Bikanír, where water cannot be got at much less than two hundred feet below the surface, and cultivation is not to be thought of. The Mahárájá of Bikanír is a young man, tall, handsome and of fair complexion. He is a major in the British Indian Army, and is very popular in military circles.

Sambhar Lake is situated on the borders of the Jodhpur and Jaipur States, in the midst of an arid and barren country. It is about twenty miles long and five miles in breadth.

The lake yields about four hundred tons of salt annually. The water, which is very shallow, dries up in the hot weather, leaving a crust of salt at the bottom. This is gathered by women with baskets, and, after the process of extraction and concentration, is shipped to various parts of the country. In 1870 the British Government leased the lake, which had been worked by the native States for two hundred years or more previously.

The salt question was at one time a bone of contention between the Government and the Mahárájá of Jodhpur. Lord Lytton, anxious to come to an agreement, invited Rám Singh to Simla, intending to discuss the matter with him. When they met, the Viceroy grasped the Mahárájá's hand, with the greatest show of friendliness, saying, "Now, Mahárájá, if there is *anything* I can do for you, don't hesitate to let me know." "There *is* one thing," answered Rám Singh, with equal suavity; "please don't mention the word salt."

Amber, the "Queen of the Pass," is set in the crutch of a rocky gorge, where it stood early enough for Ptolemy to make mention of it. It was founded by the ancient race of Mynas, and passed through many hands before it fell into those of the Rájput in 1037.

The Man Singh of Akbar's time, who did much to improve Amber, was followed by two chiefs of little or no account. It might have fared badly with the ráj under a succession of such rulers but for the intervention of Jodha Bai, the Rájput wife of Jahángír, who persuaded the Emperor to give the principality of Amber to the young Mirza Rájá, a grand-nephew of Man Singh. Under him Amber reached the height of its prosperity. He erected many fine buildings, laid out gardens, and constructed forts and fortifications.

Mirza Rájá attained to great power and a high military command under the Mughal Emperors; but Aurangzeb became jealous of his growing influence, and, so Tod says, induced his younger son to murder him. At any rate, Mirza Singh died in 1608, and from that time the ráj of Amber began to decline, and continued to do so until Siwai Jai Singh mounted the musnud, thirty years later.

Jai Singh deserted the capital of his ancestors and

built a new city, five or six miles away, on the borders of a lake, within a circle of low, red hills. Since then Amber has been forsaken; but, although the ravages of decay and the onslaughts of jungly vegetation are plainly visible about the city, the Palace is in a state of remarkable preservation, having been cared for and repaired by the successive rulers of Jaipur.

Above all is the old fort, connected with the Palace, four hundred feet lower down the hillside. Man Singh began the latter building three hundred years ago, upon a well-chosen site. The houses of the city lie round about and below the splendid piles, whose walls are reflected in the waters of the lake.

The early Rájput built nobly and with a free hand. Here are beauty, strength and ornament in plenty; magnificent gateways, spacious courtyards, pillared halls, latticed galleries, carved marble and ivory inlay, temples, pavilions, gardens, fountains, corridors and colonnades.

The Hall of Victory is beautified by the enamel-work for which Jaipur is renowned to this day; its alabaster panels are finished with delicate inlay, or carved into floral designs in high relief. Hence a passageway leads to the bathing-rooms of cream-white marble. Near by another hall, "which literally glows with bright and tender colors, and exquisite inlaid work, and looks through arches of carved alabaster and clusters of slender columns upon the sleeping lake and the silent mountains."

Truly the "Kings who took their pleasure in that now desolate pile made all their eyes rested upon royal and superb."

The road to Jaipur passes along a range of fortified hills, reminders of the stirring days when Rájputána was "the cock-pit of India." From the slope of one of the hills starts the word "Welcome," in huge letters formed of white stones. A reminiscence this of the visit of King Edward in 1876; but also a true index of Jaipur's attitude toward strangers. The city is encompassed by a crenelated wall of heavy masonry, with seven gates. The Palace is a small town in itself, and occupies one-seventh of the entire area within the walls. It is enclosed by a high battlemented wall, within which are many scattering buildings, set in beautiful gardens. The central point of the Palace, and, indeed, of the city, is the Chandra Mahál, from the topmost of whose seven stories a panoramic view of Jaipur and the surrounding country may be had.

The most modern buildings are those occupied by the present Mahárájá and his household. They are chiefly remarkable for the incongruity produced by the European furnishings and ornaments.

That remarkable combination of literateur, scientist and statesman, Jai Singh, fittingly erected the largest and most extensive of his observatories in his own capital. Others he built at Benares, Mathura, Delhi and Ujjain, "and their results were so correct as to astonish the most learned. He had previously used such instruments as those of Ulug Beg (the Royal Astronomer of Samarkand), which failed to answer his expectations. From the observations of seven years at the various observatories, he constructed a set of tables. While thus engaged, he learned through a Portuguese missionary, Padre Manuel, the progress which his favorite pursuit was making in Portugal, and he sent 'several skillful persons along with him' to the Court of Emanuel. The King of Portugal despatched Xavier de Silva, who communicated to the Rájpoot the tables of De la Hire." Referring to these tables, Jai Singh writes: "On examining and comparing the calculations of these tables with actual observation, it appeared that there was an error in the former, in assigning the moon's place, of half a degree. Although the error in the other planets was not so great, yet the times of solar and lunar eclipses he" [Jai Singh refers to himself] "found to come out earlier or later than the truth by the fourth part of a ghurry, or fifteen puls (six minutes of time)."

Here, in an open courtyard, are dials, gnomons, quadrants and other instruments designed by the royal astronomer, and used by him in the calculations and discoveries which were the wonder of his contemporaries, and have excited the admiration of modern scholars.

The present Mahárájá has recently had much

needed restoration carried out in the Observatory, and the place now bears a close resemblance to its original appearance.

The famous Hall of the Winds—an architectural fantasy—is also a production of Jai Singh. It fronts upon a broad thoroughfare, which forms a portion of the open space surrounding the Palace. The building is "of a singularly vivid rose color, rising in the form of a pyramid, bristling with a nine-storied façade composed of a hundred bell-turrets and sixty-five projecting windows, adorned with colonettes and balconies, pierced in openwork with countless flowers cut out of the stone—a vapory, impossible construction."

The first impression of Jaipur is that of a strange mixture of the old and new, of the Eastern and Western, and the more one sees of the city, the more deeply this impression is borne in on one. In the Palace, Jai Singh's Observatory is in close proximity to a modern printing plant, and an up-to-date Clock Tower stands beside an old-time Armory. In the city the streets are flanked by arched and tinted houses distinctly Hindu in style and architecture, but they run broad and straight at right angles, forming regular blocks such as we have in American cities.

The principal thoroughfares are over one hundred feet wide, paved and lighted by gas, and peopled by a brightly-clad crowd of natives, with scarce a white face among them. In one quarter a large hydraulic

The Palace—Jaipur

cotton press is kept profitably at work; in another men are engaged in the ancient way at the ancient industry of enameling.

"The houses, all of a pale pink or violet color, ornamented with paintings, look well in the bright sunshine, but we miss the gloom and shadow, the mystery and romance, of an Oriental city. The wide spaces, filled with a white and red crowd, present a gay scene, but it is merely spectacular. The Rájpoot cavaliers on their fine horses, the bullock carts, the palanquins, the camels, the donkeys, the richly caparisoned elephants making their way through the throng, merely seem to be passing over a stage. The houses, pierced with small windows filled in with slabs of perforated stone, are mere scenery—mud walls made to look like houses, and painted pink."

Outside the city walls is a splendid garden—one of the finest in India—which was laid out at a great expense, and which costs thirty thousand rupees a year to maintain. In the centre of the garden is the Albert Hall, containing a model museum. There are a hospital, a church, a school of art, a college, and, in contrast with these, the cenotaphs of passed rájás, marking the sites of satís.

In the early part of the nineteenth century the Mahárájá was a minor, and his mother a profligate. The actual control of affairs was in the hands of Jota Rámá, the paramour of the Rání. She died in 1833, and soon afterwards Jota Rámá poisoned the young Mahárájá. The British Government then installed an Agent, but Jota Rámá was still at large. "The Agent's life was attempted, and his assistant was murdered." The murderers were executed, and vigorous measures were taken to lift Jaipur out of the slough of misrule and corruption into which it had fallen.

It is now one of the most prosperous and advanced of the native States. Its sanitary conditions are good; its commerce is thriving, and its people are contented. These things, while they could not have been brought about without the countenance of the ruler, are due for their design and execution to three or four energetic Englishmen, who have at different times been connected with the State. Without witnessing the results, it is difficult to realize how much may be done, and often has been done, by one man towards the betterment of a province. But, seeing the splendid work accomplished in the face of the greatest difficulties, and sometimes under heart-breaking conditions, one is filled with admiration for the splendid men who compose that unique body—the Indian Civil Service. Kipling, who knew them well, has this to say of them:

"In the middle of all this bustle of reform, planned, achieved, frustrated, and replanned, and the never-ending underground warfare that surges in a Native State, move the English officers—that irreducible minimum of exiles.

"As a caste, the working Englishmen in Native States are curiously interesting. In the first place, they are, they must be, the fittest who have survived; for though, here and there, you shall find one chafing bitterly against the burden of his life in the wilderness—one to be pitied more than any chained beast—the bulk of the caste are honestly and unaffectedly fond of their work, fond of the country around them, and fond of the people they deal with. In each State their answer to a question is the same. The men with whom they are in contact are 'all right' when you know them; but 'you've got to know them first,' as the music-hall song says. Their hands are full of work—so full that, when the incult wanderer says, 'What do you find to do?' they look upon him with contempt and amusement. And it seemed to him that in one respect their lives were a good deal more restful and concentrated than those of their brethren under the British Government. There was no talk of shiftings and transfers and promotions, stretching across a Province and a half, and no man said anything about Simla.

"To one who has hitherto believed that Simla is the hub of the Empire, it is disconcerting to hear, 'Oh, Simla! That's where you Bengalís go. We haven't anything to do with Simla down here.' And no more they have. Their task and their interests run in the boundaries of the States they serve, and, most striking of all, the gossipy element seems to be cut altogether.

It is a backwater of the river of Anglo-Indian life—or is it the main current, the broad stream that supplies the motive power, and is the other life only the noisy ripple on the surface?

"Much can be learnt from the talk of the caste—many curious, many amusing and some startling things. One hears stories of men who take a poor, impoverished State as a man takes a wife, 'for better or worse,' and, moved by some incomprehensible ideal of virtue, consecrate—that is not too big a word—consecrate their lives to that State in all single-heartedness and purity. Such men are few, but they exist to-day, and their names are great in lands where no Englishman travels. Again the listener hears tales of grizzled diplomats of Rájputána—Machiavellis who have hoisted a powerful intriguer with his own intrigue, and bested priestly cunning, and the guile of the Oswal, simply that the way might be clear for some scheme which should put money into a tottering Treasury, or lighten the taxation of a few hundred thousand men—or both; for this can be done. One tithe of that force spent in their own personal advancement would have carried such men very far.

"Truly the Hat-marked Caste are a strange people. They are so few and so lonely and so strong! They can sit down in one place for years, and see the works of their hands and the promptings of their brain grow to actual and beneficent life, bringing good to thousands. Less fettered than the direct servant of the Indian Government, and working over a much vaster charge, they seem a bigger and a more large-minded breed; and that is saying a good deal. But let the others, the little people, bound down and supervised, and strictly limited and income-taxed, always remember that the Hat-marked are very badly off for shops. If they want a necktie, they must get it up from Bombay, and in the rains they can hardly move about; and they have no amusements, and must go a day's railway journey for a rubber, and their drinking-water is doubtful; and there is less than one white woman per ten thousand square miles."

CHAPTER XI.

CHITOR, UDAIPUR.

CHITOR was the heart of the Rájput confederation of States, and its Rána the suzerain prince of Rájputána. He was the direct descendant of Rámá, the great ancestor of the "Children of the Sun," and of the ancient sovereigns of Ayodhyá and Kanauj. When the Túrk, or Pathán, or Mughal designed to deal a death-blow to the power of the Rájput, Chitor was the point at which it was aimed. Many are the scenes of siege and sack and massacre which have been enacted upon the grim rock, for in the days of Chitor's supremacy the city was within the Fort, and only grass-cutters and water-carriers lived without the walls.

The three miles and more of isolated rock, with hardly half a mile of breadth, rising four hundred feet above the plain, looks like an enormous coffin—appropriately enough when one thinks of the history of the place. Such a site could never escape the eye of a warrior, and so tradition has the support of reason in asserting that this was a fortified place from the beginning of time. One of the first of its early rulers of whom we have any trace was Allují, who, some time in the eleventh century, built the Jain tower, which is a conspicuous object in the landscape to-day.

When Prithvi Rájá, the last of the Hindu Emperors, was defeated by Muhammad of Ghor, his kinsman Samar Singh of Chitor lost his life. The Ráni committed satí, but another wife girt on her dead lord's sword, and led his people against Kutab-ud-dín, whom she defeated. Then followed a hundred and fifty years of far from peaceful time for Chitor, and afterwards Alá-ud-dín Khiljí, the Pathán Emperor, swept the country to the Dekkan. "In those days—and these things are confusedly set down as having happened at the end of the thirteenth century—a relative of Rána Lakhsman Singh, the then Rána of Chitor, had married a Rájput princess of Ceylon, Pudmini, 'and she was fairest of all flesh on earth.' Her fame was sung through the land by the poets, and she became, in some sort, the Helen of Chitor. Alá-ud-dín heard of her beauty, and promptly besieged the Fort. When he found his enterprise too difficult, he prayed that he might be permitted to see Pudmini's face in a mirror, and this wish, so says the tale, was granted. Knowing that the Rájput was a gentleman, he entered Chitor almost unarmed, saw the face in the mirror, and was well treated; the husband of the fair Pudmini accompanying him in return, to the camp at the foot of the hill. Like Rájá Runjeet, in the ballad, *The Rájput*, he—

> "Trusted a Musálman's word—
> Wah! Wah! Trust a liar to lie.
> Out of his eyrie they tempted my bird,
> Fettered his wings that he could not fly."

Pudmini's husband was caught by a trick, and Alá-ud-dín demanded Pudmini as the price of his return. The Rájputs here showed that they too could scheme, and sent, in great state, Pudmini's litter to the besiegers' entrenchments. But there was no Pudmini in the litter, and her following of handmaidens was a band of seven hundred armed men. Thus, in the confusion of a camp fight, Pudmini's husband was rescued, and Alá-ud-dín's soldiery followed hard on his heels to the gates of Chitor, where the best and bravest on the rock were killed before Alá-ud-dín withdrew, only to return soon after, and, with a doubled army, besiege in earnest. His first attack men called the half-sack of Chitor; for, though he failed to win within the walls, he killed the flower of the Rájputs. The second attack ended in the first sack, and the awful satí of the women on the rock.

"When everything was hopeless and the very terrible goddess, who lives in the bowels of Chitor, had spoken and claimed for death eleven out of the twelve of the Rána's sons, all who were young or fair women betook themselves to a great underground chamber, and the fires were lit, and the entrance was walled up, and they died. The Rájputs opened the gates and fought till they could fight no more, and Alá-ud-dín the victorious entered a wasted and desolate city. He wrecked everything except only the palace of Pudmini, and the old Jain tower before mentioned. That was all he could do, for there were few men alive of the defenders of Chitor when the day was won, and the women were ashes underground."[1]

One son of Lakshman Singh survived, and escaped to "carry on the line" of the royal house, and not long afterwards the "Children of the Sun" were once again seated upon the rock of Chitor.

Two hundred years passed by in comparative peace and security, and the capital of Mewár throve and flourished. It was at the height of its glory under Kumbha Rána, who built the stately Tower of Victory to commemorate his reign. But after him its glory waned. The rulers of Chitor gave themselves up to luxury and ease, and the chiefs, for want of other outlet to their energies, took to quarreling among themselves. In 1535 Bahadur Sháh of Gujarát noted these things and deemed the occasion favorable for an invasion of Mewár. The Rána was in no condition to withstand the attack. His chiefs were disaffected, and the State totally unprepared. He left Deola,

[1] "Letters of Marque," Kipling.

where, for the better pursuit of pleasure, he had made a new capital, and took refuge in Chitor, the old-time rallying point of the Mewárís.

Rána Bikrmajit knew that the situation was hopeless, and it only remained to die hard, after the immemorial manner of the Rájput. Bahadur Sháh mined one of the bastions, and in the explosion five hundred of the defenders were killed. The Rána's mother headed a desperate sally, but she was slain and her followers driven back behind the walls. Then the Rájputs prepared for another johur, which was to be even more dreadful than that of the time of Alá-ud-dín. Thirteen thousand died within the Fort before the gates were thrown open and the rush made upon the besiegers in the final sacrifice. From the ensuing sack and massacre was saved

> "A motherless infant, the heir of that race of pride;
> The heir of the peacock banner, of the five-colored flag of the throne
> Which traces its record of glory from days when it ruled alone."

In course of time this Rájput prince succeeded to the Ráj of Mewár. But Udai Singh was a weakling, and, what was almost more to the point, the irresistible Akbar was by that time upon the throne of Delhi. Jaipur and Jodhpur had bowed to Fate, and each had given a daughter to the Great Mughal in marriage. Other rájás followed their example. The Rájput league was broken up and Chitor stood alone—the trunk lopped of its branches.

Udai Singh was a Rájput, and the honor of his house was dear to him, so he refused to yield to Akbar; but he was also a coward, and so when Akbar appeared before his walls, he fled to the Arávallis and left a woman to defend his capital.

For the third time Chitor was the scene of a magnificent johur. Akbar's hand fell heavier upon the city than that of any previous conqueror. "He killed everything that had life upon the rock, and wrecked and overturned and spoiled."

That was the end; Chitor sank into the desolation of abandon. Udai Singh made a new capital at Udaipur, and his grandson recovered the dominion of his fathers; but no head of the house has had the heart to resuscitate the dying city on the rock. Indeed, only in recent years has any attempt been made to save the place from sinking unchecked into absolute ruinous decay. Ruins of palaces, temples and houses lie thick upon the summit, but the principal buildings are tended and kept in repair, thanks to the interest of a few English officials. Dense jungle now covers the slopes which were formerly scraped bare to frustrate ascent.

The approach to the rock is by a good, broad road which passes over the Gamberi by a massive stone bridge, built by one of the sons of Rána Lakshman, who was killed in the attack by Alá-ud-dín. At the foot of the hill is the modern town of Chitor, whose walls enclose mean houses, crowded along dirty, narrow streets.

The ascent is by a zigzag road, a mile in length, and interrupted at intervals by seven strong gates, with guard rooms. One wonders "how much life has flowed down this sluice of battles, and been lost at the Padal Pol, the last and lowest gate—where, in the old days, the besieging armies put their best and bravest battalions," and whence the desperate garrison issued forth in the final act of the ghastly johur. Just outside this gate an erect stone marks the spot where the Chief of Deola Pratapgarh fell in the siege of Bahadur Sháh.

Farther up the slope two chattris commemorate those knightly heroes, Jaimal of Bednor and his clansman Kalla, who figure in the story of Akbar's sack. Kalla carried his already wounded chief down to this spot that he might get at close quarters with the enemy while he yet had strength to strike a blow, and here they both died in the good old fashion of Rájputs. There are other memorials of valor, but if one tithe of the deeds of heroism which have been performed upon this slope were commemorated with stones the size of cocoanuts the road would be hidden by them.

Passing through the handsome Ram Pol, which is the uppermost and main gate, one enters the city. Hard by is the chattri of Patta. Akbar coupled Jaimal and Patta as the heart and strength of the defence of Chitor. He took no account of Udai Singh, but had two enormous stone elephants made to commemorate his victory, and on their backs were sculptured presentments of Jaimal and Patta. Some part of these monuments one may see in the Queen's Gardens at Delhi.

The ancient Jain Tower of Fame stands prominently forth upon the eastern rampart. Fergusson describes it thus: "One of the most interesting Jaina monuments of the age (the first or great age of Jaina architecture, which extended down to about the year 1300, or perhaps a little after that) is the tower of Sri Allat (Rána Allují). It is a singularly elegant specimen of its class, about eighty feet in height, and adorned with sculptures and mouldings from the base to the summit. An inscription once existed at its base, which gave its date as 896 A.D., and, though the slab was detached, this is so nearly the date we should arrive at from the style that there seems little doubt that it was of that age. It was dedicated to Adnath, the first of the Jaina tirthankars, and his figure is repeated some hundreds of times on the face of the tower; but, so far as I could perceive, not that of any other Jaina saints."

The seventh and topmost story, which is reached by a narrow and winding stair, is open and surrounded by pillars supporting the roof, from which bushes are growing.

Standing co-sentinel over the deserted city is Kumbha's Tower of Victory, also a Jain edifice, but strangely crowned with a Muhammadan dome. Is it possible that Alá-ud-dín, or Bahadur Sháh, may have been satisfied to spare the building after working a significant change in its roof?

"To Kumbha, who reigned from 1418–'68, we owe this tower, which was erected to commemorate his victory over Mahmúd, King of Malwa, in 1439. It is a Pillar of Victory, like that of Trajan at Rome, but of infinitely better taste as an architectural object. It has nine stories, each of which is distinctly marked on the outside. A stair in the centre leads to each story, the two upper ones being open and more ornamented than those below. It stands on a base forty-seven feet square and ten feet high, and is thirty feet square, rising to a height of one hundred and twenty-two feet, the whole being covered with ornaments and sculptures to such an extent as to leave no plain part, while the mass of decoration is kept so subdued that it in no way interferes with the outline or general effect."

Inside, the walls are covered with carvings, in relief, of Hindu deities, with their names inscribed below each figure. In the top story are two slabs with long inscriptions—two others have been lost—from which it is learned that the tower was from seven to ten years in the course of construction.

Out of the mass of ruins on every hand one may pick a few palaces and temples in a fair state of preservation, some of them beautiful specimens of Hindu architecture and ornamentation; but for the most part the ancient capital of Rájputána is a mass of indistinguishable ruins.

From Chitorgarh a branch line runs to Debari, and there the railroad ends. The eight miles thence to Udaipur is covered in a tonga, passing on the way Dabok, where Colonel Tod, the first Resident of Rájputána and the author of the "Annals," lived.

The situation of Udaipur is beautiful in the extreme. The surrounding landscape is made up of a combination of lakes and mountains. A bastioned wall, with several fine gateways, encircles the city. On the west side it abuts upon a lake, whose waters supply a moat which runs around the other sides. The lake owes its origin to Udai Singh, but successive rulers have added to its extent and beauty. Its surface is broken by several islands, on which are palaces and gardens. The traveler who is fortunate enough to secure, through the mediumship of the Resident, the use of one of the Mahárájá's boats may enjoy good fishing and shooting amid superb scenery. In one of these delightful island retreats Prince Salím found refuge when hiding from the wrath of his father, Akbar. During the Mutiny, forty or more refugees sought the protection of the Rána, and were lodged by him among these island groves until all danger was past. It is said that Outram, stung by a taunt uttered by the young ruler of Udaipur, jumped from a terrace of one of these palaces into the lake, which swarmed with crocodiles, and swam ashore.

The Palace of the Maháránas of Udaipur overhangs the lake. "It is a most imposing pile of granite and marble, of quadrangular shape, rising at least one hundred feet from the ground, and flanked by octagonal towers, crowned with cupolas. Although built at various periods, uniformity of design has been well preserved; nor is there in the East a more striking structure. It stands upon the very crest of a ridge, running parallel to, but considerably elevated above the margin of the lake. The terrace, which is at the east and chief front of the Palace, extends throughout its length, and is supported by a triple row of arches from the declivity of the ridge. The height of this arcaded wall is fully fifty feet, and although all is hollow beneath, yet so admirably is it constructed that an entire range of stables is built on the extreme verge of the terrace, on which all the forces of the Mahárána—elephants, cavalry and infantry—are often assembled. From this terrace the city and the valley lie before the spectator, whose vision is bounded only by the distant hills; while from the summit of the Palace nothing obstructs the view over lake and mountain."

Udaipur is in striking contrast to Jaipur. In the former city are few, if any, of the indications of advance along the lines of modern civilization which are so strikingly evident in the latter place. It is said that the Rána discourages "improvements," and —here again is marked contrast to Jaipur—extends but a scant welcome to European visitors. His refusal to have the railroad extended to his capital is also attributed to a desire for continued isolation. Under the circumstances, Udaipur could not be expected to enjoy a great degree of commercial prosperity. As a matter of fact, it has no trade. The sole manufacture is swords, and every man goes armed, more from force of habit, however, than from any need.

A rude presentment of a horseman and an elephant, which is painted on wall and gateway everywhere, and puzzles every visitor, is thus accounted for by Kipling: "A highly intelligent priest grunted that it was a picture; a private of the Mahárána's regular army suggested that it was an elephant; while a wheat-seller, his sword by his side, was equally certain that it was a rájá. Beyond that point his knowledge did not go.

"The explanation of the picture is this: In the days when Rájá Maun of Amber put his sword at Akbar's service, and won for him great kingdoms, Akbar sent an army against Mewár, whose then ruler was Pertap Singh, most famous of all the princes of Mewár. Selim, Akbar's son, led the army of the Toork; the Rájputs met them at the Pass of Huldighat, and fought till one-half of their band was slain. Once, in the press of battle, Pertap, on his great horse, Chytak, came within striking distance of Selim's elephant, and slew the mahout; but Selim escaped, to become Jahángír afterwards, and the Rájputs were broken. That was three hundred years ago, and men have reduced the picture to a sort of diagram, that the painter dashes in in a few minutes, without, it would seem, knowing what he is commemorating."

The State supports a well drilled and equipped force of about six thousand of all arms. The cavalry are well mounted, and the infantry unusually efficient for irregulars. This satisfactory condition of the army of Udaipur is due to a retired British non-commissioned officer, who, with the local title of Major-General, held, and possibly does so yet, the virtual position of Commander-in-Chief.

At Ahar, about three miles from Udaipur, is a modern village and the ruins of an ancient city. Here, among the chattris of their ancestors, are interred the ashes of the Maháránas of Udaipur. "Here they go down in their robes of state, their horse following behind, and here the Political saw, after the death of a Mahárána, the dancing-girls dancing before the poor white ashes, the musicians playing among the cenotaphs, and the golden hookah, sword, and water-vessel laid out for the naked soul doomed to hover twelve days round the funeral pyre, before it could depart on its journey toward a fresh birth. Once, in a neighboring State, it is said one of the dancing-girls stole a march in the next world's precedence and her lord's affections, upon the legitimate queens. The affair happened, by the way, after the Mutiny, and was accomplished, with great pomp, in the light of day. Subsequently those who might have stopped it, but did not, were severely punished. . . . It would be curious to know whether satí is altogether abolished among these lonely hills in the walled holds of the Thakurs."

The native State of which the Mahárájá Holkar is the ruler is one of the most prosperous and promising in the country. Indore, like Jaipur, is open to the reception of modern ideas and the adoption of modern methods. The natural advantages of an elevated and healthy situation have been much enhanced in recent years by improvements effected at the instigation of the British Resident, and with the hearty support of the Mahárájá. The water supply is ample at all seasons, and the drainage system unusually good. The roads have been extended and metaled, facilitating the trade with outlying districts. The streets of the city are kept in repair and lighted. There are good schools, a library, a dispensary and—the never absent mission —in this case an outpost of the Presbyterian Church of Canada. Indore exports a considerable amount of grain raised in the State, is one of the centres of the opium belt, and keeps a large cotton mill busy. The State coins its own money, and issues its own postage stamps.

The Sarsati River intersects the city, and the Palace of the Mahárájá stands almost in the centre of it. It has an imposing gateway of several stories, facing an open square. Near by is the quarter inhabited by the Marwárí money lenders—Itwar Street, where a market is held every Sunday—and the Haldi Bazaar, in which the opium dealers congregate. On the bank of the river is the Lal Bagh. The garden contains a menagerie, and an attractive villa, in which the Mahárájá often receives guests. In the lower story is a handsome audience hall, looking up the Sarsati, which is dammed at this point so as to form a sort of lake.

The old capital of the Holkars was at Maheswár, to the south of Indore, and there a magnificent chattri commemorates the memory of one of the Mahárájá's most renowned ancestors, and, probably, the most remarkable of the many women who figure prominently in the history of India. Ahalia Bai left the impress of her character upon the State she served so faithfully, and the evidences of her philanthropy are all over India. Everywhere the traveler goes he will find temples, gháts and wells built by this estimable woman. Sir John Malcolm says of her: "The character of her administration was for more than thirty years the basis of the prosperity of the dynasty to which she belonged. She sat every day for a considerable period in open durbar, transacting business. Her first principle of government appears to have been moderate assessment and an almost sacred concern for the native rights of village officers and proprietors of land. She heard every complaint in person, and, although she constantly referred cases to courts of equity and arbitration, and to the ministers, for settlement, she was always accessible, and so strong was her sense of duty on all points connected with the dispensation of justice that she is represented as not only patient, but unwearied in the investigation of the most insignificant causes when appeals were made to her decision. It appears, above all, extraordinary how she had mental and bodily powers to go through the labor she imposed upon herself, and which, from the age of thirty to that of sixty, when she died, was unremittent. The hours gained from the affairs of State were all given to acts of devotion and charity, and a deep sense of religion appears to have strengthened her mind in performance of her worldly duties. Her charitable foundations extend all over India, from the Himálayas to Cape Cormorin, and from Somnáth to the Temple of Jagaunáth."

When one considers the condition of Hindu women, with tradition, custom, heredity—every factor, in short—unfavorable to the development of strength of character, the life of Ahalia Bai presents a phenomenon which defies explanation.

A divergence from the route of travel is necessary in order to visit Mandu, the ancient capital of Malwa, which was founded in 313 A.D. The first ten miles from the railroad is done in a tonga, which brings one to Dhar. From here an elephant, or horse, is used to complete the journey over the remaining twenty miles. The ruins extend along about eight miles of a ridge of the Vindhyas, and have long since been swallowed up by the jungle.

There is a village in the vicinity, but no accommodation for the traveler, and, unless he has provided himself with a tent, he must share one of the ruins for the night with bats and creeping things. Pathways have been cut through the jungle to the principal buildings and points of chief interest. Even seen under the most disadvantageous conditions, the edifices accessible impress one with their magnitude and grandeur. The least injured is the Jamá Masjid, which is said to be the largest and finest specimen of Afghán architecture existing in India. There are palaces of old-time Kings of Malwa, notably that of Hoshang Ghorí. He reigned in the fifteenth century, and, besides fortifying the city, erected several of its grandest buildings.

It was during the time of Hoshang that Mandu reached the zenith of its splendor. The wealth of the place excited the cupidity of Bahadur Sháh of Gujarát, the same who sacked Chitor, and in 1526 he besieged and took Mandu, which remained an appanage of the kingdom of Gujarát until Akbar came upon the scene with his irresistible army.

Sir Thomas Roe was in Mandu at the time he was dancing attendance upon Jahángír, in his fruitless mission. In his "Memoirs," Roe complains of the "lions" that infested the district, and one of which carried off a pack animal belonging to him.

Ujjain, the ’Οζήνη of the Greeks, is situated in Malwa, upon a tributary of the Chambal. It is the spot which marked the first meridian of Hindu geographers. Ujjain is even more ancient than Mandu, and was no less famous in the days of its power and glory. Asoka was Viceroy here when his father reigned in Magadha; so that Ujjain must have been a great city then, and that was at least two hundred and fifty years before Christ. About three hundred years later Ujjain was the capital of the great King Vikrámaditya. Legend, which perpetuates some extraordinary stories of this monarch, attributes the expulsion of the Indo-Scythians to him. It is tolerably certain that his kingdom extended over the greater part of Hindustán, and that he had no considerable rival in India.

Alá-ud-dín conquered Malwa in time, and Ujjain became the seat of a line of viceroys, one of whom asserted his independence at the end of the fourteenth century, and founded the Ghorí dynasty, which ruled over Malwa until dispossessed by the Sultán of Gujarát.

It was near Ujjain that the wily Aurangzeb, in alliance with Murad, defeated their eldest brother Dara. The subsequent history of this unhappy prince—his futile effort to regain his birthright, his treacherous betrayal and barbarous murder—is one of the most romantic and pitiful chapters in the annals of India.

Holkar and Sindhia have both held Ujjain, and it was the capital of the latter until the British turned Gwalior over to him. The modern city lies a mile or so to the south of the ruins of ancient Ujjain. A massive stone wall, along which at intervals are placed watch-towers, makes a six-mile circuit of the city. The environs are park-like, groves of trees and gardens surrounding the walls on every side.

Near the Palace of the Mahárájá is an old isolated gateway, which, if tradition be reliable, is a vestige of one of Vikrámaditya's buildings. At the southern end of the city is one of the several astronomical observatories erected by Jai Singh in different parts of the country.

Bhilsa stands upon a rock fifteen hundred feet high, whose base is washed by the river Betwa, which rises near Bhopal, a few miles to the south, and flows almost due north, until it joins the Jumna not far from Cawnpur.

Bhilsa has been a town of some political importance in its time, but at present is chiefly noteworthy as a popular place of pilgrimage, and on account of the famous Buddhist Topes, which are in the vicinity. There are five or six groups of these peculiar structures, comprising in all twenty-five or thirty separate topes, the farthest less than ten miles from the city. Fergusson considers the Bhilsa Topes to be the most extensive and interesting in India. We have very little accurate information as to the history and purpose of these curious monuments.

The finest specimens are to be found at Sanchi, about five miles from Bhilsa. The little village is perched upon an isolated flat sandstone hill, about three hundred feet above the level of the plain. The topes, or stupas, are at the top of this eminence, and although the situation is a conspicuous one, they seem to have escaped the willful damage so often inflicted by Muhammadan fanatics upon the religious monuments of the Hindus.

The great champion of Buddhism, Asoka, lived for some time at Bessagar, in this neighborhood, and married Devi, the daughter of the chief of Sanchi, by whom he had twin sons, Ujenia and Mahinda. This fact forms a basis for the reasonable hypothesis that Asoka raised these huge spherical mounds, to mark burial place or depository of sacred relics. If that much is probable, it is a fair surmise that the Great Tope was erected as a memorial to the royal mother of Asoka's twin sons. This tope has been tunneled, but nothing of significance was discovered in the interior. It is one solid mass, the bulk consisting of bricks laid in mud on a foundation trodden hard by elephants. The outside was covered with a casing of stone, smooth-faced, and finished with a coating of plaster. On the top is a flat space, thirty-four feet in diameter, which was once surrounded by a railing. In the centre of this space is a receptacle, which is believed to have been designed for a relic casket. The tope is almost hemispherical. The mound rises from a base one hundred and twenty feet in diameter and fourteen feet high, projecting sufficiently to form a broad, processional path around the stupa. The latter is one hundred and six feet in diameter, and rises to a height of forty-two feet. The circumference of the base is five hundred and fifty feet. The tope is surrounded by a stone railing nine feet high. The large, cut stones have been mortised and fitted in the manner of the Druidical remains at Stonehenge, in England. There were four lofty gateways, facing the cardinal points of the compass; only two of these are now standing. The stones of which the gateways are constructed are beautifully carved, and with great elaboration of detail. Sculptures of elephants, lions and human beings are the most prominent objects in the ornamental design. The date assigned to the tope is about 250 B.C., but the rails and gateways were added at intervals afterwards. Fergusson is inclined to believe that the gateways were erected as late as the first century of the Christian era.

CHAPTER XII.

JHANSI, GWALIOR.

Bundelkhand has from time immemorial been distinguished for the turbulence and lawlessness of its people. It has been styled "the classic land of brigandism," and it is said that "in its sombre forests was born the terrible religion of the Thugs." After the aboriginal Bundelas were driven out or submerged in the immigrant population, their successors maintained the old reputation of the province, and it is only within very recent years that it has been reduced to a condition of peacefulness.

Early in the seventeenth century Bir Singh built the fort of Jhansi a few miles to the north of his capital. Instigated by Prince Salím, this chief murdered the notorious Abúl Fazal, the favorite of Akbar, who flattered the Emperor by proclaiming him the "Lord of the Age," who was to bring about the Muhammadan millennium. Akbar sent an army into Bundelkhand and ravaged the country, but Bir Singh made his escape. From that time on, the province was, with brief intervals of comparative peace, the arena of armed conflicts. In 1732 the ruler called upon the Maráthás to aid him in a campaign. Such a summons never failed of a prompt response. The usual result followed. The Maráthás secured a cession to themselves of one-third of the Rájá's territory, and soon annexed the remainder of it, which they held until it passed to the British in 1817. Native rulers were allowed to occupy the throne, although, without exception, they abused their power shamefully.

When the Mutiny broke out the State was ruled by a woman. The Rání of Jhansi was smarting under two bitter grievances. The British would not permit her to adopt an heir, and they allowed cattle to be killed in the territory, which she held as their deputy. It was with her open encouragement that the native troops broke into revolt, and slew as many Europeans as could be taken unawares. Several of the officers, with their families, took to the Fort, where they stood a siege of a few days. The situation was hopeless, however, and upon the sacred oaths of the rebel leaders, sworn upon the Kurán and upon Ganges water, that their lives would be spared, they surrendered. No sooner were the men unarmed than the entire party—sixty-six in all, mostly women and children—were massacred.

Following this, quarrels broke out between the mutineers at Jhansi, and a contest for supreme authority ensued. For well nigh a year a condition of anarchy prevailed. But at length the British, having relieved the strain at more important points, were enabled to send a force into the district. The Ránì fled with Tantia Topí, and met her ultimate fate at Gwalior.

The Fort of Jhansi is an extremely strong position. It stands upon a lofty rock rising abruptly from the plain. The walls are of solid granite, from sixteen to twenty feet in thickness. The outworks are of similar massive construction, with embrasures for front and flanking artillery fire, and tier upon tier—in some places as many as five lines—of loopholes for musketry.

The city, which is completely commanded by the Fort, lies on the north and east sides of it. A strong, fortified wall, rising from eighteen to thirty feet in height, surrounds the city. It is strengthened by numerous bastions furnished with heavy guns. The fortifications and armament are being improved according to modern standards. The result will be to make Fort Jhansi one of the strongest, as it is one of the most important, strategetical positions in India. It came into the possession of the British in 1886 as the result of an exchange with the Mahárájá Sindhia for the fortress of Gwalior.

Gwalior, the capital of the territory of Sindhia, is one of the most ancient and renowned strongholds in India. Native historians are greatly at variance as to the date of the foundation of the place. One of them gives 3101 B.C. as the year, but two others, with whom the most reliable European authorities agree, assign 275 A.D. as the time of the foundation.

According to Cunningham, Toramana was a tributary prince under the Guptas, against whom he rebelled and established a great kingdom, including all the country between the Jumna and the Nerbudda.

During the reign of the son of Toramana the Sun Temple was erected and the Suraj Kund excavated, and Gwalior founded by a Kachhwaha chief, who was a leper. This chief, Suraj Sen by name, came to the rock of Gopagírí on a hunting expedition. Upon this hill dwelt a holy hermit, who cured the chieftain of his leprosy. Suraj Sen determined to build a city upon the spot. In this design he was encouraged by Gwalipa, the recluse, who gave him a new name—to wit, Suhan Pál—with the promise that so long as his descendants should retain the cognomen Pál, they should retain their kingdom.

So Suraj Sen, or Suhan Pál, built a fort upon the hill, and called it Gwaliawar out of compliment to his benefactor; and he prospered, and founded a long line of kings, eighty-three of whom bore the surname Pál, but the eighty-fourth called himself Tej Kura, and lost his kingdom.

Then followed a Parihara dynasty, which lived for one hundred years, when Altamsh captured Gwalior. This capture was commemorated by an inscription over the gate of the Urwahi. The Emperor Bábar, in his "Memoirs," says he saw it, and the date was

630 A.H., which would be 1232 A.D. according to our method of reckoning.

Timúr invaded the State, and Hoshang Sháh of Malwa laid siege to Gwalior, but without success. Sikandar Lodi failed to reduce the Fort, and Bábar only succeeded by a stratagem. Many an attack the old stronghold has withstood, and more than once it has fallen.

When the Mutiny broke out, Gwalior was in the hands of Sindhia, then an energetic young man, with a considerable talent for soldiering. Besides ten thousand troops of his own, he had a force of the Company's soldiers, numbering seven thousand of all arms, including about seven hundred and fifty artillerymen and twenty-six guns. The entire body consisted of well-equipped and thoroughly-trained men, under British officers. There is no doubt that had Sindhia, with this army at his command, thrown in his lot with the rebels, he might, at an early stage of the struggle, have easily marched upon Agra, and have captured the city. Such a disaster would have seriously added to the difficulties with which the British had to contend.

Fortunately for all parties concerned, Sindhia and his astute Minister determined to keep faith with the British. It was impossible for them to have saved the officers who were killed, but the few who, together with some women and children, escaped to the Palace were conveyed by the Mahárájá to a place of safety.

By evasion and subterfuge Sindhia contrived to restrain the troops for several months, and when Tantia Topí and the Ráni of Jhansi approached Gwalior, the Mahárájá went out with his army to oppose them. In the engagement which ensued all the Gwalior troops, with the exception of Sindhia's body-guard, went over to the enemy, and the Mahárájá only saved his life by flight. His loyalty was unquestionable, but all his efforts to hold the Fort for the British proved futile. The Ráni then seized the Fort, but was almost immediately attacked by Sir Hugh Rose. The Ráni was in the thick of the hot fighting which followed. "Clad in the attire of a man, and mounted on horseback, the Ráni of Jhansi might have been seen animating her troops throughout the day. When inch by inch the British troops pressed through the pass, and when reaching its summit, Smith ordered the hussars to charge, the Ráni of Jhansi boldly confronted the British horsemen. When her comrades failed her, her horse, in spite of her efforts, carried her along with the others. With them she might have escaped, but that her horse stumbled and fell. A hussar, close upon her track, ignorant of her sex and her rank, cut her down. She fell to rise no more. That night her devoted followers, determined that the English should not boast that they captured her, even dead, buried her body."

The Fort was carried by two young subalterns, with a handful of men. The fortune that favors the bold attended upon the audacious enterprise. Of the series of six gates which protected the approach, five were unguarded, and the storming party gained the last before they were discovered. This was forced in the face of a heavy fire. Led by the two British officers, the assailants rushed into the Fort and a desperate hand-to-hand fight ensued. Lieutenant Rose, the leader of the enterprise, fell mortally wounded, but the Fort was won.

When at the end of the eighteenth century, Daulat Ráo Sindhia got possession of Gwalior he did not take up his abode in the Fort, nor in the city, which lies about the northeast end of the rock, but pitched a camp to the south of it. The camp remained, and, as not infrequently happened in olden times, the city of canvas became gradually transformed into a city of stone. So they called the place Lashkar, meaning camp, and that is the name of the modern city of Gwalior to-day. A considerable portion of the area enclosed by the fortified wall which encircles Lashkar is occupied by the park, in which stands the residence of the Maháráját. The Palace is quite modern—there is an old one near the centre of the city—and quite commonplace. It is not open to visitors in ordinary. This is simply because the Maháráját objects to having his privacy intruded upon by the tourists, who in the cold weather pass through Gwalior in a continual stream. That His Highness is not lacking in reasonable hospitality is evidenced by the fact that he maintains one of the best rest-houses in India for the accommodation of travelers, and places at their disposal carriages and elephants from the royal stables.

The Mahárájá Sindhia's Palace is one of those which called forth Lord Curzon's timely protest against "Tottenham Court Road furniture." Under the shadow of the historic rock, and within sight of the Tomb of Tansen, one cannot fail to be impressed with the incongruity of Lincrusta Walton and gilt willow-ware, and in the garden the turbaned guards are not in harmony with the miniature railroad. But the white Palace has a smart, well-kept appearance, and makes a not unattractive picture in its setting of fine trees, with its surrounding garden, whose flower-beds and paths and lamps are a little too precise, perhaps.

Lashkar is a clean, growing city, with some particularly fine streets. Its white, artistic houses make an admirable background to the brilliant costumes of the people on the streets. It is unequivocally Hindu in appearance and in population. Its Maráthá origin is everywhere in evidence.

Old Gwalior, fast lapsing into disregarded decay, is in striking contrast with Lashkar. Every invader—and they were not a few—who was foiled by the strength of the well-watered rock, wreaked his vengeance upon the city which lay at its foot, so that time and again Gwalior has been rebuilt from the ruins of a terrific sack. Its small, squat stone houses, along whose flat roofs one might walk with almost as much ease as upon the ground, are huddled together along narrow streets and crooked lanes.

The palaces and the better residences are deserted, for the well-to-do people have long since abandoned the place, and those who live there now are the poorest and the lowest castes. Just without the gates the Jamá Masjid stands, the only object about Gwalior that has not the impress of neglect and decay stamped forcibly upon it, and yet a large portion of it, at least, dates back to 1665 A.D. It is a beautiful building, fashioned from the white sandstone of the fortified rock above, and "looks as fresh as if it had not been finished a month."

Beyond the river, but still in the immediate vicinity of the city, is the grand mausoleum of the pír Muhammad Ghaus, the same whose subtle scheme enabled Bábar to win Gwalior. He had a great reputation for sanctity in his life, and his memory is still revered by Musalmáns. The tomb was built some time in the early part of Akbar's reign, probably by order of that monarch. It is a massive square stone structure, one hundred feet each way, surmounted by a lofty dome, and with a tower at each angle.

Close by the mausoleum of the Muhammadan saint is a small open pavilion containing the tomb of the celebrated Hindu musician, Tansen. The leaves of the tamarind tree, which throws its shadow over the spot, are believed to have the property of imparting an extraordinary quality to the voice. Dancing-girls resort to the place, and strip the branches, and in this way the tree with which this superstition was first associated, and probably more than one successor, has been killed.

The Fort may only be visited on an order from the Mahárájá. This is a little concession to the Mahárájá's authority—a little intimation to the traveler that he is not in British territory. The request is invariably granted, and an elephant from the royal stables is generally placed at the disposal of the visitor, in order to facilitate the steep ascent.

The road, which was formerly a series of flights of steps terminating in landings, is guarded by six gateways, after the fashion of ancient Hindu rock fortresses. This is the main approach, and is at the northeast corner of the rock, but there are entrances on the northwest and southwest.

The Ganesh Gate, which is the fourth of the series in ascending, was built some time in the earlier half of the fifteenth century. Close to it stand a little Hindu temple and a small mosque. The former is sacred to Gwalipa, the patron saint of the Kachhwaha dynasty of rájás. The mosque bears an inscription of date corresponding to 1664 A.D.:

> "In the reign of the great Prince Alamgír,
> Like the full-shining moon,
> The enlightener of the world,
> Praise be to God that this happy place
> Was by M'utamad Khán completed
> As a charitable gift.
> It was the idol temple of the vile Gwali.

He made it a mosque
Like a mansion of Paradise.
The Khán of enlightened heart,
Nay, light itself from head to foot,
Displayed the divine light like that of mid-day."

He closed the idol temple; from which it may be surmised that the hermit from whom the rock took its name was at an early period apotheosized. The temple in which he was then worshiped was destroyed by "the Khán of enlightened heart," and the mosque built upon its site. The adjacent temple of "the vile Gwali," which is comparatively modern, must have been built when the Hindus came unto their own again.

This is a typical little bit of religious history. Similar instances of Muhammadan fanaticism and Hindu persistence are to be found all over India, and the singular feature of these cases is that the latter appear to have seldom, if ever, retaliated by destroying the erections which usurped the places of their own buildings.

Before arriving at the Lakshman Gate, about five hundred feet farther on, one of Gwalior's famous rock temples is passed. It is an excavation dedicated to Vishnu, and dating, according to an inscription upon its walls, from 876 A.D. Along the face of the rock there are bas-reliefs of gods and goddesses, and a number of lingams. A colossal group of the Boar Incarnation is believed to be the oldest sculpture in

Gwalior. It is almost obliterated, and a carving of an elephant which surmounted it is also mutilated beyond any semblance of its original form. The natural strength of the rock, enhanced by an unfailing water supply, has been augmented from time to time by engineering works, so that even in this age of powerful siege guns it would be, if adequately garrisoned, an almost impregnable position.

The rock is an isolated, flat-topped mass of sandstone, rising precipitously out of the plain to a height of three hundred feet. It is nearly two miles in length from north to south, and varies in breadth from two hundred to nine hundred yards. The upper portion of the hill is steeply scarped all around below the embattlemented wall, which is thirty feet or more high.

The famous rock-sculptures of Gwalior are excavations in the cliff beneath the wall of the fortress. Wherever the rock presented a tolerably smooth surface, advantage has been taken of the fact to cut out a temple-cave or alcove-shrine. These minor excavations are innumerable, but irrespective of them, there are five distinct groups. Of these groups the Urwahi and southeastern are the most important, on account of their extent and the character of their sculptures. Most of these colossal carvings were mutilated by order of the Emperor Bábar, and he records the fact, with apparent satisfaction, in his "Memoirs," "They have hewn the solid rock of this

Adwa, and sculptured out of it idols of larger and smaller size. On the south part of it is a large idol, which may be about forty feet in height. These figures are perfectly naked, without even a rag to cover the parts of generation. Adwa is far from being a mean place; on the contrary it is extremely pleasant. The greatest fault consists in the idol figures all about it. I directed these idols to be destroyed."

The Emperor's orders were not carried out to the extent of destruction, probably because nothing short of explosives would have been effective to destroy those gigantic rock forms, but they were badly mutilated. The Jains have since done what they could to repair the damage with stucco, with the result, at least, of giving an idea of the original form, if not of the precise effect.

The Urwahi Group of sculptures is situated about the middle of the western face of the rock. It consists of twenty-two nude figures, including the one of which Bábar makes particular mention. This colossus is, however, fifty-seven feet high—not forty, as stated in the "Memoirs." There is a huge statue of Adinath, the first Jain pontiff, and one of Nemnath, his twenty-first successor.

The southeastern group includes a number of figures from fifteen to thirty feet in height, ranged along the cliff for a distance of half a mile. Some caves are occupied by Birajís, who refuse admittance and resent the approach of strangers. The caves vary in size, the largest being eighty across by eight feet deep, and thirty feet high; some are mere niches. Many of them bear inscriptions, and the dates range from 1440 A.D. to 1473 A.D. The sculptures are mentioned by Father Montserrat, who visited Gwalior, on his way to Delhi, during the reign of Akbar.

Within the Fort are five or six palaces, and a greater number of Hindu temples, all of which show signs of the destructive proclivities of the Musalmáns.

The Palace of Man Singh, which was built at the end of the fifteenth century and the beginning of the next, is also called "The Painted Palace," by reason of the fact that "the walls are covered with a profusion of colored tiles—bands of mosaique, candelabra, Bráhman ducks, elephants and peacocks —enameled blue, green and gold, giving to this massive wall an unsurpassed charm and elegance. The tiles of this great windowless wall possess a brightness and delicacy of tint unblemished by the ten centuries which they have weathered. . . . The secret of these enameled tiles has not yet been discovered."

From the Teli-ka-Mandir, the highest building upon the rock, and occupying a position in the centre of the Fort, there is a fine view of the surrounding country.

The neighboring plain is brown and arid, but the villages which dot its surface proclaim the possibility of wresting subsistence from it. Low sandstone hills bound the horizon in almost every direction. Far away in the north the red hills of Dholpur form a background to the white walls of the great Temple of Sahamiya. On the west, within easy distance, the whitewashed Temple of Hanuman stands out against the dark flank of the flat-topped hill to which it gives a name. In the south the conical peak of Ráipur dominates over the lower ranges beyond. Within the shadow of the northern end of the rock old Gwalior lies in comatose repose; and about a mile to the south of it the "Camp" carries on the commerce of the district. The chief products are grain, cotton and opium.

The territory of Sindhia, like that of Holkar to the south, is within the opium belt. While opium is cultivated for local consumption throughout Ráj-putána, there are two special tracts in which the poppy of commerce is grown—namely, the table-land of Central India and the valley of the Ganges, round abont Patná and Benares. In the former district, which is under the rule of native princes, the cultivation of the plant is free; but duty is levied upon the manufactured article when it enters British territory. In Bengal, opium is a Government monopoly. Throughout the rest of India it is absolutely prohibited.

The total annual exports of the drug are valued at about one hundred millions of rupees, upon which the Government nets about six per cent. profit. By far the greater quantity goes to China and the Straits Settlements.

In Bengal the Government enters into yearly contracts with the cultivators to devote a certain area to the growth of the poppy. "It is a fundamental principle that they may engage or refuse to engage, as they please." Before he commences operations the cultivator receives an advance payment, the amount of which is deducted from the settlement when he delivers the opium at the collecting agency. He is paid for the produce at a fixed rate, according to quality, and is bound to make over the entire output.

The cultivation of the poppy returns large profits to the ráyat, but it is a delicate process, requiring the most careful attention in all its stages. The best soil is high land, with facilities for artificial fertilization and ample irrigation. From the commencement of the rains, in about the middle of June until October, the ground is treated by several plowings, thorough and constant weedings, and two or three applications of manure. The seed is sown in the early part of November, and the fields require to be frequently irrigated between that time and February, when the plants reach maturity. After the poppies have fully flowered, the petals are picked off and laid away, to be used ultimately as wrappers for the cakes of opium.

The following operation is the most important and delicate of the whole process, and that upon which the quantity of the output depends: In the afternoon the cultivator lightly scrapes the outer skin of the capsules with an iron instrument, and the following morning collects the juice which has exuded from the scarifications. This is the opium in a rough state.

At the beginning of the month of April the cultivators take their produce to subordinate agencies, where it is examined and weighed, and the accounts settled.

The final process of making the opium up into balls for the Chinese market is performed at the central agencies of Patná and Ghâzipur. The spherical cakes are dry and in condition to be packed in chests by October.

The natives of India are not, as a general thing, addicted to the use of opium. Indeed, the difficulties in the way of securing the drug would be well-nigh prohibitive for the great mass of the people, even though the desire existed. In Rájputána and the native States in which the cultivation of opium is free, considerable quantities of it are consumed, especially by the rájás and thakúrs.

CHAPTER XIII.

AGRA, FATTEHPUR-SIKRI.

On a day in one of the closing years of the sixteenth century a little party of four persons—father, mother and two young boys—found themselves in the heart of the Thar, or Great Indian, Desert. Attracted by the reputation for liberality of the greatest monarch of Hindustán, the man had left his home in Western Tartary, with the intention of seeking his fortune at the Court of Akbar. The little band of lonely wayfarers had been two days without food, and exhaustion threatened to make farther progress impossible.

Under these perilous conditions, the woman gave birth to a child. In their dire straits, the parents determined to abandon the babe. Laying it in the shade of a dwarf oak, and covering it with leaves, they pursued their way, the mother mounted upon the one bullock left to them. They had proceeded scarce a mile when the maternal instinct overcame the dictates of prudence, and the woman, in a paroxysm of grief, threw herself to the ground, crying, "My child! my little one!"

Unable to resist this piteous appeal, the father returned to the spot where the infant had been left, and in so doing came in sight of a caravan, by which the party was succored and enabled to reach its destination.

The "daughter of the desert," thus narrowly snatched from the jaws of death, was destined to become Empress of India, with the title of Núr Jahán—the Light of the World. Each of her brothers lived to occupy a prominent place in the pages of Indian history. One of them was the father of Mumtáj-i-Mahál, to whose memory Sháh Jahán erected the Táj Mahál.

The head of this, perhaps, the most remarkable family that ever emigrated to India, made his way by sheer talent to the highest post in the Empire—that of Itmad-ud-daulá, or High Treasurer. He died at an honorable old age in possession of the high office. His daughter, the Empress, erected over his remains the beautiful tomb which stands upon the left bank of the Jumna, overlooking the city of Agra.

The building is square, with an octagonal tower, surmounted by a cupola, at each corner, and in the centre of the roof a small structure, in its principal lines not unlike the main building. The exterior is entirely of white marble, carved into lattice-work of the delicacy of lace. The same material and treatment are conspicuous in the interior, the ceiling of which is laid with plaster profusely painted in floral and geometrical designs.

The central hall contains the tombs of Khwajah Accas, the Itmad-ud-daulá, and his wife, and in the pavilion above are counterparts of these tombs. The mausoleum is rich in marble panels, wrought in the most elaborate designs, which have been executed by piercing the material so as to produce the appearance of some delicate textile. Flowers and leaves on tortuous tendrils surround scrolls bearing texts from the Kurán.

Nothing which the Empress could command of genius, wealth, or labor was spared to make this shrine a thing of beauty incomparable. It is said that her original intent was to use solid silver in the construction, but that her purpose was changed by the consideration that marble would be a more lasting material, and one less calculated to excite the cupidity of future generations.

From the garden, which, according to the custom of the Mughals, was planted around the tomb, one may reach the city by way of the pontoon bridge.

Agra first began to be a city of prominence at the beginning of the sixteenth century, when a monarch of the Afghán dynasty of Lodi made it his capital. After his conquest of Hindustán, Bábar took up his residence at Agra, and there he died in his forty-eighth year, legend says voluntarily, in order that by the sacrifice of his own life he might save that of his beloved son Humáyun, who was at the point of death.

The first of the Mughal dynasty was, with the possible exception of his grandson Akbar, the most illustrious of all the Indian Emperors. Erskine graphically sketches his character in the following terms: "His character was compounded of most of the qualities that go to form a great prince and a good man. He was bold, enterprising, full of ardor, and possessed of the commanding talents that sway and lead the mind of man. His temper was frank, confiding and gay, and he maintained through life the freshness of youth. He had strong affections, the warmest of domestic feelings, was devoutly attached to his relations and friends, and ready to sympathize with the pleasures and the sufferings of human beings of every class. Keenly alive to whatever was grand and beautiful, he cultivated knowledge of every kind with unwearied assiduity, and with proportionate success. Glory in every shape inflamed his imagination, and he attained a rare eminence of power and renown. Yet no man's success could be more entirely his own."

When one reflects upon the splendid characters of the early Mughal Emperors, it is difficult to account for the despicable qualities displayed by their direct descendants.

Humáyun was a man of strong intellect and endowed with the characteristic courage of his race, but he lacked the commanding influence of his father. He never had his subjects well in hand. Bábar had reduced Bengal and Behar, but Humáyun foolishly allowed the former Afghán Viceroy of those provinces to hold the fortress of Chunar, and that act of fatuitous confidence was his undoing. Now Chunar was the key to Bengal, and when Humáyun returned from his chivalric expedition to Chitor, he found his passage to the capital barred by Shir Khán. During a campaign extending over twelve months the Afghán wore down the Emperor's army, and in the end decisively defeated him at Kanauj. With a few followers, Humáyun fled to Persia. In the Thar—the desert in which Núr Mahál was born—Hamida, the Sultána, gave birth to Akbar. After an exile of fifteen years, Humáyun returned to India and regained his throne. Akbar made Agra the capital of his Empire, and built a new fort upon the site of the old citadel, but to Sháh Jahán, who reigned at Agra during five years, and was imprisoned there by his son Aurangzeb, the city owes its finest buildings. Of him might be said literally, what was figuratively said of Augustus: he found cities of brick and left them of marble.

Agra has undergone many changes of masters by force of arms. In 1764 it was taken by the Jats, who lost it six years later to the Maráthás; in 1774 it was captured by the Patháns, and in 1784 by Mahádají Sindhia. In 1803 it fell into the hands of the British.

The old city covered an area of more than ten square miles, about half of which is now occupied by the native town; to the south lie the cantonment and European quarter. At the apex of the triangular boundary of the cantonment stands the Fort, upon a bed of red sandstone. Within its confines are some of the principal buildings of old Agra, and the remains of several others.

The Moti Masjid, the "Pearl Mosque," built by Sháh Jahán in 1655, is a building of surpassing beauty; probably it is without a superior in its class. The exterior is of red sandstone; the interior of variegated marble slabs. Along the entire length of the entablature of the east façade runs an inscription inlaid with black marble, to the effect that this mosque may justly be likened to a pearl on account of the beauty and the extent of its marble work.

The Diwán-i-Am and Diwán-i-Khás, the Halls of Public and Private Audience respectively, are both remarkable structures.

Upon an open terrace, fronting the river, is a large block of black marble, formerly the throne of Akbar. When the Bhurtpur rájá usurped the throne, legend says this block split and spurted blood, in evidence of which the natives point to a reddish stain upon its surface. Hawkins tells us that Jahángír used this stone as a *prie-dieu.* "In the morning, at break of day, the King is at his beads, praying, on his knees, upon a Persian lamb-skin, having some eight rosaries, or strings of beads, each containing four hundred. The beads are of rich pearl, ballare rubies, diamonds, rubies, emeralds, aloes, wood, eshem and coral. At the upper end of a large, black stone on which he kneels there are figures graven in stone of the Virgin and Christ; so, turning his face to the west, he repeats thirty-two hundred words, according to the number of his beads."

Near by is the exquisitely carved marble Jasmine Tower, the pavilion of the Empress, from which a subterranean passage affords a secret outlet. Its original appearance must have been marvelously lovely, with gilded roof, and walls inlaid with gold and mother-of-pearl, and marble screens of the most delicate lattice-work. Much of the lighter decoration has been injured or destroyed.

The Angari Bagh, the "Grape Garden," holds the Shish Mahál, "Mirror Palace," and the Khás Mahál, "Private Palace." The latter was restored about thirty years ago, and contains some fine specimens of frescoing. Here Sháh Jahán died, within view of his beloved Táj.

Hard by, in an enclosure, stand the reputed Gates of Somnáth. After the sack of the famous temple, Mahmúd carried the gates to Ghazní in 1025. During the Afghán war of 1842 they fell into the hands of the British, by whom they were brought back to India, and set up on this spot. The gates are of finely carved deodar. They stand twenty-five feet in height, and bear a Kufic inscription. There is serious doubt

Palace within the Fort, Agra

about the genuineness of this relic. The best authorities support the opinion that the gates in question are but replicas of the original.

Toward the southern end of the Fort is the palace of Jahángír, a two-storied redstone edifice, which, although it is fast falling into decay, still displays many grand and beautiful features. An inlaid design of frequent occurrence upon the outer gateway represents the symbolic double triangle, but whether it has any connection with the Masonic emblem it is impossible to determine. Near the northwest corner of the palace is an enormous sixteen-sided well, two hundred and twenty feet in circumference, lined with masonry and capped by a heavy coping.

Immediately to the south of the Jahángír Mahál are the ruins of another palace, attributed to Akbar. Without the Delhi Gate stands the Jamá Masjid, erected, so announces an inscription upon its face, by Sháh Jahán, the master builder of India, in honor of his daughter Jahánara, who shared the captivity of his last years. The most striking feature of this structure consists of three large inverted domes of red sandstone, encircled by serrated bands of white marble, giving the appearance of huge rusty ornamented kettle-drums. As the grand gateway, by reason of the shelter it afforded, was a menace to the Fort, it became unfortunately necessary to destroy it during the Mutiny.

No other city affords so many and excellent

examples as does Agra, of the harmonious blending of vigor and delicacy which is characteristic of Mughal architecture. It is this peculiarity that elicited from Bishop Heber the apt epigram: "These Patáns built like giants, and finished their work like jewelers." The masterpiece of that, and every other age, is without question the Táj Mahál. This most beautiful of all buildings stands upon the right bank of the Jumna, so that the river laps the northern wall of the enclosure. At one end of this wall is a mosque of many minarets, which in any other spot would hold the attention by its beauty and elegance, but here the Táj fills the eye to the exclusion of all else. At the other extremity of the river wall is an exact duplicate of the place of worship. The latter building was until recent years used as a rest house for visitors.

The Táj should be seen from different points and at different times: from the opposite bank of the river; from the gateway; from one of the wings; at night and at noon; at dawn and at sunset. And with each varying condition it will assume a fresh aspect. One never tires of it. It grows on one. It is like an oft-read poem that discloses new beauties with each repetition. It is like a lovely face expressing the emotions of a pure and rich mind, ever changing, ever attracting.

Come to the Táj at the full of the moon, when the dewy blossoms give forth their richest perfumes, to mingle with the odors of aromatic trees; when the surface of the shrine has the softness and sheen of satin, and the gradual shadows give the graceful curves of falling drapery; when the cupolas seem as giant pearls, and the minárs as polished ivory; when the splash of waters breaks gently upon the silence, as the runlet, feeding a score of fountains on its way, pursues its silvery course adown the stately lines of cypress that fittingly beset the pathway to the tomb; when the spirit of the place insistently whispers:

> "Ugur Firdousi ba-roo-i zameen ust,
> Ameen ust, ameen ust, ameen ust!"[1]

and the refrain is taken up from a neighboring tamarind, in the sweet contralto of the bulbul, "Ameen ust, Ameen ust."

Then abandon yourself to the sedative influence of the scene. Dream if you will; the place was made for dreams. Or let your thoughts stray through the pages of history amongst those strange characters who lived in Agra amidst barbaric splendor, and in sensuous ease—men hard enough to murder their own flesh and blood, and soft enough to surrender their wills to those of women; men with the artistic sense that

[1] A Persian inscription inscribed upon an alabaster slab at the entrance of the Diwán-i-Khás at Delhi. A correct translation, which differs from the rendering in Lalla Rookh, is:

> "If there be a paradise on the face of the earth,
> This is it, this is it, this is it!"

could plan a Táj Mahál, or Pearl Mosque, yet capable of destroying the finest specimens of Hindu architecture; curiously disjointed characters, but perhaps in harmony with the disjointed times in which they lived. Picturesque, at least, though not amiable, and, in the main, strong men, if not intellectual.

As the rustling boughs respond to the sudden chilly wind that tells of the dawning day, turn back to the gateway and mount to the gallery at its summit. "The moon has just hidden her face beneath the western horizon, and the darkness, at its deepest, presages the approaching break of day. You look down upon the immense enclosure, crowded with trees mingled together in one indistinguishable mass, gently surging and moaning in the night breeze. Above rises, apparently in the distance, a huge gray-blue mass, without shape or form, which rests like a cloud on the gloomy sea of foliage. Soon a faint glimmer of light appears in the eastern horizon. As the darkness flies away before its gradually increasing power, the cloud changes first to pale blue and then develops into shape and proportion; and the minarets and the cupolas and the dome define themselves in clearer lines upon the still dark sky beyond. Soon the first rosy tint of the dawn appears, and, as if by magic, the whole assumes a roseate hue, which increases as the sun makes his appearance, and the Táj stands before you, dazzlingly brilliant in the purest white—absolutely perfect in its fairy proportions."

Táj Mahál, Agra

It stands in the centre of a marble terrace, about twenty feet in elevation and three hundred and thirteen feet square. At each corner is a tapering minaret one hundred and thirty-three feet in height. The Táj covers one hundred and eighty-six square feet of ground. Its central dome is eighty feet in height and one hundred and seventy-five feet in circumference. The extreme altitude, including the spire surmounting the dome, is two hundred and seventy-five feet from the level of the terrace.

The main building and the supporting minarets are made of the finest white marble, embellished with precious stones, including diamonds, sapphires, amethysts, turquoises, crystal, onyx, lapis lazuli, chalcedony, carnelian, jasper and others. These materials were drawn from China, Persia, Tibet, Bagdad, Ceylon and many parts of the Indian peninsula, while the marble was carried three hundred miles.

Outside and in, the building is covered with texts from the Kurán, the Arabic characters being formed with the most perfect precision in black marble or valuable stones. It is said that the entire book has been reproduced in this manner.

The actual tombs are in a vault below the floor of the central chamber; that of Mumtáj Mahál occupies the centre, with that of the Emperor beside it.

The Táj is but the partial realization of a design which included a mausoleum of at least equal splendor to have been erected on the farther bank of the river, and connected with the shrine of the Empress by a bridge. Sháh Jahán commenced work upon the separate mausoleum for his remains, but was probably diverted from the completion of the project by the death of the architect and the stormy events of the later years of his reign.

Exactly above the real tombs are the cenotaphs of the Emperor and Empress, enclosed by an octagonal trellis-work screen of white marble, wrought into beautiful floral forms, its borders inlaid with similar designs in precious stones. These latter forms are executed with such exactness and cunning that scores of stones are frequently found united in a single flower or leaf, and so exquisitely joined that at a distance of a few feet they look like a single piece.

The same treatment has been applied to the tomb of the Empress, but with greater success, if possible. Butler notes thirty-five different specimens of carnelian in a single leaf of a carnation, and Long asserts that he counted no fewer than three hundred different stones in one flower.

A mosaic inscription of the same character upon the side of the tomb records in Arabic the virtues of the Empress. Among other inscriptions is one at the foot of the tomb, which reads, "And defend us from the tribe of Kafirs"—that is, infidels. In accord with this invocation, a guard of two thousand soldiers was in constant possession of the building and all its approaches, with orders from the Emperor to exclude all but true Muhammadans.

The tomb of Sháh Jahán is decorated in a similar manner, but less elaborately than that of his consort.

Above these *chef d'œuvres* of mosaic art rises the magnificent dome. This structure, in combination with other portions of the building, exhibits the most extraordinary acoustic properties. It is said to emit the purest and most prolonged echo ever heard. Butler quotes "a competent judge" in the following terms: "Of all the complicated music ever heard on earth, that of a flute played gently in the vault below, as the sound rises to the dome amid a hundred arched alcoves around, and descends in heavenly reverberations upon those who sit or recline upon the cenotaphs above, is perhaps the finest to an inartificial ear. It is to the ear what the building itself is to the eye, but unhappily it cannot, like the building, live in our recollections. All that we can in after life remember is that it was heavenly, and produced heavenly emotions."

Butler adds: "Let us imagine if we can the *effect* produced here when the funeral dirge was chanted over the tomb of the lovely Empress, and the answering echoes in the pauses of the strains would seem to fall like the responses of angel choirs in paradise."

It is remarkable, in view of the perfectly patent facts of history, that so many writers state that the

Táj was built to the memory of the notorious Núr Mahál, who was the wife of Jahángír, and the aunt of Mumtáj Mahál, whom she outlived by fifteen years. That Bishop Heber and Montgomery Martin, both of whom had extended acquaintance with India, and a wide knowledge of its history, should fall into such a crass error is indeed surprising.

Few of the numerous accounts of the Táj Mahál make any mention of the architect, to whom surely the chief credit must be due. True, Sháh Jahán employed twenty thousand men for twenty-two years upon the work, and expended the equivalent of sixty million dollars upon the edifice, as Tavernier tells us; but all this would have been as naught without the poetic genius of Austin de Bordeaux, whose master mind designed and superintended the most perfect building the world has ever seen. This Frenchman held the office of Naksha Nuwes, or Chief Architect, under Sháh Jahán, who bestowed upon him the fanciful title of Zurrier Dust, the Jewel-handed. He designed the palaces of Delhi and Agra, as well as less important buildings.

Austin de Bordeaux died at Cochin, while on a political mission for his master. He is said to have been poisoned by the Portuguese, who were jealous of his influence at the Court of the Mughal.

Akbar's mausoleum is at Sikandra, about five miles out from Agra. On the way one passes many other tombs and an ancient serai, and, lastly, a two-storied

"Akbar's Tomb," Fattehpur-Sikri

red sandstone building, which is said to have been erected by Sikandar Lodi, at the end of the fifteenth century. The building, which is now occupied as an orphan asylum, is supposed to contain the remains of the Begam Miriam, Akbar's Portuguese wife, Mary. The remains were interred in the vault below, and there is a cenotaph in the upper story.

The garden surrounding Akbar's tomb is entered through a magnificent gateway of massive blocks of red sandstone, inlaid with white marble. From each corner of the gateway rises a two-storied minaret. A paved pathway leads up, through masses of flowering trees and shrubs, to the vast mausoleum of "The Guardian of Mankind." Three stories of light red sandstone, with exterior galleries, are surmounted by one of marble, within the fretted walls of which is the splendid cenotaph of the Emperor. On one side of it is carved the text, "Allahu Akbar," "God is Greatest," and on the other, "Jalla Jalallahu," "May His Glory Shine." Within a few feet of the cenotaph is a white marble pillar, with a dish upon the top of it, in which the Koh-i-núr was found by Nadír Sháh. In the crypt directly below the sarcophagus is the grave of Akbar. It is in a dark and dirty vault, neglected and squalid. The restoration which has been effected in other parts of the building might well have been extended to this chamber, whose once illuminated walls have been soiled and defaced.

Fattehpur-Sikri was Akbar's own city, founded and finished by him. Inhabited by him alone of the Great Mughals, and deserted after his death, it stands to day in excellent preservation, almost as he left it. He gave it the name of "City of Victory," to commemorate the conquest of Gujarát; but it was evidently built with a well-defined plan, and probably as a place of quiet retirement and domestic pleasure. The design of the buildings is admirably adapted to privacy and convenience. From his own quarters the Emperor could overlook all the principal streets and structures. By a covered way he could reach unobserved the house of the Begam Miriam, or that of his Turkish Sultána, or the pavilion of his Hindu wife, the Council Chamber, and other important points.

In front of the Hall of Audience is a broad veranda, from which Akbar delivered his judgments, in the hearing of the crowd assembled below.

The walls of the Emperor's sleeping apartment, or "House of Dreams," which were originally painted, display some Persian verses, referring to the Great Mughal in highly flattering terms. It is quite probable that they were the composition of Abúl Fazal. Of course, that close companion of the Emperor was not absent from the holiday expeditions to Fattehpur-Sikri. His house is pointed out, at the southern end of the city.

The Turkish queen must have been very luxuriously

Pillar in Throne Room—Fattehpur-Sikri

lodged. All that remains of her palace is a small chamber, fifteen feet square, but it is a gem of decorative architecture. "Every square inch is carved, including the soffits of the cornices. The ceiling and decoration of the veranda, pillars, and pilasters are exceptionally fine. Inside is a most elaborate dado, about four feet high, consisting of eight sculptured panels, representing forest views, animal life, etc. Above, the wall takes the form of a stone lattice screen, the divisions of which were used as shelves. Much of the carving is curiously like Chinese work."

Akbar's pachísi-board is laid out on the colored pavement of an open square. In the game, slave girls were at once the pieces used and the prizes played for.

In a building containing three large rooms, surrounded by a number of narrow, dimly-lighted passageways, the Prince Salím is said to have played hide-and-seek with the ladies of the Court.

The palace built by Rájá Bir Bal for his daughter, who was one of Akbar's wives, is the most beautiful of the many beautiful dwellings in Fattehpur-Sikri. Bir Bal was one of the Emperor's favorite Rájputs, and he was killed whilst commanding one of his armies. The palace is constructed entirely of stone, and is carved inside and out in the most exquisite manner.

In the quadrangle of the Mosque is the tomb of Salím Chisti, the celebrated saint whom Akbar held in great esteem, and after whom the Emperor's son is said to have been named. Before Fattehpur-Sikri was thought of, the sheik lived in a cave near by—to which childless women still make pilgrimage—and it is said that Akbar built the city at his suggestion.

The tomb is a beautiful little building of white marble, hardly more than large enough to hold the sarcophagus. It is surmounted by a graceful cupola, and its walls are formed of lattice-work screens. The doors of solid ebony are ornamented with brass. Over the cenotaph is a canopy, inlaid with mother-of-pearl, and from it pendent a number of ostrich eggs.

Near the Mosque building is the tomb of an infant, said to have been the son of the sheik, whose life was sacrificed in order that Akbar's son might live.

At the southern end of the quadrangle is the magnificent "Gate of Victory," which Fergusson describes as "noble beyond that of any portal attached to any mosque in India, perhaps in the whole world." From the outside, the gateway is reached by a grand flight of steps rising thirty feet from the ground. The gateway towers to a height of one hundred and thirty feet above the steps. On one side of the archway is the following curious inscription, apparently coincident with the erection of the structure: "Isa (Jesus), on whom be peace, said, 'The world is a bridge; pass over it, but build no house on it. The world endures but an hour, spend it in devotion.'"

Akbar was the actual founder of the Mughal line. He securely planted the Imperial musnud upon a solid foundation of conquest and sound policy. He conciliated his natural enemies by making concessions to their pride and by toleration of their religions. He had a genuine regard for the welfare of the common people, and displayed a wise consideration for the Hindu nobility. He made an effort to suppress satí, and is said to have personally rescued a princess of the House of Jodhpur, who was about to become an unwilling victim of the practice.

In his youth Akbar began to display those remarkable qualities which in later life distinguished him above all his fellows. To a handsome person and commanding presence he added an affable manner and gracious magnanimity. Vigorous and unyielding in war, he was lenient to a fallen foe, and neither cruel nor revengeful.

Jahángír describes his father as "of middling stature, but with a tendency to be tall, wheat-colored complexion, rather inclining to dark than fair, black eyes and eyebrows, stout body, open forehead and chest, long arms and hands. There was a fleshy wart, about the size of a small pea, on the left side of his nose, which appeared exceedingly beautiful, and which was considered very auspicious by physiognomists, who said it was the sign of immense riches and increasing prosperity. He had a very loud voice, and a very elegant and pleasant manner of speech. His manners and habits were quite different from those of other persons, and his visage was full of godly dignity." Akbar was skilled in all manly exercises, and possessed extraordinary strength. His great courage and wide knowledge of the science of warfare made him the most formidable general of his time.

He displayed in early manhood the exuberance of spirits which characterized the youth of his illustrious grandfather. In early life both Bábar and Akbar freely violated the Kuránic prohibition against indulgence in strong drink, but, unlike Jahángír, both in manhood observed strict temperance, if not abstinence. Akbar was pre-eminent as a statesman and legislator. He lightened taxation, proclaimed religious toleration, and enacted laws for the equal benefit of his subjects, regardless of race or religion.

Akbar was a liberal patron of science, the arts and letters, and gave active encouragement to intellectual pursuits on the part of his nobles. "Learned men of various kinds and from every country, and professors of many different religions and creeds, assembled at his Court, and were admitted to converse with him. Night and day people did nothing but inquire and investigate. Profound points of science, the subtleties of revelation, the curiosities of history, the wonders of Nature, of which large volumes could only give a summary abstract, were ever spoken of. His Majesty collected the opinions of every one, especially of such as were not Muhammadans, retaining whatever he approved of, and rejecting everything which was against his disposition and ran counter to his wishes. From his earliest childhood to his manhood, and from his manhood to old age, his Majesty has passed through the most diverse phases, and through all sorts of religious practices and sectarian beliefs, and has collected everything which people can find in books, with a talent of selection peculiar to him, and a spirit of inquiry opposed to every (Islámic) principle. Thus a faith based on some elementary principles traced itself on the mirror of his heart, and as a result of all the influences which were brought to bear on his Majesty, there grew, gradually as the outline on a stone, the conviction in his heart that there were sensible men in all religions, and abstemious thinkers and men endowed with miraculous powers, among all nations."

Jahángír tells us that his father was "illiterate; yet, from constantly conversing with learned and clever persons, his language was so polished that no one could discover from his conversation that he was entirely uneducated. He understood even the elegancies of poetry and prose so well that it is impossible to conceive any one more proficient."

After a brilliant reign of forty-nine years, the greatest Mughal of them all died two years after the accession of James I. to the throne of England. Jahángír has left a record of Akbar's last moments. All his omrahs had been summoned to his bedside, and, after looking wistfully round, he begged them, the companions of his glory, to forgive any offences of which he might have been guilty toward any of them. He desired to die under the ægis of Islám, and repeated the Muhammadan confession of faith in the presence of a priest.

He addressed his son in terms of affectionate admonition and advice. Then, turning to those about him, he said, "My servants and dependents, when I am gone, do not forget the afflicted in the hour of need." And so he died in peace.

CHAPTER XIV.

CAWNPUR.

DELHI, Lucknow and Cawnpur were the great storm centres of the Indian Mutiny. At these three points the struggle waged most fiercely. At Delhi, where the English were on the aggressive, many deeds of valor were performed; but, for patient heroism under heart-rending conditions, the stories of Lucknow and Cawnpur have no parallels in the splendid annals of British warfare.

In February, 1857, "it was reported to the authorities that the chowkidars, or village policemen, were speeding from Cawnpur through the villages and towns of the peninsula, distributing on their way a symbol, of the origin of which no European could at the time form an intelligible idea, or conjecture the purpose. The manner of effecting this singular movement, which later events have shown to be somewhat analogous to that of the Fire-cross of our own Highland clans in earlier times, was as follows: One of the chowkidars of Cawnpur ran to another at Futteghar, the next village, and placing in his hands two chupatties (small unleavened cakes), directed him to make ten more of the same kind, and give two of them to each of the five nearest chowkidars, with instructions to perform the same service. He was obeyed, and in a few hours the whole country was in a state of excitement through these policemen running from village to village with these cakes. The wave spread over the provinces with a velocity of speed never yet equaled by the bearers of government dispatches. The English officials in the districts through which this extraordinary and mysterious operation progressed with the rapidity of light, were bewildered; some of the messengers were arrested, and themselves and the cakes examined by the magistrates and superior police, who looked at, handled and tasted the latter, but could arrive at no satisfactory conclusion respecting them. The chowkidars professed to be ignorant of the source whence they originated, or of the object in view by their transmission and distribution over the country, which they believed to be by the order of the Government. The magistrates thereupon reported the occurrence as a strange but harmless affair . . . but no one appeared capable of elucidating the mystery in which it was involved. Some thought it might be a superstitious act of Hindu faith; others who, more penetrating than their neighbors, ventured to suggest the possibility of a plot against the Government, were laughed at for their apprehensions."

When the storm burst with such unexpected

suddenness in May, 1857, Cawnpur, like most of the stations of Upper India, was almost defenceless against an uprising of the native army. There were but sixty European artillerymen, with six guns, to oppose three thousand native troops of all arms.

The station was without any fort or place of refuge, and when Sir Hugh Wheeler had entrenched a few buildings on the ground which is now the European parade, it was a sorry shelter, though the best that could be provided, for the women and children. In those entrenchments the sturdy veteran terminated an honorable life and over fifty years of splendid service in the Indian Army.

During the month of May, and before the native regiments had broken into actual revolt, the garrison at Cawnpur was reinforced by fifty-five men of the Thirty-second and two companies of the Eighty-fourth, Queen's regiments. Despite his critical position, the gallant old soldier responded promptly to a call for aid from a comrade by detaching from his meagre force a full company. On June 3d he telegraphed to the Governor-General—and this was his last report—as follows:

"Sir Henry Lawrence having expressed some uneasiness, I have just sent him by dák gharries, out of my small force, two officers and fifty men of Her Majesty's Eighty-fourth Foot. Conveyance for more not available. This leaves me weak, but I trust to hold my own until more Europeans arrive."

That same night indications of an outbreak were so apparent that the women and children, to the number of about four hundred, were ordered to assemble within the entrenchment, and the next morning the native corps were in open mutiny.

For twenty-three days—until the fateful 27th of June—the eight hundred Europeans within their slim defences bore the incessant fire and the repeated attacks of the besiegers, whose ranks had been swelled to the number of twelve thousand. Time and again the defenders repulsed assaults, and even sallied forth from their breastworks and routed the enemy. It was in the sortie of June 22d that Sir Hugh Wheeler received his death wound. But the sorest trials of the garrison were the lack of water and food in a tropical summer. The suffering of the women and children and the wounded was intense. Many lives were laid down in attempts to relieve them. The only well was kept under an incessant fire, day and night. Its woodwork, and even the brick coping, was shot to pieces, and to-day it stands a mute monument of the heroic courage of John Mackillop and others, who daily ran the gauntlet of a thousand bullets to get a few buckets of its precious fluid.

Before the capitulation two hundred and fifty souls found a fortunate release in death. Each night, through three long weeks, the bodies of those who had passed away during the day were carried to a

Memorial Well—Cawnpur

well outside the entrenchment and silently lowered into it. The spot, near by the modern barracks, is now enclosed, and marked by a cross, which bears an inscription running thus: "In a well under this Cross were laid, by the hands of their fellows in suffering, the bodies of men, women and children, who died hard by during the heroic defence of Wheeler's Entrenchment, when beleagured by the rebel Náná—June 6th to 27th, A.D. MDCCCLVII."

Where now stands a church was the hospital building, which, taking fire from a shell, burned to the ground on the eighth day of the siege. W. J. Shepherd, a non-combatant, who owed his life to the fact that he volunteered, with magnificent daring, to carry dispatches through the enemy's lines, thus narrates the circumstance:

"The enemy now commenced firing live shells, well heated, with the intent of setting fire to the tents of officers in the compound, as also to the thatched barracks (hospital). . . . The tents, therefore, had all to be struck, as several had been thus burnt; and at last, on the 13th of June, the barrack also took fire; it was about five P.M.; and that evening was one of unspeakable distress and trial; for all the wounded and sick were in it, also the families of the soldiers and drummers. . . . The flames spread out so quickly that it was a hard matter to remove the women and children, who were all in great confusion; so that the helpless wounded and sick could not be removed, and were all burnt to ashes (about forty or upwards in number). . . . It was perfectly impracticable to save any of the wounded or the medicines, in consequence of the insurgents collecting in very large bodies in the adjacent compounds and buildings, with their muskets and swords, ready every moment to pounce down upon us; and the men were compelled to keep their places under the walls of the entrenchment, and could not bear a helping hand to those in the barracks."

Thus two hundred and fifty women and children, many of them delicate and unused to the least privation, were robbed of shelter and forced to pass the remaining twelve days of the siege upon the bare ground in the open. Sunstroke, exhaustion, bursting shells, and bullets mercifully terminated the sufferings of many; but all bore themselves, as eye-witnesses have testified, with the firm courage becoming the wives and daughters of soldiers.

"It is beyond description to attempt to give a detail of the innumerable troubles and distresses to which all in the entrenchment were subjected. The poor wounded and sick were objects of real commiseration; for their state was extremely wretched. The stench also from the dead bodies of horses and other animals that had been shot in the compound, and could not be removed, as also the unusually great influx of flies, rendered the place extremely disagreeable. Thus it will not be wondered at when I say that many persons were extremely anxious to get out of the entrenchment;" and so, when the Náná offered safe conduct to the garrison, and boats to take them down the river to Allahábád, they unfortunately agreed to the proposition and placed themselves in his hands.

The terms of capitulation were solemnly ratified by "Dhoondu Náná Pant, Peshwá," over his seal and signature, with the usual oaths, that, until violated in this instance by himself, had been held sacred by the whole Hindu race—his principal officers joining in the ceremony.

As eloquent testimony to their heroic defence they left two buildings, of which an officer, who subsequently visited the spot, wrote, "The walls are pitted with cannon-shot like the cells of a honey-comb. The doors, which seem to have been the principal points against which the Náná's fire was directed, are breached and knocked down into huge shapeless openings. Of the verandas which surrounded both the buildings, only a few splintered rafters remain; and at some of the angles the walls are knocked entirely away, and huge chasms gape blackly at you. Many of the enemy's cannon-shot had gone through and through the buildings; portions of the interior walls and roof had fallen; and here and there are blood gouttes on wall and floor. Never yet had I seen a place so terribly battered."

On the morning of the 27th of June, the garrison, reduced to less than half its original number, passed along the avenue of trees that leads to the river, by the Temple of Siva, now fast falling into ruin, and so down the steps of the ghát, which was the scene of as foul a deed of treachery as any in the history of the world.

Hardly half a dozen men survived the massacre at the ghát. The fate of the women and children was yet worse. They had three weeks more of untold suffering to endure before the butchery of July 15th terminated their miseries. Their last resting place is marked by an enclosed mound, over which is the somewhat trite figure of an angel. It is not adequate —nothing could be adequate—to the great tragedy it commemorates. One cannot help but think that a simple slab had been more fitting.

The inscriptions read, "Sacred to the perpetual memory of a great company of Christian people, chiefly women and children, who near this spot were cruelly murdered by the followers of the rebel Náná Dhúndu Pant, of Bithúr, and cast, the dying with the dead, into the well below, on the xvth day of July, MDCCCLVII."

"These are they which came out of great tribulation."

Of all the scenes associated with the Mutiny, none conjures up such sad thoughts as does Cawnpur and its Memorial Well. Keen as the horror of the tragedy is the regret that so brave a defence should have gone for naught—and yet, not for naught surely, when it left so grand a lesson of heroism to the world.

A few miles from Cawnpur stands the remnant of the palace of Bithúr, in which Bájí Ráo passed the last years of a life so foul that it seemed impossible that it could be surpassed in bestial ferocity and sensual indulgence, until eclipsed by the supreme villainy of his adopted son Sírík Dhúndu Pant, generally known as Náná Sáhib.

On the death of the ex-Peshwá, Náná Sáhib, then about thirty years of age, inherited his immense private fortune, but failed to induce the Government to continue the pension of four hundred thousand dollars a year, which had been allowed to Bájí Ráo. Satisfied that there was nothing to be gained by application to the authorities in India, the Náná determined to prosecute his claim in England, and for that purpose dispatched an agent to the British capital.

The man chosen for this mission was a shrewd and talented scoundrel named Azí Múllah. In early life this Muhammadan had been a khitmatgar, or table-waiter. He appears to have had a facility for the acquirement of languages, and learned to read and write both English and French with fluency. He was plentifully supplied with money by the Náná, and in London contrived to cut a considerable figure, and to create a sensation in social circles. He arrived at the height of the London season of 1854, and seems to have been accepted without question, on his mere statement that he was a prince of good birth and enormous wealth. Society lionized him, and the women pronounced him "perfectly charming." His handsome person, native wit and marvelous jewels made a deep impression, and one young lady of good family came perilously near contracting marriage with the pretender. It is needless to say that Azí Múllah's errand on behalf of his master was futile, but he lost nothing in the regard of the latter, to whom he continued to be, after his return, companion, councilor and general factotum. Under a show of extreme cordiality these two nursed their deep hatred to the English. The Náná affected the society of the English residents of Cawnpur, entertained them at Bithúr, and was by them considered a very agreeable and friendly neighbor.

The palace was furnished in European style, in a most extravagant manner, but not in the best of taste. The stable was extensive, and contained the finest horses, elephants and camels obtainable. There was a fine kennel, and a menagerie "which would have done credit to any Eastern monarch, from the days of Solomon downward." The armory was a comprehensive collection of the weapons of all ages and countries. The equipages were imported from London, at great cost, and were the best productions of the metropolitan manufacturers.

The Náná's plate, jewelry and wardrobe were of fabulous worth, his sword of state alone having cost, it is said, one hundred and fifty thousand dollars.

All this for public display; but the palace, like its owner's character, had a secret side of which few were aware. In it were apartments "horribly unfit for any human eye, where both European and native artists had done their utmost to gratify the corrupt master, who was willing to incur any expense for the completion of his loathsome picture-gallery."

How successfully this fiend contrived to veil his real character may be judged from the statement of one who had an extensive acquaintance with him. "I knew Náná Sáhib intimately," he says, "and always regarded him as one of the best and most hospitable natives in the Upper Provinces, and certainly one of the last men to have been guilty of the atrocities laid to his charge." He is described as "very fat . . . his face round, his eyes very wild, brilliant and restless; his complexion, as is the case with most native gentlemen, scarcely darker than a dark Spaniard; his expression, on the whole, of a jovial, indeed somewhat rollicking, character."

After the massacre at Cawnpur, there was no individual in the whole length and breadth of the country upon whom the British soldiers were more keenly eager to lay hands; but the Náná, with cunning dexterity, evaded them to the end.

When his army fell back before Havelock, the Náná was already in flight, and the burning of his palace was but meagre satisfaction to the men who had seen the fresh blood of his victims. He joined the insurgents at Lucknow, but again fled in the face of danger, and was at large, a hunted fugitive, during the closing operations of the following year.

The ultimate fate of Náná Sáhib is a matter of conjecture. He probably died in the jungle, a prey to wild beasts, or the victim of starvation.

CHAPTER XV.

LUCKNOW.

Lucknow, the capital of Oudh, lies on both sides of the Gúmti. It is the fourth in size of the cities of India, having a population of about two hundred and seventy thousand, contained in an area of thirty-six square miles.

About six miles distant is the ancient Ayodhyá, one of the principal scenes of the Rámáyana, and the capital of the great Solar race, the ancestors of the families of Udaipur and Jodhpur.

During the revolutionary period of the latter half of the eighteenth century, the Persian Sádat Khán established an independent kingdom in Oudh. "Ayodhyá (the ancient capital) and Lucknow were the places at which he chiefly resided, and having assumed for his crest the fish, which is still, so to speak, the arms of Oudh, he changed the name of the well-known fort of Lucknow from Kila Likna (so called after the founder, one Likna Ahur) to Machi Bhawan, or the fish-house."

The successive rulers of Oudh were notoriously incompetent, and with few exceptions hopelessly depraved. Worst of them all was the Nawáb Nazír-ud-dín, who "might one hour be seen in a state of drunken nudity with his boon companions and the low menial who was his chief confidant; at another he would parade the streets of Lucknow, drunk at mid-day, driving one of his own elephants. All decency and propriety were banished from the Court" during the reign of this profligate, who died in 1837. Ten years later, Wajid Alí, "the last, and, with the exception of Nazír-ud-dín, perhaps the most despicable, of his line, mounted the throne." After repeated and futile warnings, he was deposed in February, 1856, and passed the balance of his life in splendid ease as a pensioner of the British Government.

Oudh was annexed, and the condition of its millions became immediately bettered; but this could only be achieved at the expense of the grandees and land-holders, who had previously robbed and oppressed the peasantry. Thus it happened that at the time of the Mutiny the province of Oudh contained a large and influential element which was highly discontented and ripe for mischief. Sir Henry Lawrence was the Commissioner, and to his wise and energetic measures is due the fact that Lucknow was not the scene of such a disaster as befell Cawnpur.

The Residency was the main point of a cluster of buildings which Sir Henry entrenched and fortified as far as possible. The position extended about seven

Ruins of the Residency—Lucknow

hundred yards from northwest to southeast, and four hundred yards from east to west.

The entrenchment was commanded on all sides by buildings which gave shelter to the enemy's riflemen, who, after the outbreak, ceased to have any compunctions about using the defiling cartridges, which afforded the chief excuse for the Mutiny. The difficulties and disadvantages of the position are made apparent by a very perfect model of the Residency contained in the Museum of Lucknow.

The building, which has given its name to the entire entrenchment, was an imposing three-story structure, standing upon the greatest elevation in the neighborhood. It has a subterranean apartment, in which a number of women found shelter. From the first, and throughout the siege, the Residency was a particular target for the enemy's guns, and its present ruined condition speaks more eloquently than words of the fearful storms of lead that beat upon it.

"After repeatedly facing the perils of treason, and the more honorable dangers of the battle-field, it was the fate of Sir Henry Lawrence to be stricken down in a moment of comparative repose, and beneath the shelter of his own roof. It had happened, during the morning of the 1st of July, that an eight-inch shell, from a battery of the rebels, entered a small apartment of the Residency, in which at the time Sir Henry Lawrence was sitting, in conversation with his private secretary, Mr. Couper. The missile burst between them without injuring either, and now, as the Residency seemed to have become a special target for the round shot and shells of the insurgents, the officers of Sir Henry's staff earnestly besought him to remove his personal quarters to another and more secure part of the building. He, however, declined to accede to their wishes, jestingly observing that the room was so small another shell would certainly never pitch into it. Unfortunately, his error was a fatal one. On the very next day, while resting on a couch in the same apartment, after several hours of severe and exhausting labor, another shell penetrated the wall and burst, one of the fragments inflicting a wound upon Sir Henry that was immediately known to be mortal."

The dying chief was removed to the house of Doctor Fayrer—now a ruin—near the Bailey Guard Gate. By some means the rebels learned of his presence there and his plight, and concentrated their fire upon the place.

"In the veranda, with the shells hissing through the air and the pillars crashing to the stroke of the bullets," the Last Sacrament was administered, in the presence of a grief-stricken circle of subordinates.

Sir Henry approached his end with the calm fortitude of a Christian and a soldier, his mind filled with concern for others. Although suffering extreme agony, he spoke with perfect self-possession during his last hours, dictating farewell messages to his children, commending the Lawrence Asylum for soldiers' orphans to the support of the Government, insisting that "no fuss" should be made over his burial, and that his tombstone should bear only the simple epitaph which is chiseled upon it, "Here lies Henry Lawrence, who tried to do his duty. May God have mercy on him"; and almost with his last breath urging upon his officers never to surrender.

A few yards from Doctor Fayrer's house is one of a number of pillars which have been set up to mark the sites of the several posts by which the Residency was surrounded. "Anderson's" and the "Cawnpur Battery" Posts were perhaps the most exposed of all. Duprat's Post was commanded by a gallant Frenchman, who had been an officer in the army of his native country.

Before the ruins of Gubbin's House stands the scarred and battered trunk of an old tree, which displayed a verdant vigor at the time of the siege, when "its colossal trunk and massive branches interrupted many a roundshot; day by day the boughs were shot away, till little but the stem remained."

Near Ommaney's House is the Begam Kothi, in whose underground apartments a number of women passed the weary days of the siege in comparative safety, but extreme discomfort. There they crowded together in a small room, "perfectly dark," and so "always obliged to light a candle for breakfast and dinner." They had "only room for very few chairs" down there, and those were assigned to invalids. They slept upon the ground, "packed into each other like bits in a puzzle." But even such cramped and loathsome quarters afforded a grateful exemption from the terrors of the bullet-swept entrenchment above.

When the enclosure was first made about the Residency, there were within the entrenchments seven hundred and ninety-two Europeans. Of that number no less than five hundred and twenty-two were women and children, and one hundred and thirty-eight civilians, to whom, however, the technical term "non-combatant" could not be applied with literal truth.

At a subsequent period, when the Machi Bhawan had been blown up and all outlying posts abandoned, the Residency—that is, be it understood, the lines surrounding it—became the shelter for a much greater number of people, including, besides the British troops, natives, some of whom remained faithful to the end.

The place was invested on the 1st of July; Havelock's reinforcement effected an entry on the 25th of September, and on the 17th of November Sir Colin Campbell's relief column raised the siege. Every day of those long months was "marked with some vicissitudes." They were days to try men's souls, and the story of gallant deeds done, and hardships endured with patient stoicism, would fill many volumes such as this.

One day the Bailey Guard would be fiercely attacked; the next, Anderson's point would be assailed. Then a general assault would be made at every point. Meanwhile a shower of lead swept the entrenchment day and night. After a hard day, a few of the defenders would lie down at midnight, only to be aroused in an hour or two by the report of an attack on the Cawnpur Battery or Sago's Post. Fire had to be fought from time to time, as the enemy's shells set alight buildings, and incessant mining necessitated constant watch and countermining. Men worked like Titans and fought like demons. At Anderson's, eighty men are attacked by "several thousands of merciless, bloodthirsty fanatics. They well know what they have to expect if they are defeated," and therefore each individual fights for his very life. At Innes' House, Lieutenant Loughnan maintains "a long and fierce contest against a body of insurgents twenty-fold more numerous" than the little band that is entrusted with the defence of the place; and before the rebels desist a hundred of their number are laid low. Captain Mansfield and three other officers sally forth, spike a gun and kill about forty of the enemy. Captain Fulton makes a sortie and blows up a number of houses which had afforded shelter to the insurgents' marksmen.

After days such as these, officers had to employ themselves at night in burying dead bullocks and horses, the stench from whose carcasses became overpowering, and, together with "the hot vapors from stagnant pools, engendered fevers, cholera and other diseases." The children died rapidly, and the hospitals were "so crowded with wounded and dying that there was no room to pass between them." Officers and men lay together upon the ground, "covered with blood and often with vermin."

In the day, flies; in the night, mosquitoes; but the latter were bearable, the former intolerable. "The mass of putrid matter that was allowed to accumulate, the rains, the commissariat stores, the hospitals, had attracted these insects in incredible numbers. They swarmed in millions." Each day hundreds of thousands were blown into the air with gunpowder, but their numbers did not appear to diminish. "The ground was still black with them, and the tables were ever covered" with them. The beef, of which each person "got a tolerably small quantity each day, was usually studded with them."

Eight weeks of struggle and suffering dragged through without any aid or encouragement, only a letter from Havelock saying that three weeks at least must elapse before he could reach them. With every day the conditions became worse. As the bullet-riddled houses known as Anderson's, Gubbin's and Duprat's ceased to afford shelter to the women and children lodged there, they were removed to the already over-crowded refuges in the centre of the entrenchment. "A few little creatures ('siege babies,' as their poor mothers called them) came into the world during this stormy period; and with them each day was a struggle for life."

Death laid many low; disease and wounds prostrated a still greater number, and those who survived were prey to apprehensions that weakened body and mind.

Now and then, "when an officer is struck down to death," an auction is held of the few trifling comforts he may have remained in possession of. Thus £7 is paid for a ham; £4 for a quart bottle of honey; £5 for two small tins of preserved soup; and £3 for a cake of chocolate. "And these prices were moderate compared with those given towards the close of the siege." The tea and sugar were exhausted, save for a small store reserved for the sick. The tobacco was all gone, and "the soldiers, yearning for a pipe after a hard day's work, smoked dry leaves, as the only substitute they could obtain."

As the time lengthened out toward the twelfth week the enemy displayed increased activity. The musketry fire increased; mining and open assaults became almost incessant, and the endurance of the garrison was well nigh exhausted, when, one morning, a cry arose from the British soldiers, "The Minié! The Minié!" Amidst the rattle of musketry on the outside they had detected the familiar whistle of the bullet of the Minié rifle, with which only European troops were armed, and the sound told the weary watchers that "Havelock's Saints" were fighting their way through the streets of Lucknow.

Northwest of the Residency stands the great Imambara, the "largest room in the world which has an arched roof without supports." This hall is one hundred and sixty-three feet long and fifty feet broad. Fergusson thus describes its curious construction: "This immense building is covered with vaults of very simple form, and still simpler construction, being of rubble or coarse concrete several feet in thickness, which is laid on a rude mould or centreing of bricks and mud, and allowed to stand a year or two to set and dry. The centreing is then removed, and the vault, being in one piece, stands without abutment or thrust, apparently a better and more durable form of roof than our most scientific Gothic vaulting, certainly far cheaper and far more easily made, since it is literally cast on a mud form, which may be moulded into any shape the fancy of the architect may dictate." The Imambara was built by the Nawáb Asuf-uddaulá, in order to afford relief to the people in the great famine of 1784. It was once splendidly decorated, but all its ornamentation has disappeared. A plain slab, without inscription, marks the spot where the Nawáb was buried. The western entrance, called the Rúmi Darwazah, or Constantinople Gate, is said to have been built in imitation of the famous gate from which the title of "Sublime Porte" is derived. The Kaiser Bagh, or Cæsar's Garden, was constructed

The Kaiser Bagh—Lucknow

at great cost by the last King of Oudh. It was the scene of hard fighting and great slaughter during the relief operations. At the gateway of the Kaisar Bagh the gallant Neill fell dead.

The Farad Bakhsh Palace was erected by Sádat Alí Khán, a brother of Asuf-ud-daulá. The portion of it that overlooked the river had belonged to the celebrated French adventurer Claude Martin. The ceremony of accession to the throne took place here, and is thus described by a woman who was present on one such occasion: "The Resident, with all due form, having taken off the King's turban, placed the crown upon his head, and he ascended the musnud.

"I was standing next to the Resident and the Prime Minister, when, during a part of the ceremony, a shower of precious stones was thrown over us. I looked at the Resident, and saw him move his arm to allow the valuables that had fallen upon him to drop to the ground; I imitated his example by moving my scarf, on which some were caught; it would have been *infra dig.* to have retained them; they fell to the ground and were scrambled for by the natives; the shower consisted of emeralds, rubies, pearls, etc."

The Sháh Najif was built by Ghazí-ud-dín Haidar, the first King of Oudh, and is his mausoleum. It is a white mosque, surrounded by a high, strong wall.

The Sháh Najif marks one of the most critical stages of Sir Colin Campbell's relief operations. After "fighting every inch of ground from the first streak of dawn," the troops reached the mosque in the late afternoon, and found their way to the Residency barred by it. "For three hours the bombardment lasted, and no impression was made upon the stout walls. For three hours the Sháh Najif sent forth a perennial stream of fire. To remain was sheer death. To retreat by the narrow defile blocked by troops was out of the question. The moment was decisive. Colin Campbell, collecting the Ninety-third around him, said unto them, 'I had no intention of employing you again to-day, but the Sháh Najif must be taken. The artillery cannot drive the enemy out, so you must with the bayonet.'" And when their old chief declared his intention of leading them in person, a cheer went up from the ranks of the weary Highlanders, and every man braced himself for the coming struggle. "The gray-haired veteran of many fights rode, with his sword drawn, at their head. Keen was his eye as when, in the pride of youth, he led the stormers at Sebastian. They went on steadily till before them towered a wall twenty feet high, from whose parapets and countless loopholes came in blasts a storm of musket balls. Many fell. The assailants replied to their slayers with musketry, yet with little effect, and no ladders were available for escalading the ramparts. Nothing was to be done but to breach them. Peel poured his broadsides into the stout, massive walls; but no impression was made on the solid masonry. Never did English soldiers and sailors distinguish themselves more than on this afternoon. They worked the guns, though every moment many were killed, and more were wounded. But while their own losses were terrible, they could inflict but little in return. They were being destroyed by bullets, and that was all. Day was fast turning into night. The rocket tubes were brought up, and while they discharged their fiery missiles into the building, Peel, with the reluctance of a brave man, slowly withdrew his guns. At this moment fifty Highlanders, creeping stealthily through the brushwood, guided by Sergeant Paton, of the regiment, reached a rent in the wall, which Paton had discovered. A soldier was pushed up with some difficulty. Several men immediately followed. The small party, pushing on, gained the main gateway, and threw it open for their comrades. The white dresses of the last of the garrison were just seen gliding away amidst the rolling smoke in the dark shadows of the night."

The relief column received another check at the Sikandar Bagh, which is a garden enclosure about one hundred and twenty yards square. The high wall is loopholed throughout its length, and strengthened with bastions at every angle. Sir Colin Campbell said, "There never was a bolder feat of arms than the storming of the Sikandar Bagh."

Lieutenant Cooper, of the Ninety-third, was the first in, diving head-foremost through a small breach, "like a clown in a pantomime." A Sikh got his arm within the gate; it was immediately cut off, but he quickly substituted the other, and held it there until his comrades had effected an entrance. This Lord Roberts qualifies as the bravest deed he ever witnessed.

When the Bagh was taken, two thousand Sepoys lay dead and dying within the enclosure.

Within the lines of the entrenchment, and near Anderson's Post and the Cawnpur Battery, is a "whimsical pile," which was formerly the residence of Claude Martin, and is now, in accordance with his will, a well-endowed school for boys.

Martin, a man of obscure origin, came to India as a private soldier in the French service. He was attached to the garrison of Chandinágar, and when that place was captured by Clive, Martin enlisted in the army of the East India Company, and rose to the grade of captain. He subsequently entered the service of the King of Oudh, and gained high rank, as well as great wealth. He enjoyed the implicit confidence of the people for his integrity and wisdom. "His character in that respect became so established that the natives who had amassed money and dreaded the rapacious grasp of the sovereign, entrusted their riches to the care of General Martin. Such amplitude of funds enabled him to take advantage of many favorable opportunities, and to make many advantageous speculations, so that he gathered extraordinary wealth. He expended some of it in erecting this house, on a plan entirely his own. The idea of it was probably taken from those castles of pastry, which used to adorn desserts in former days. The mansion consisted of three stories, gradually diminishing in the size of the square, so as to leave to the two upper stories a broad space between the apartments and the parapet which covered the wall of the story below it. This was for the purpose of defence, with a view to which the building was constructed.

"The doors of the principal floor were plated with iron, and each window was protected by an iron grate. Loopholes from passages above gave the means of firing in perfect security upon any persons who should force their way into these lower apartments. The spiral stone staircases were blocked at intervals with iron doors; in short, the whole was framed for protracted and desperate resistance. The parapets and pinnacles were decorated with a profusion of plaster lions, Grecian gods and Chinese figures, forming the most whimsical assemblage possible. Still, the magnitude of the building, with its cupolas and spires, gave it a certain magnificence."

For Englishmen, and indeed for all who are familiar with the story of Havelock's noble life, the ruins of the Dilkúsha must have a touching interest. Here, in what was then a handsome villa, they carried him from the Residency to die only a few days after the final relief of Lucknow. A lofty obelisk marks the spot where, "on the low plain by the Alum Bagh, they made his humble grave; and Campbell and Outram and Inglis, and many a stout soldier who had followed him in all his headlong march, and through the long, fatal street, were gathered there to perform the last rites to one of England's noble dead. As long as the memory of great deeds, and high courage, and spotless self-devotion, is cherished among his countrymen, so long will Havelock's lonely tomb in the grove beneath the scorching Eastern sky, hard by the vast city—the scene alike of his toil, his triumph and his death—be regarded as one of the most holy of the many holy spots where her patriot soldiers lie."

CHAPTER XVI.

THE HOLY LAND OF BUDDHISM.

At least five hundred years before the battle of Actium, Prince Gautama was born at his father's capital, Kapilavastu, situated on the northeastern boundary of Hindustán. A Rájput of the ancient Solar line, and chief of the noble Sakya clan, King Suddhodana hoped to find in his son and heir a warrior worthy of the martial traditions of his house. But from his earliest years the little prince was prone to solitary day-dreams, and given

> "To meditate this deep disease of life,
> What its far source and whence its remedy;
> So vast a pity filled him, such wide love
> For living things, such passion to heal pain,
> That by their stress his princely spirit passed
> To ecstasy, and, purged from mortal taint
> Of sense and self, the boy attained thereat
> Dhyána, first step of 'the path.'"

However, in open Swayamvara, he proved his superiority in manly exercises by defeating in turn every one of the champions of the kingdom. And thus he won the fair Yasodhara, and for a time forgot "his world" in a "calm home of happy life and love."

After ten years, Yasodhara bore a son, thus completing for her husband the second stage of the ancient Hindu saintly life. Then

> "Once again the spirit of the Prince
> Was moved to see this world beyond his gates,
> This life of man, so pleasant if its waves
> Ran not to waste and woful finishing
> In Time's dry sands."

It cost him grief unutterable to tear himself away forever from his beloved wife and babe, but because his "heart beat with each throb of all the hearts that ached," he determined to sacrifice all—kin and kingdom, ease and happiness—for the sake of mankind. With

> "Tearful eyes raised to the stars, and lips
> Close-set with purpose of prodigious love,"

he turned his back upon the palace, and discarding his royal robes for beggar's rags, went forth into the world alone.

Thus, in the twenty-ninth year of his life, did Gautama effect the Great Renunciation. He retired to the depths of the jungles in the Gáya district, and there gave himself up to meditation and self-discipline. Gradually it was borne in upon him that "the way" was not through fasting and penance, the self-seeking methods of the Bráhmans, but by active work in the world.

"Thou who wouldst see where dawned the light at last,
Northwestwards from the 'Thousand Gardens' go
By Gunga's valley, till thy steps be set
On the green hills where those twin streamlets spring,
Nilájan and Mohána; follow them,
Winding beneath broad-leaved mahúa trees,
'Mid thickets of the sansár and the bir,
Till on the plain the shining sisters meet
In Phalgú's bed, flowing by rocky banks
To Gáya and the red Barabar hills."

There, behind the temple, you may see the tree, or a lineal descendant of it, sacred to five hundred millions of mankind, beneath which Buddha sat when "Enlightenment" came to him, and "when the conflict began between the Saviour of the World and the Prince of Evil."

"The ten chief Sins came—Mara's mighty ones,
Angels of evil— . . . .
But Buddha answered, 'What thou bidd'st me keep
Is form which passes, but the free Truth stands.
Get thee unto thy darkness!'"

And as the soul of the "Enlightened" wrestled with the "Mighty One of Evil," the elements were convulsed, "the earth shook, the sea uprose from her bed, the rivers turned back to the mountains, the hill-tops fell crashing to the plains, the sun was darkened, and a host of headless spirits rode upon the tempest." This was Buddha's second birth.

Two months after the temptation in the wilderness Buddha commenced his ministry by teaching in the

Deer Park, on the outskirts of the great city of Benares.

At the outset he rejected the exclusiveness of the Bráhmans, and made his appeal to all classes alike, women and Súdras being among his earliest converts. In a few months he had drawn to himself sixty disciples, and these he sent abroad, saying, "Go ye now and preach the most excellent Law." It was a doctrine of self-renunciation, and peace and goodwill toward all men—a sublime philosophy, capable of an intensely practical application.

Through Behar, Oudh, and the country of the Northwest, Buddha traveled widely, preaching unceasingly, "converting nations, withstanding kings, eluding assassins, and sifting out false disciples." In after ages monasteries and temples marked the principal points upon his route. After forty-six years of unremitting ministry, he died, at the age of eighty, at Kasia, in the District of Gorackpur.

He passed his last night in prayer, and in comforting a weeping disciple. The parting words of Siddártha—that is, "He who has fulfilled his end"—to those about him were, "Work out your salvation with diligence."

Sarnath is associated with the earliest ministry of Buddha. Here was the Deer Park, in which he first "turned the wheel of the Law." The Chinese pilgrims Fa Hian and Hiouen Thsang visited the place, the former at the end of the fourth century, and the latter in the middle of the seventh century.

Hiouen Thsang gives a detailed description of Sarnath as he found it: "Its precincts are divided into eight portions (sections), connected by a surrounding wall. The storied towers, with projecting eaves, and the balconies, are very superior work. There are fifteen hundred priests in this convent. In the great enclosure is a vihara (monastery), about three hundred feet high; above the roof is a golden covered figure of the Amra (An-mo-lo-mango) fruit. The foundations of the building are of stone, and the stairs also; but the towers and niches are of brick. The niches are arranged in the four sides in a hundred successive lines, and in each niche is a golden figure of Buddha. In the middle of the vihara is a figure of Buddha, made of native copper. It is the size of life, and he is represented as turning the wheel of the Law (preaching)."

There was a stupa of brick, with one hundred niches encircling it, and in each niche "a statue of Buddha, in embossed gold. To the southwest of the vihara was a stone stupa, raised by Asoka, having in front a column seventy feet high, on the spot where Buddha delivered his first discourse. West of the monastery was a tank in which Buddha bathed; to the west of that another, where he washed his monks' water-pot; and to the north a third, where he washed his garments. Close to the tanks was a stupa, then another, and then, in the midst of a forest, a third. To the southwest of the monastery was a stupa, three hundred feet high, resplendent with jewels, and surmounted by an arrow." In front of this was a lofty pillar of stone, "as bright as jade. It is glistening, and sparkles like light; and all those who pray fervently before it see from time to time, according to their petitions, figures, with good and bad signs." A high mound of solid brickwork is all that remains of the stupa, which was once adorned with "precious substances."

Guided by the precise description of Hiouen Thsang, excavations were made in the vicinity, and resulted in bringing to light the ruins of the monastery. "The final destruction of the large monastery, which took place towards the ninth or tenth century, was, no doubt, sudden and unexpected; for among the calcined beams of the roofs, and beneath the ashes, have been found, as in Pompeii, household utensils, corn, and remains of wheaten cakes. The monks must have been surprised by their foes, and the conflagration so swift that they had to fly for life as they were preparing their daily food. Many must have perished in the flames."

The Dhamek Stupa, the only one now existing, rises to a height of over one hundred feet above its stone base. It was explored by General Cunningham, who found no relics in it, but at a depth of about ten feet from the summit came upon a

Buddhist Tope—Sarnath

large stone bearing the usual Buddhist formula, "Ye dharma hetu," etc.[1] The weight of antiquarian opinion assigns this stupa to the seventh century.

In all the wide world there is no place that is held sacred by so many of mankind as is Buddh Gáya. What Jerusalem was to mediæval Europe; what Mecca became to the Muhammadan countries, it is the scene of the "Enlightenment" to the people of China, Tibet, Burma, Japan, Ceylon, and many islands of the Indian Archipelago. Nor are the Buddhists alone in their reverence for the place. The Bráhmans venerate Buddha as an incarnation of Vishnu in his ninth avatar, and numbers of Hindus make the pilgrimage to Buddh Gáya.

The temple lies in a depression of the ground, which detracts somewhat from its appearance. It is, nevertheless, an imposing building, rising to a height of one hundred and seventy feet from the ground. It is a nine-storied pyramid, embellished in the usual manner with crowded forms and figures. The structure is in a remarkable state of preservation, con-

[1] Sir Edwin Arnold, in "The Light of Asia," gives the following rendering of the formula:

"Ye dharma hetuppabhawá
Yesan hétun Tathágató;
Aha yesan cha yo nirodhó
Ewan wadi Maha samano."

"What life's course and cause sustain
These Tathágato made plain;
What delivers from life's woe
That our Lord hath made us know."

sidering that it probably dates from the third or fourth century of the present era. In fact, it is difficult to associate its appearance with the thought of such extreme old age.

King Asoka, the convert, built a temple on the spot, and the present structure probably covers its site. In one of the earliest years of the nineteenth century the King of Burma sent an expedition to Buddh Gáya for the purpose of restoring the temple. The place was then in the possession of a colony of Sivaite priests, who had obtained some sort of title from the Court of Delhi.

In 1861 the Archæological Survey made explorations with important results. Amongst other things, was unearthed a considerable portion of the stone railing which had been erected by Asoka. The posts and rails are carved with flowers and figures, the most ancient sculptures in India.

In 1877 permission was again given to the Burmese to engage in the work of restoration. This was an unfortunate concession; for, as an official report states, "the Burmese carried on demolitions and excavations, which in a manner swept away most of the old landmarks." The damage they did was irreparable. Finally the work of restoration reverted to the Archæological Survey, and was completed under the supervision of General Cunningham.

The famous Bo tree, literally, "The Tree of Enlightenment," stands upon an enclosed platform in

Temple of Buddh Gáya

close proximity to the temple, and undoubtedly upon the very spot which has, from the time of Asoka's conversion (257 B.C.), been identified with the "Enlightenment." Indeed, there is no good reason to question the assertion that the present tree is one of a succession of offshoots from the original Bo tree.

The pípul (*Ficus religiosa*) has been deemed sacred by all classes of Hindus from time immemorial. It is found in all parts of the country, and in the most extraordinary places. It will take root under the most unpromising conditions, and may sometimes be seen forcing its way through bricks and mortar. "No wonder," says Colonel Sleeman, "that superstition should have consecrated this tree, delicate and beautiful as it is, to the gods. The palace, the castle, the temple, and the tomb, crumble to dust beneath her withering grasp. She rises triumphant over them all in her lofty beauty, bearing high in air, amidst her green foliage, fragments of the wreck she has made, to show the nothingness of man's efforts."

Oaths are taken, and invocations made, upon the leaves of the pípul. A Hindu dare not lie within its shadow. The perpetual rustling of its leaves is to him a manifestation of the mysterious presence by which he believes it to be inhabited. The roadside idol and village deity are placed at the foot of the pípul, and the ground round about is kept swept and clear.

CHAPTER XVII.

BENARES.

It is impossible to say when Benares became the religious capital of the Hindus, but such it certainly was many centuries before the Christian era, and there has been a city on or near the present site since an early period of the Aryan occupation. When Buddha came to Benares it was the principal city of a powerful Hindu kingdom, and so it continued until Kutab-ud-dín took it for the Ghorí monarchs at the close of the twelfth century. According to their usual practice, the Moslems immediately commenced the destruction and conversion of the Hindu buildings. Hundreds of edifices were razed to the ground; others were damaged beyond repair, and one thousand temples were turned into mosques. As a result of all this very few indeed of the ancient buildings of the city exist at the present day. The old temple of Siva, one of the finest in Benares, was pulled down by Aurangzeb, and a mosque was erected upon its foundation.

But through all the centuries of Muhammadan rule and Muhammadan iconoclasm Benares maintained its position as the centre of Hinduism. To-day it contains more than twelve hundred Hindu temples, and there are probably at least twenty thousand priests in the city. A considerable proportion of the population, which approximates a quarter of a million, is, however, Muhammadan. The followers of the rival creeds bear no good will toward each other, and serious conflicts between them have occurred. About fifty years ago two religious processions, one Muhammadan and the other Hindu, happened to meet in the street, and a fracas followed. This quickly developed into a bloody riot, involving the greater part of the population. The Musalmáns overthrew a sacred monument of the Hindus, who retaliated by burning a mosque. The Muhammadans then slew a cow, and poured its blood into one of the temple tanks of the Bráhmans. This outrage aroused every Hindu in the city, and, being in the majority, they would probably have annihilated the Muhammadans but for the intervention of the sepoys.

Then ensued a remarkable exhibition of discipline. By far the greater part of the troops were Hindus, and perhaps one-half of them were Bráhmans. "Any one of them, if he had been his own master, would have rejoiced in an opportunity of shedding his life's blood in a quarrel with the Musalmáns; and of the mob who attacked them, Bráhmans, yogís and other religious mendicants formed the front rank, their bodies and faces covered with chalk and ashes, their long hair untied as devoted to death, showing their caste-strings and yelling out to the sepoys all the bitterest curses of their religion, if they persisted in waging an unnatural warfare against their brethren and their gods. The sepoys, however, were immovable. Regarding their military oath as the most sacred of all obligations, they fired at a Bráhman as readily as at any one else, and kept guard at the gate of a mosque as faithfully and fearlessly as if it had been the gate of one of their own temples. Their courage and steadiness preserved Benares from ruin."

Aurangzeb's Mosque, which was, with design, erected in one of the most sacred portions of the city, has been the cause of much malevolence. The Hindus have established a claim to the courtyard between the building and the wall, and this prevents the Muhammadans from entering except by the side. The gateway in front has been bricked up and rendered useless.

"Benares is bounded by a road which, though fifty miles in circuit, is never distant from the city more than five kos (one and a half miles); hence its name, Panch-Kos Road. All who die within this boundary, be they Bráhman or low caste, Muslim or Christian, be they liars, thieves or murderers, are sure of admittance into Siva's heaven. To tread the Panch-Kos Road is one of the great ambitions of a Hindu's life. Even if he be an inhabitant of the sacred city, he must traverse it once in the year to free himself from

Bathing Ghát—Benares

the impurities and sins contracted within the holy precincts. Thousands from all parts of India make the pilgrimage every year. By the roadside, lined with noble trees, there are tanks where the pilgrim must perform the sacred ablutions, and there are numerous shrines to which he may offer his prayers. The journey must be made on foot, and the luxury of shoes is not permitted. On the way the pilgrim must not quarrel or use harsh language, and he must not give or receive any gift from a friend—nay, not even a handful of grain, nor a cup of water. But along the last stage he scatters barley on the ground, in honor of Siva, the emblem of creation. Arrived at the Manikaranika Ghát, from whence he started, he bathes in the river, makes an offering of money to the priest in attendance, and then goes to the temple of Sakshi-Binark, or the witness-bearing Ganesa, to have his pilgrimage attested and recorded by the deity."[1]

The pilgrims come from every part of the country, and even from Tibet, China and Burma; for Benares is sacred also to the Buddhist. The ceremonies in the Holy City are, perhaps, the culmination of a long journey on foot, occupying a year or more, and involving various penitential features.

On the occasions of special festivals pilgrims crowd into the cities in vast numbers; but at all times they are numerous, pilgrims, priests and beggars being met

[1] "Cities of India," G. W. Forrest.

at every turn. The ghâts are daily thronged with tens of thousands of devotés, who bathe in the holy Ganges for purification, and drink its filthy waters. Bottles are filled with the sacred fluid and carried home to distant villagers, to be prized beyond all other possessions.

Fákírs, who are only too numerous in every part of the country, abound in Benares. It is said that India harbors over two millions of these loathsome pests. One comes across them everywhere—on the highways, at the bathing ghâts, in the temples and bazaars. Some wander about from place to place, collecting alms and food without any difficulty; indeed, it is deemed a duty and a privilege to minister to their wants. Others station themselves in one spot, and there receive the superstitious attentions of their votaries, who include all classes of society. They are frequently naked, and always repulsive. Their hair, quite often infested with vermin, hangs in filthy, matted strands about their shoulders. Their faces and bodies are hideously smeared with ashes or mud. Generally they make a parade of some self-imposed penance, which is accepted by the people as a token of surpassing saintliness. Thus some move about only by rolling over the ground; others drag heavy chains, attached to the body, or perhaps a weighty iron frame about the neck. Not infrequently some absurd practice is persisted in, with the result of atrophy of a limb, or the entire destruction of certain physical functions, as when the arms are held above the head until they become immovable in that position.

The worst, and by no means infrequent, exhibitions of these scarcely human beings will not admit of description. To say that they transcend the bounds of decency is putting it too mildly; they surpass all conception of obscene bestiality. Nevertheless, since time immemorial these "poor men"—for such is the significance of the word fákír—have exercised an extraordinary influence over the minds of the whole people of India. They are exempted from the laws affecting the seclusion of women, and a princess will deem it an honor to wait upon the vilest gymnosophist. It is no uncommon thing to see a rájá rise in the howdah of his state elephant and salaam to a filthy fákír by the roadside.

Undoubtedly some of these so-called saints are sincere ascetics, but at best their motives are selfish; for the sole object of their devotions is to "acquire merit," by which they hope to profit in the next transmigration. The majority, however, are unquestionably hypocritical impostors; lazy vagabonds, who enjoy the life of ease and the condition of consequence which the calling insures. It goes without saying that large numbers of the fákír class are insane; indeed, they must all be more or less unbalanced.

The yogís are a sort of superior grade of fákírs, or perhaps they may be more exactly described as fákírs who have attained to the highest degree of saintliness. Professor Wilson thus describes their practices and alleged powers:

"These practices consist chiefly of long-continued suppression of respiration; of inhaling and exhaling the breath in a particular manner; of sitting in eighty-four different attitudes; of fixing their eyes on the tips of their noses, and endeavoring by the force of mental abstraction to effect a union between the portion of vital spirit residing in the body and that which pervades all Nature, and is identical with Siva, considered as the supreme being and source and essence of all creation. When this mystic union is effected, the yogí is liberated in his living body from the clog of material encumbrance, and acquires an entire command over all worldly substance. He can make himself lighter than the lightest substances, heavier than the heaviest; can become as vast or as minute as he pleases; can traverse all space; can animate any dead body by transferring his spirit into it from his own frame; can render himself invisible; can attain all objects; become equally acquainted with the past, present and future; and is finally united with Siva, and consequently exempted from being born again upon earth. The superhuman faculties are acquired in various degrees, according to the greater or less perfection with which the initiatory processes have been performed."

That some of these yogís acquire wonderful powers will not be denied by any who have seen the apparently

Itinerant Fákirs

supernatural feats they commonly accomplish. Their performances have been the wonder of every traveler in India, and theories without end have been advanced in explanation of the extraordinary control of the forces of Nature seemingly exerted by these strange men. The yogís and their manifestations are not to be confused with the traveling jugglers and their tricks, which are, however, generally more clever and striking than the exhibitions of Western "magicians."

Every one has heard of the miracle of the mango tree, and that of the rope held suspended in air from nothing, whilst a man slides down it from nowhere. These and similarly startling phenomena are thoroughly authenticated, and have defied the investigation of the shrewdest observers. Thousands have testified to seeing these miracles, and if we deny that such things can be, we must look for the explanation of the mystery in some form of hypnotism. The yadú-wallahs, or ordinary jugglers, apply the term nazarbund—that is, "closing the sight" (of the spectator)—to a certain class of feats which involve extraordinary deception. To take a very common case in illustration. A person is requested to hold fast in his closed hand a coin, say an English half-crown piece; after a brief interval he is asked to open his hand, when the coin is found to have been changed to an American dollar. Not only the person holding the coin, but the spectators also will receive the impression that such is the case. In the same way the coin will be carried through a series of transformations back to its original form. In the meantime the yadú-wallah will not approach within ten feet of the subject of the experiment. This is one of the most simple and common of the tricks professedly performed by means of nazarbund.

The sámpri, or snake-charmers, may be included in the category of traveling jugglers, although their vocation has some claims to practical utility; for if, as frequently happens, especially in the mofussil, there are snakes about the compound of a house, the musical blandishments of the sámpri will usually entice them from their retreats and enable them to be caught.

The calling of the snake-charmer is as old as the hills, but it is still an open question whether the reptiles that dance—the word precisely describes the action—to the weird strains of the sámp-wallah's magic flageolet have been rendered innocuous by the extraction of the poison bags. The sámpri invariably aver that the snakes are in their natural state, and the careful investigations of several Europeans bear out the assertion. Furthermore, it is an unquestionable fact that many snake-charmers are killed by their pets, which are rather uncertain of temper. When performing, the sámpri appears to be very solicitous of the safety of the spectators, and careful in handling the snakes.

There are about fifty ghâts at Benares, backed right along the river front by crowded temples. Taking a boat, one may be rowed slowly down stream, and so get the best view of this curious conglomeration of sacred buildings and superstitious people.

At one of the landings is a huge prostrate figure of a god, which is said to be washed away annually, and to be as regularly restored to its place by miracle. At the Sivala Ghát is the well-preserved fort of Cháit Singh, who was Rájá of Benares at the latter end of the eighteenth century. It was here that Warren Hastings so nearly lost his life when he came to Benares to exact from the Rájá the fulfillment of an agreement entered into with the Government. Cháit Singh failed to respond with satisfactory alacrity, and Hastings ordered him to be seized. In this proceeding the usually astute Governor-General acted impulsively, and without calculating the probable consequences.

"The handful of sepoys who attended Hastings . . . were unequal to a conflict with the hardy rabble of Benarés. The streets surrounding the palace were filled by an immense multitude, of whom a large proportion, as is usual in Upper India, wore arms. The tumult became a fight, and the fight a massacre. The English officers defended themselves with desperate courage against overwhelming numbers, and fell, as became them, sword in hand. The sepoys were butchered. The gates were forced. The captive prince, neglected by his jailors during the confusion, discovered an outlet, which opened on the precipitous bank of the Ganges, let himself down to the water by a string made of the turbans of his attendants, found a boat and escaped to the opposite shore.

"If Hastings had, by indiscreet violence, brought himself into a difficult and perilous situation, it is only just to acknowledge that he extricated himself with even more than his usual ability and presence of mind. He had only fifty men with him. The building in which he had taken up his residence was on every side blocked by the insurgents. But his fortitude remained unshaken." He held the place, and contrived to have news of his predicament conveyed to Calcutta.

"The officers, and even the private men, regarded the Governor-General with enthusiastic attachment, and flew to his aid with an alacrity which, as he boasted, had never been shown on any other occasion."

The old palace of Cháit Singh has long been unoccupied, and is spoken of by the natives as the "empty palace."

Passing a ghát which is the particular rendezvous of the Danda, or staff-bearing sect of ascetics, and another where corpses lie in a row, with their feet in the water, awaiting cremation, the Kedar Ghát is reached. The neighboring temple is especially patronized by the Bengalís. The prevailing colors are red and yellow and white. Near by is a large tank, surrounded by fifty or sixty shrines. A large circular stone on the bank is said to grow daily to the extent of a sesamum seed.

At the next ghát serpent worship is carried on, and here the long-haired, repulsive Nágás congregate beneath a pípul tree about their peculiar idols. Then come in succession the ghát where every possible disease may be cured; the ghát built by the Mahárána of Udaipur, which is frequented by Muhammadans, and a ghát dedicated to the goddess of small-pox.

Jai Singh's Observatory comes into view at the Man Mandir Ghát, and tends to make an imposing picture at this point. A broad flight of steps leads to the summit of a huge, massive building, a terraced height well suited to the watchers of the stars. The apparatus is remarkable in design and purpose. The mural quadrant is a wall, eleven feet in height and over nine feet in breadth, by means of which are determined the sun's altitude and zenith distance, and its greatest declination, and hence the latitude of the place. "There is a gigantic gnomon, thirty-six feet long, sloping and pointing to the north pole, which is rightly termed Yantra-Samrat, or prince of instruments. On each side of it are arcs of a circle, so divided as to act as a sun-dial. Near to the dial is a small mural quadrant, and to the east is a gigantic equinoctial circle, made of stone. Then we come to an instrument called Chakrajantra. It consists of a circle of iron turning on an axis fastened to two walls, and pointing to the north pole. It was intended to show the declination of any star or planet. Not far from this is an azimuth compass, consisting of an outer and inner wall surrounding a broad pillar. The upper part of both walls is graduated into three hundred and sixty degrees, and shows the points of the compass with iron spikes to mark the cardinal points."

At the Bhairava Ghát is a Sivala, whose idol is said to be the magistrate of the city. Beside him is the image of his dog, upon which he is believed to ride about. In the neighboring sweetmeat shops sugar dogs are sold, and are offered at the shrine.

The Manikaranika is the most sacred of all the ghát s, and at certain times, especially on the occasion of a solar eclipse, is visited by millions of pilgrims. The place derives its name and much of its sanctity from the belief that Deví dropped an ear-ring into the tank at the top of the steps. Into the tank are thrown the offerings of flowers, milk, sweetmeats and other things, which, putrefying, create an insufferable stench. This ghát boasts one of the charana-padukas, which are so highly prized in Upper India. It is a stone pedestal set in the pavement. Upon its marble top are the impressions of two feet, supposed to have been made by Vishnu.

The temple of Visweswara, or Lord of the Universe, under which name Siva is the principal object of worship in Benares, is one of a group of three temples which stand in a row in the centre of a quadrangle. It is sometimes called the Golden Temple, on account of the gilt tower which surmounts it. The embellishment resembles the gilding of the Golden Temple of Amritsar, and the copper and gold plates were laid at the expense of Ranjít Singh.

Beside the Temple of Visweswara is that of Mahádeo—Siva again as the "Great God" of modern Hinduism. The building owes its erection to Ahalia Bái, the Mahárání of Indore. The entire group is commonplace in the matter of architecture and sculpture.

Between the Temple of Visweswara and the adjacent Mosque of Aurangzeb is the Gyan Kup, or Well of Knowledge, within a colonnaded quadrangle. The dirty, sloppy enclosure is always crowded with men, women, children and cows. The last are treated with the greatest deference. They meander about, lazily nuzzling their way through the throng, nibbling the votive blossoms, and submitting to the extravagant attentions of fanatic worshipers with an almost intelligent expression of boredom.

The well, or tank, owes its extreme sanctity to the belief that when Aurangzeb destroyed the old Temple of Visweswara a priest cast the image of Siva into the water here.

The votaries throw vast quantities of flowers into the well, and from it arises an overpowering stench, notwithstanding which pilgrims draw the fetid water and drink it with ecstatic fervor.

Benares is not a pleasant city. As the centre of Hinduism it is curious and interesting, but one is brought into too close contact with idolatry in its most repulsive aspects, and superstition in its grossest manifestations. To the Hindu, idolatry is as "the air he breathes. It is the food of his soul. He is subdued, enslaved, befooled by it. The nature of the Hindu partakes of the supposed nature of the gods whom he worships. And what is that nature? According to the traditions handed about among the natives, and constantly dwelt upon in their conversation, and referred to in their popular songs—which perhaps would be sufficient proof—yet more especially according to the numberless statements and narratives found in their sacred writings, on which these traditions are based, it is in many instances vile and abominable to the last degree."

The gods, at least of the masses, have been endowed with all the gross, sensual and cruel characteristics of the non-Aryan deities, and much of the ceremonial which attends their worship has been derived from the same source, so that the Hinduism of to-day is largely a survival of the dark superstitions and practices of prehistoric times. "It had to provide for the non-Aryan as well as for the Aryan elements of the Indian people, and it combined the Bráhmanism and the Buddhism of the Aryans with the fetish-worship and religion of terror which swayed the non-Aryan races."

It is true the religion of the Bráhmans, and the more intellectual among the Hindus, still partakes largely of the philosophical character imparted to it by the Vedas. Take, for instance, the case of Siva, the Mahádeo, or Great God, who is the chief object of worship in Benares, and that of his wife Deví, the Goddess. They are worshiped in various forms, with widely different attributes. "The Bráhmanical conception is represented by his attitude as a fair-skinned man, seated in profound thought, the symbol of the fertilizing Ganges above his head, and the bull (emblem alike of procreation and of Aryan plough-tillage) near at hand. The wilder non-Aryan aspects of his character are signified by his necklace of skulls, his collar of twining serpents, his tiger skin, and his club with a human head at the end. His five faces and four arms have also their significance from this double aspect of his character, Aryan and non-Aryan. His wife, in like manner, appears in her Aryan form as Umá, 'Light,' the type of high-born loveliness; in her composite character as Durgá, a golden-haired woman, beautiful, but menacing, riding on a tiger; and in her terrible non-Aryan aspects as Kálí, a black fury, of a hideous countenance, dripping with blood, crowned with snakes, and hung round with skulls. As an Aryan deity, Siva is Pasu-pati, the Lord of Animals and the Protector of Cows; Sambhu, the Auspicious; Mrityunjaya, the Vanquisher of Death; Viswanátha, Monarch of all. In his non-

Aryan attributes, he is Aghora, the Horrible; Virúpáksha, of Mis-shapen Eyes; Ugra, the Fierce; Kapála-málin, Garlanded with Skulls. So also Deví, his female form, as an Aryan goddess is Umá, the lovely daughter of the mountain King Himavat; Aryá, the Revered; Gaurí, the Brilliant, or Gold-colored; Jagad-gaurí, the World's Fair One; Bhavaní, the Source of Existence, and Jagan-mátá, the Mother of the Universe. Her non-Aryan attributes appear in her names of Kálí, or Syámá, the Black One; Chandí, the Fierce; Bhairaví, the Terrible; Rakta-dantí, the Bloody-Toothed.

"The ritual of Siva-worship preserves, in an even more striking way, the traces of its double origin. The higher minds still adore the Godhead by silent contemplation, as prescribed by Sankara, without the aid of external rites. The ordinary Bráhman hangs a wreath of blossoms around the Sivaite linga, or places before it offerings of flowers and rice. But the low-castes pour out the lives of countless goats at the feet of the terrible Kálí, and, until lately, in times of pestilence and famine, tried, in their despair, to appease the relentless goddess by human blood."[1]

The compactness and cohesiveness of Hinduism, with its octopus-like embrace of the people, are discernible in Benares as nowhere else. The deep-seated effects of caste, and the powerful influence

[1] "The Indian Empire," Sir W. W. Hunter.

of the priesthood, are more apparent here than elsewhere. But of all the many repulsive manifestations of religious feeling which meet the eye in Benares, none is so disgusting as the shameful deference shown to the loathsome fákírs who infest the place.

CHAPTER XVIII.

CHRISTIANITY IN INDIA.

THE precise date and manner of the introduction of Christianity to India is obscure. Early tradition, which is fully accepted by the Roman Catholic Church, and doubtfully by Protestants, ascribes its origin to direct apostolic agency. According to the tradition in question, Saint Thomas the Apostle preached extensively at the southern end of the peninsula, founded several churches, and was finally martyred near Madras in the year 68 A.D. The researches of latter-day scholars have shaken the foundation of this story, if they have not actually destroyed it.

A second legend assigns the conversion of India to Thomas the Manichæan, or disciple of Manes, some time towards the end of the third century. Yet another version ascribes the honor to Thomas Cana, an Armenian merchant, who settled in Malabar in the eighth century, and became the archbishop of the Christian Church. "On his death, his memory received the gradual and spontaneous honors of canonization by the Christian communities for whom he had labored, and his name became identified with that of the apostle." Whatever may be the claims of Thomas the Armenian to credit as a rebuilder of the Church in Southern India, he may not be considered as its founder, for there is ample evidence of its existence before his time. Indeed, the arrival of a missionary from Alexandria in the second century appears to be well authenticated.

The claims of Saint Thomas the Apostle have weighty support, but they will not bear the test of modern criticism.

The apocryphal history of Saint Thomas, by Abdias, which probably dates from the second century, tells that the Indian King, Gondaphorus, sent a merchant to Christ, seeking a skillful architect to build him a palace. Jesus, so the narrative goes, sold Thomas to the King as a slave and an expert in architecture. The Apostle converted Gondaphorus, and afterwards journeyed into another part of the country, where he was slain. The difficulties in connection with this story are found in the facts that Gondaphorus was an Indo-Scythic monarch, whose kingdom was remote from Malabar, being in the territory now known as the Punjab, and his coins, which have been found in great number, would place him in the last century before Christ, or early in the first century of the present era.

Probably a misconception is due to the ancient use of the word "India." At the period in which the early Fathers of the Church lived, the term was applied to the countries of Central Asia, and perhaps to

Hindustán proper, but certainly never to the southern peninsula. It was in the restricted sense of the word, no doubt, that the Apostle's labors in "India" were referred to in the ancient records. "Candid inquiry must therefore decline to accept the connection of Saint Thomas with the 'India' of the early Church as proof of the Apostle's identity with Thomas the missionary to Malabar."

In the second century a large fleet of Roman merchant ships had established a regular route between Myos Hormus, a port of the Red Sea, and Arabia, Ceylon and Malabar. Previous to this time a Jewish colony existed upon the Malabar coast, an outcome of the Dispersion, or of some later emigration. The remnants of this settlement are found at this day in the Beni-Israels of the Bombay coast and the Poona district.

It is highly probable that the Roman trading vessels had communication and commercial relations with this colony, and that Jewish merchants and others familiar with the doctrines of Christ, and the story of the infant Church, took part in these voyages. Moreover, the course of the fleet was along the Asiatic coast, and a part of it touched at Aden and other points which were early seats of Christianity. Of several hundred Roman coins found at Coimbatore, Calicut, and other points on the western littoral, many were silver denarii, of Augustus and Tiberius, and all pre-dated the death of the Emperor Nero. Thus,

Alamgir's Mosque—Muttra

ascertained facts, and probability alike, point to the conclusion that the Christian faith had become known to some portion of the Indian people at latest early in the second century.

At this period Buddhism was supreme in Southern India, and had the support of the rulers, as well as of the masses. Its extreme tolerance must have been favorable to the introduction and growth of the new faith. Moreover, there was so much in the teachings of Buddha entirely in accord with the doctrine of Christ, that it is easy to imagine the two religions existing peaceably side by side, and the story of Jesus, with its almost contemporary Messiah, gaining converts from the ranks of Buddhism.

Before the close of the second century news had reached some of the Christian centres of a community of co-religionists existing upon the Malabar coast of India. Excited by the prospect of a vast field for evangelization, Pantænus of Alexandria set out for the East, and he is the first authentic missionary to India. Doctor Kennet, quoting Eusebius, in his monograph on *St. Thomas, the Apostle of India*, relates that Pantænus "found his own arrival anticipated by some who were acquainted with the Gospel of Matthew, to whom Bartholomew, one of the Apostles, had preached, and had left them the same Gospel in the Hebrew, which also was preserved at this time." In the *Liber de Viris Illustribus* Jerome writes of Pantænus as "a man of such learning, both in the sacred

Scriptures and in secular knowledge, that Demetrius, the Bishop of Alexandria, sent him to India, at the request of ambassadors of that nation; and there he found that Bartholomew, one of the twelve Apostles, had preached the advent of our Lord Jesus Christ, according to the Gospel of Matthew written in Hebrew, which he brought away with him on his return to Alexandria."

Saint Hippolytus, Bishop of Portus, writing about 220 A.D., also ascribes the conversion of India to Saint Bartholomew. To Saint Thomas he assigns the countries of Central Asia; but he mentions Calamina, "a city of India," as the place in which that Apostle met his death.

The orthodox Bishop Frumentius was sent by Athanasius to India in the middle of the fourth century; but there is no substantial evidence connecting him with Malabar, nor, indeed, with Southern India.

The Alexandrian monk, Cosmas Indico-pleustes, writes, about 540 A.D., of a Christian Church in Ceylon, and of one on the Malabar seaboard; but he makes no mention of Saint Thomas in either connection, and we must suppose him to have been well informed.

Considering the lack of corroborative evidence, and the conflicting facts, it must be concluded that the traditional connection of either Saint Thomas or Saint Matthew, or of any other missionary of the early apostolic age, with the Indian peninsula (that is to say, with India in the modern sense of the word) must be regarded as apocryphal.

The early tradition of the Catholic Church, already referred to, narrates that a persecution arose soon after the martyrdom of Saint Thomas; that all the Christian priests were slain, and the infant church reduced to sore straits; that the Patriarch of Babylon, while still in communion with Rome, sent bishops to the languishing church in India, who caused a revival; and that Nestorianism was carried from Babylon to Malabar about 486 A.D.

Cosmas, the Alexandrian, states that the Bishop of Malabar was consecrated in Persia, which would create the inference that the church of Southern India had by that time (circa 540 A.D.) been incorporated with the Nestorian body.

When Indian Christianity emerges from the fog of tradition into the clear light of history, it is as a branch of the Nestorian Church. "At a very early date in our era, Edessa, the Athens of Syria, had become a centre of Christian teaching, whence missionaries issued to the Eastern world. In the fifth century, Nestorianism, driven forth from Europe and Africa, became definitely the doctrine of the Asiatic Church, and Syriac became the sacred language of Christian colonies far beyond the geographical limits of Syria."

From that country authorized emissaries of the Nestorian Church carried the doctrine, ritual and literature of that institution through Persia and over the Arabian coast country, and thence to the Christian settlements in Southern India.

The history of these Syrian Christians "forms the longest continuous narrative of any religious sect in India, except the Buddhists and Jains.

"The Syrian Church of Malabar had its origin in the period when Buddhism was still triumphant; it witnessed the birth of the Hinduism which superseded the doctrine and national polity of Buddha; it saw the arrival of the Muhammadans, who ousted the Hindu dynasties; it suffered cruelly from the Roman Catholic inquisitors of the Portuguese; but it has survived its persecutors, and has formed a subject of interest to Anglican Inquiries during the past eighty years."

The Syrian Jacobites still number three hundred thousand, and until within the past twenty years they had a larger native following in India than all the Protestant sects combined.

The life of the Nestorian Church in India was checkered and troublous. The Patriarch Jesajabus, who died in the year 660 A.D., wrote to the Metropolitan of Persia, complaining that the Christians in Malabar were destitute of a regular ministry.

About a hundred years later, Thomas, the Armenian, found them taking refuge in the mountain fastnesses.

In the fourteenth century they were pronounced by

Friar Jordanus to be Christians merely in name, lacking the essential of baptism. "They even confounded Saint Thomas with Christ."

In some districts of Southern India the Church drifted back into heathenism; in others it perished from sheer inanition. But, on the other hand, there were Christian communities that banded themselves into military brotherhoods, somewhat analagous to the Sikh confederacy, and had their own chiefs and even kings. They were the first to learn the use of gunpowder and firearms, and so became the most important elements in the forces of the local rulers. Before the arrival of Vasco de Gama, in 1498, the Saint Thomas Christians (as the Malabar Nestorians called themselves, in imitation of the mother church) had established their position as a powerful military caste in Malabar.

The Portuguese chanced to land in that portion of India where Christianity had long been established, and where its adherents were at that time established as "a recognized and established caste." This should have been a happy circumstance for the newcomers, as well as for the native Christians. As a matter of fact, however, nothing could have been less fortunate, for "the downfall of the Nestorian Church in India was due neither to such reversions to paganism (as have been referred to), nor to any persecutions of native princes, but to the pressure of the Portuguese Inquisition, and the proselytizing energy of Rome. . . . That energy was vigorously directed both against the natives and the ancient Christian communities. Indeed, the Nestorian heresy of the Saint Thomas Christians seemed, to the fervor of the friars, to be a direct call from heaven for interference by the Orthodox Church." The strenuous efforts of the Portuguese, resisted as long as possible by the Saint Thomas Christians, at length resulted in the incorporation of the latter with the Roman Catholic Church. In 1599, "the sacred books of the Saint Thomas congregations, their missals, their consecrated oil, and church ornaments, were publicly burnt; and their religious nationality as a separate caste was abolished."

After the overthrow of the Portuguese by the Dutch in 1663, the Nestorians reasserted their spiritual independence. Since that time the Syrian Church of India has been divided into two sects. The Old Church, although it revolted from incorporation with the Roman Catholics, resumed allegiance to that body in 1656. Its members are known as Catholics of the Syrian Rite. It acknowledges the supremacy of the Pope and his Vicars-Apostolic. It still employs the Syrian language in its services, and to some extent retains the old Syrian ritual. The New Church, which embraces the other section of the Malabar Christians, adheres to the Jacobite tenets introduced by the first Jacobite bishop, Mar Gregory, in 1665. It finds condemnable errors in the doctrines of Arius, Nestorius, and the Bishops of Rome. Its members "reject the use of images; honor the Mother of Jesus and the saints only as holy persons and friends of God; allow the consecration of a married layman or deacon to the office of priest, and deny the existence of purgatory."

Both these sects maintain their differences with a "high degree of religious vitality at the present day." Their congregations do not affiliate with the Catholics of the Latin Rite, nor with any of the Protestant sects.

The Syrian Churches in India—that is to say, the successors of the early Malabar Christians—"owe their survival as organic bodies in no small measure to the fact that they practically formed themselves into castes, dwelling in the territories of a Hindu dynasty —that is to say, with all their surroundings in favor of the perpetuation of any hereditary aggregate of persons who can constitute themselves into a recognized caste. If the Buddhists had in like manner amalgamated into a coherent caste, they would now be numbered probably by millions, instead of hundreds of thousands, on the continent of India."

While individual friars of the Roman Catholic faith had visited India since the thirteenth century, the first regularly equipped mission of that Church arrived from Portugal in the year 1500. The early missionaries met with the antagonism of the natives, sometimes amounting to attacks attended with bloodshed. These popular assaults were sometimes reprisals for the cold-blooded barbarities of the Portuguese soldiers, whose acts the Hindus, not unnaturally, believed to be prompted, or at least sanctioned, by their priests; sometimes they were the direct results of the ill-judged zeal of the missionaries, and their inconsiderate conduct in the treatment of objects of native veneration. Similar conduct at this day is provided for by the clauses of the Anglo-Indian Penal Code, "which deal with words or signs calculated to wound the religious feelings of others."

The arrival of Saint Francis Xavier in 1542 marked the commencement of the labors of the Society of Jesus in the East, and a resultant acceleration of the progress of Christianity in India. The name of Saint Francis, whose relics repose in a silver shrine at Goa, is closely associated with Malabar.

The history of this period of Jesuit endeavor is highly interesting. Among the noble workers of that Order, the names of De Nobili, Beschi, Arnauld and Calmette stand prominently forth. Many of them met with martyrdom, and all underwent severe hardship. Apart from their labors in the direct line of conversion, they performed notable services in the cause of education and in printing books in various native languages. "Their priests became perfect Indians in all secular matters, dress, food, etc., and had equal success among all castes, high and low.

"The Jesuits worked to a large extent by means of

industrial settlements. Many of their stations consisted of regular agricultural communities, with lands and a local jurisdiction of their own. Indeed, both in the town and country, conversion went hand in hand with attempts at improved husbandry, or with a training in some mechanical art."

The guiding policy of these early Jesuit pioneers in the missionary field of the East was expressed in the statement that "The Christian religion cannot be regarded as naturalized in a country until it is in a position to propagate its own priesthood."

This, which is undoubtedly true, and especially so with regard to India, "is the secret of the wide and permanent success of the Catholic missions; it was also the source of their chief troubles. For, in founding Christianity on an indigenous basis, the Fathers had to accept the necessity of recognizing indigenous customs and native prejudices in regard to caste. The disputes which arose divided the Jesuit missionaries for many years, and had to be referred, not only to the General of the Order, but to the Pope himself. . . . In the end, one division of the missionaries was told off for the low castes, while another ministered to the Indians of higher degree. A similar distinction was rigidly maintained in some churches. Pére Bertrand gives the plan of a Madura church as laid before the Sovereign Pontiff in 1725, which shows a systematic demarcation between the high and low castes even during divine service. Whatever may have been lost of the primitive Christian equality by this system, it had the merit of being adapted to native habits of thought, and it was perhaps unavoidable in an Indian church which endeavored to base itself upon an indigenous priesthood."

For some time past—in fact, since the re-establishment of the Society of Jesus in the early part of the last century—the Roman Catholic Church in India has enjoyed a steady growth. Its stronghold is now, as formerly, the southern portion of the peninsula. The work is carried on under severe conditions and with slender pecuniary resources. "The priests of the Propaganda deny themselves the comforts considered necessaries for Europeans in India. They live the frugal and abstemious life of the communities among whom they dwell."

In 1891 there were in India and Burma thirty archbishops and bishops, and upwards of two thousand priests, of whom about fourteen hundred were natives. The Roman Catholic population in the same territory numbered about one million six hundred thousand.

There are a large number of important Catholic educational institutions in India. "In nearly every diocese or mission there is a college; in some more than one." In 1891 these establishments numbered upwards of fifteen hundred, with nearly sixty-four thousand pupils. In addition to these, there were one hundred and seventeen orphanages, which partake more or less of the character of schools.

The Protestant missionary movement in India owes its inception to the Lutherans. In 1705 Ziegenbalg and Plutschau began work in the Danish colony of Tranquebar, under the patronage of the King of Denmark. Many of the early Lutheran missionaries were men of great ability and scholarship. Their translations of the Bible were notable additions to the Christian literature of India.

Owing to hindrance by the local authorities and lack of funds, the first Lutheran mission made but little progress, and it is probable that after the death of Ziegenbalg it would have become extinct but for the support extended to it by the British Society for Promoting Christian Knowledge. "This body of British philanthropists helped the King of Denmark to support Ziegenbalg. On Ziegenbalg's death in 1719 funds from Denmark failed, and the Danish missions were adopted by the Society," and they incurred the entire maintenance of the Lutheran missions until they were handed over in 1824 to the Society for the Propagation of the Gospel.

The British institution seems to have been unable to induce any Englishmen, who were qualified for the work, to go out to India, and so they selected their representatives from foreign Lutherans, who at that time were the only Protestant sect imbued with the missionary spirit. Thus Schwartz, Kiernander and other notable missionaries were sent into the Indian field. "The Society for Promoting Christian Knowledge thus claims to have preceded even the Baptist Carey by about eighty years, although the fact has been obscured by the Danish names of its agents."

Carey arrived in 1793, and established the Baptist missionary centre at Serampur, then a Danish possession, in order to avoid the opposition of the East India Company. "Then began that wonderful literary activity which has rendered illustrious the group of 'Serampur missionaries.' In ten years the Bible was translated and printed, in whole or part, in thirty-one languages; and by 1816 the missionaries had about seven hundred converts."

The London Missionary Society entered the field in 1798, since when its work has steadily progressed. The opposition of the East India Company to missionary endeavor was removed in 1813. A bishopric of the Church of England was established in Calcutta, and an archdeaconry in each Presidency. Up to that time the Established Church had taken no official part in the missionary movement in India, although many of its chaplains had zealously aided the extension of that movement. Since 1814, however, the Church of England has been active in the Indian missionary field through its two great societies—the Church Missionary Society and the Society for the Propagation of the Gospel.

Their greatest success has been achieved in Southern India.

Missionaries of various other Protestant societies, mainly British and American, have since entered India, and have established a large number of churches, schools, hospitals, dispensaries, and other institutions for the benefit of the natives. A notable adjunct to this work is the zenana movement carried on by female missionaries.

The first half-century of Protestant missionary work, from 1830 to 1881, may be summarized as follows: In 1830 there were nine societies at work, and about 27,000 Protestants in all India, Ceylon and Burma. In 1870 there were no fewer than thirty-five societies at work; and in 1871 there were 318,363 converts (including Ceylon and Burma). In 1852 there were 459 Protestant missionaries, and in 1872 there were 606. Between 1856 and 1878 the converts made by the Baptist societies of England and America, in India, Ceylon and Burma, increased from about 30,000 to between 80,000 and 90,000. Those of the Basle missions of Switzerland multiplied from 1060 to upwards of 6000 from 1856 to 1878; those of the Wesleyan Methodist missions of England and America from 7500 to 12,000; those of the Presbyterian missions of Scotland, England, Ireland and America, connected with ten societies, from 821 to 10,000; those of the missions of the London Missionary Society from 20,000 to 48,000; and those of the Church Missionary Society and of the Society for the Propagation of the Gospel from 61,442 to upwards of 164,000, from 1856 to 1878.

Between 1851 and 1890 the number of mission stations increased threefold; while the number of native Protestant Christians multiplied more than fivefold, and the number of churches or congregations by sixteenfold. The native ordained pastors increased from 21 in 1851 to 797 in 1890, and the native lay preachers from 493 to 3491.

"According to the missionary returns, therefore, the Christian population of all India, British, Feudatory, French and Portuguese, in 1890, was as follows: Syrian Jacobites, say, 300,000; Roman Catholics, 1,594,901; Native Protestants, 648,843, thus leaving a balance of, say, 57,611 for European Protestants and others to make up the census total of 2,601,355 for all India."

The great increase in later years of conversions by the Protestant missions is distinctly traceable to the more extended use of native agents. The activity of the Protestant missions in utilitarian works, apart from the propagation of the faith, has been very marked. Between 1851 and 1890 the number of pupils in Protestant mission schools rose from 64,043 to 295,401. Female education and the zenana movement have been prosecuted with much labor and great success by the agents of the Protestant societies.

The ecclesiastical establishment maintained by the Government of India, for the benefit of its European soldiers and officials, is quite distinct from the missionary body. In 1892 the Indian ecclesiastical staff consisted of eight bishops and one hundred and fifty-nine chaplains of the Church of England, and thirteen Presbyterian chaplains. There are no Roman Catholic chaplains upon the establishment, but several priests of that Church are remunerated by the Government for spiritual services rendered to the troops.[1]

[1] The contents of this chapter have been mainly drawn from Sir W. W. Hunter's able summary of the subject in "The Indian Empire."

CHAPTER XIX.

CEYLON.

THE island of Ceylon, having an area nearly equal to that of Ireland, lies off the southern portion of the Coromandel coast of India. Between the island and the mainland extends a reef, or isthmus, called Adam's Bridge, through which there is but one passage, and that navigable only by vessels drawing not more than ten feet of water.

The northern portion of Ceylon is covered with dense forest and jungle, broken at wide intervals by small patches of sparse cultivation. This wild region, however, includes the sites of two ancient capitals.

The middle of the lower portion of the island is occupied by a mass of granite mountains, rising in places to a height of nine thousand feet or more. Between these mountain groups and the coast lie stretches of low, fertile land.

Ceylon has been noted from time immemorial for the luxuriance of its vegetation and the beauty of its scenery. In the ancient Bráhmanic books it is termed Lanká, the "Gorgeous"; the Buddhists called it the "Pearl of India"; to the Chinese it was known as the "Isle of Gems," and to the Greeks as the "Land of the Hyacinth and the Ruby." There is every reason for believing that Ceylon is the country from which the ships of Solomon brought "gold and silver, ivory and peacocks." These and the almug trees and precious stones of Ophir are not only all products of the island, but the terms applied to some of them in the Hebrew Bible are identical with the Tamil names by which they are designated to-day.

Ceylon is the loadstone island of Sindbad's adventure, and the "Araby the blest" of Milton's great epic.

In the Rámáyana, Lanká is the abode of the demon King Rávana, who abducts Sítá, the wife of Rámá, and carries her to his stronghold upon the island. Her rescue is effected by the aid of Hanuman, the Monkey-god, who reaches the island, not by way of Adam's Bridge, but by leaping across sixty miles of intervening water.

The chronicles of the island are contained in two books—the Dipáwansa and the Maháwansa. From these we learn that for four hundred years after the beginning of the seventh century, Ceylon was a prey to piratical incursions from the Malabar coast. The natives do not appear to have been capable of withstanding the invaders, whose acts and influence are said to have been invariably evil. On the other hand, the incursions of people from farther north seem to have tended toward the enlightenment of the inhabitants of the island and the improvement of their condition.

The reign of Prakrámá Bahu is still spoken of as the halcyon period of Ceylon's history. This benign ruler occupied the throne some time in the middle of the twelfth century. Under his protecting care, peace reigned throughout the island; religion and agriculture flourished; temples were built and tanks were constructed; life and property were so secure that "a girl, decked with gold, might traverse the island in safety."

In 1505 the Portuguese effected a landing in Ceylon, and soon established settlements at various points along the coast. If there were any Christian communities on the island before this time, they were probably offshoots of the Nestorian Church of Malabar. The Portuguese commenced proselytizing with energy, and appear to have made many converts; but it is asserted that this was accomplished by themselves practically becoming "converts to Hinduism," and adapting their ritual and doctrine to those of the local religions.

The Portuguese held territory in Ceylon for one hundred and forty years. The Dutch arrived in 1602, and at once commenced a system of antagonism to the Portuguese, which culminated in the latter being driven from the island. The Dutch established the Reformed Church of Holland in Ceylon, and carried on a systematic persecution of the Roman Catholics,

Native Fruit Sellers, Ceylon

but without the result of suppressing them. In 1796 the Dutch colonies in Ceylon were ceded to the British, and in 1815 the latter annexed the Kingdom of Kandy, and so became masters of the entire island.

The northern portion of the island is mainly inhabited by Tamils, a black, hardy race, of Dravidian descent, who profess a Bráhmanic religion. They are from Southern India, and may be the descendants of the Malabar invaders, so bitterly complained of in the chronicles.

The Singhalese are of two distinct types. The natives of the Kandyan provinces of the interior are, as might be expected of highlanders, active, robust, frank, and of a fair complexion. The Singhalese of the coast districts are dark, slight of form, and timid. Their effeminacy of character is accentuated by the habit of wearing skirts, and of rolling the hair into a knot, which is held at the back of the head by a large tortoise-shell comb.

The Singhalese are almost wholly Buddhists. Buddhism was brought to the island at least two hundred years before the Christian era, and Ceylon has ever since been a stronghold of that religion. One of the dagobas, which is attributed to King Tissa, is believed to date from 200 B.C., and there are many whose erection is placed between that time and the birth of Christ. The sacred books of the Buddhists, inscribed in the ancient Páli character upon palm leaves, are called the Pítakas, or Three Baskets.

The Moormen, a people of Persian, or mixed Moslem descent, who are engaged as hawkers or shopkeepers in the cities, adhere to the Muhammadan faith.

"It is impossible to exaggerate the natural beauties of Ceylon. Belted with a double girdle of golden sands and waving palm groves, the interior is one vast green garden of Nature, deliciously disposed into plain and highland, valley and peak, where almost everything grows known to the tropical world, under a sky glowing with an equatorial sun, yet tempered by the cool sea-winds. Colombo itself, outside the actual town, is a perfect labyrinth of shady bowers and flowery streams and lakes. For miles and miles you drive about under arbors of feathery bamboos, broad-leaved bread-fruit trees, talipot and areca palms, cocoanut groves, and through stretches of rice fields, cinnamon and sugar-cane, amid which at night the fireflies dart about in glittering clusters. The lowest hut is embosomed in palm-fronds and the bright crimson blossoms of the hibiscus; while, wherever intelligent cultivation aids the prolific force of Nature, there is enough in the profusion of nutmegs and allspice, of the india-rubbers and cinchonas, of cannas, dracænas, crotons, and other wonders of the Singhalese flora, to give an endless and delighted study to the lover of Nature."

In Kalambhu the Portuguese found a word which was pronounced almost precisely like the name of the discoverer of America, and so they changed the spelling to Colombo, which name the port has retained ever since. It is a city of nearly one hundred and thirty thousand inhabitants. Its buildings straggle along four miles of coast, and extend for three miles inland. In the European quarter the houses, and some of the public buildings, show traces of the Dutch occupation, but otherwise they are uninteresting, and in not a few instances unsightly.

There is nothing attractive in Colombo itself, but its suburbs are charmingly picturesque. The Cinnamon Gardens and the Museum are well worth a visit. Along the road one passes numerous native huts, and here and there a little Roman Catholic chapel, almost buried in thick vegetation. Every dwelling is surrounded by close ranks of cocoanut palms. These trees are bountiful providers to the poor peasant. The meat of the nut is nourishing food, and its milk refreshing drink. The shell makes a convenient vessel, and it also forms the water-bowl of his peculiar pipe. The juice yields sugar, and the sap, when allowed to ferment, becomes an intoxicating liquor. The trunk furnishes building material. The leaves are used for thatching roofs, for making baskets and as writing material. Rope and matting are made from the fibre. The supply of these palms is practically inexhaustible. It has been estimated that there are at least twenty millions of them upon the island.

The Museum in the Cinnamon Gardens, or the

Victoria Park, as they are now called, is devoted to an exhibition of the natural and manufactured products of the island, its natural history and antiquities. There are many archæological remains of interest, notably a colossal figure of King Prakrámá Bahu, of date 1153 A.D., and a huge stone lion, upon whose back the ancient kings sat in audience and administered justice.

At Colombo the raw coffee, brought down from the plantations, is received at the mills, and put through the processes which prepare it for the market. The berries are here dried and "peeled"; the damaged beans are eliminated by women and children; the assortment into different sizes is contrived by means of sieves, and the product is then packed in large barrels for exportation.

The cultivation of coffee is confined to Southern India and Ceylon. "Unlike tea, coffee was not introduced into India by European enterprise, and even to the present day its cultivation is largely conducted by natives.

"The Malabar coast has always enjoyed a direct commerce with Arabia, and yielded many converts to Islám. One of these converts, Bábá Búdan, is said to have gone on a pilgrimage to Mecca, and to have brought back with him the coffee berry, which he planted on the hill range in Mysore still called after his name. According to local tradition, this introduction of the berry into Mysore happened in the seventeenth century. The shrubs thus sown lived on, but the cultivation did not spread until the beginning of the nineteenth century."[1]

For many years after its introduction to Ceylon, coffee was extensively cultivated in the island with profit. In 1870 the plant was attacked by a fungus, which, in the course of ten years, wiped out large coffee districts, and ruined the majority of planters. Many of the owners of coffee lands substituted tea with great success, and whereas in 1875 the exports of that commodity amounted to less than half a dozen chests, in 1893 upwards of eighty-four millions of pounds of the leaf was shipped from Ceylon.

The site selected for a coffee plantation is forest land at an elevation of from twenty-five hundred to thirty-five hundred feet above sea level, with a warm, moist climate. The land should be subject to an ample rainfall, but sheltered from the full force of the monsoon. The chosen site is cleared of jungle and undergrowth, but a sufficient number of trees are left standing to afford a generous shade. In the last month of the year the berries are sown in a nursery which has been carefully weeded and dug over, and plentifully manured and watered. In about six months the seedlings are removed to holes which have been made in prepared ground. The planting is done with the greatest care, in order to avoid injury to the delicate roots.

[1] Sir W. W. Hunter.

During the first year nothing more is done than to keep the garden well weeded. In the second year the plants are "topped," and kept down to a height of three feet. In the third year the plants begin to bear berries, but it is not until four or five years later that the planter harvests a full, mature crop, which should yield five or six hundredweight to the acre. In March and April the plants break forth in masses of snow-white blossoms, which throw off a pleasant fragrance. The crop ripens in October and November.

The berries are picked by hand, and collected in baskets, to be "pulped" on the spot. This operation is performed by means of an iron cylinder, which separates the beans from the husks. After fermenting for about twenty-four hours, the beans are divested of their saccharine coating by washing. They are then dried in the sun for seven or eight days, after which they are put into gunny sacks and shipped from the plantation.

The distance from Colombo to Kandy by rail is about seventy-five miles. The road winds its way through the most beautiful and diversified scenery, and amidst luxuriant vegetation, gradually ascending until the city is reached at an elevation of about seventeen hundred feet above sea level. Kandy first appears as a place of importance at the beginning of the fourteenth century, when a temple was erected there to hold the precious Buddha's tooth, which had previously been kept at the ancient Yapahú, whose remains are among the most interesting of Ceylon's antiquities. The possession of the sacred tooth and other relics made Kandy one of the most important centres of the Buddhist hierarchy, and it became at length a royal residence. After the defeat of Rájá Singha the Second, by Wimala Dharma in 1592, and the destruction of Kotta, the city of Kandy was made the capital of the island. During the conflicts between the Dutch and Portuguese Kandy was frequently the point of attack, and the city has been more than once committed to the flames. As a consequence, with the exception of a few temples and the royal palace, nothing remained of the old city when the English came into possession of the place in 1815.

Kandy occupies an extremely picturesque site amidst the most lovely surroundings, and enjoys an exceptionally agreeable climate. The city lies upon the bank of a long, artificial lake, which was constructed by the last of the kings of Ceylon. On every side rise thickly wooded hills to a height of several hundred feet about the city. The Maháwelli Ganga pursues its course, over a rocky bed, through the valley of Dumbera, the whole "presenting a scene that in majestic beauty can scarcely be surpassed. In a park, at the foot of this acclivity, is the pavilion of the Governor, one of the most agreeable edifices in India, not less from the beauty of its architecture than from its judicious adaptation to the climate."

The Palace was built by Wimala Dharma in the

early years of his reign. The employment of Portuguese prisoners in the construction of the building resulted in giving an European character to the architecture. This peculiarity is particularly noticeable in the octagon tower which adjoins the temple containing the sacred relics. The principal civil officer of the district occupies a wing of the Palace.

The Temple of the Dalada has little to recommend it in the matter of architecture, but as the headquarters of modern Buddhism it is a place of extreme interest. The library includes several valuable Páli manuscripts, and the Buddhist scriptures traced upon wood and bound with sumptuous elegance.

Chief of all the relics is the so-called tooth of Buddha. The history of this treasure is remarkable. It is said to have been secured from the funeral pile of Guatama, and carefully treasured in India during several centuries. Shortly before the visit of Fa Hian to Ceylon in 311 A.D. the relic was surreptitiously conveyed to the island by a princess of Kalinga, who hid it in her hair. The Malabars captured it early in the fourteenth century and carried it back to India, but it was recovered by the great Prakrámá Bahu. Despite every care to conceal its hiding-place, the Portuguese, in 1560, discovered the treasure and took it to Goa. There it was formally condemned as an instrument of heathen idolatry, and was publicly burned by the Archbishop in the presence of the officials and the populace of the city. The civil and ecclesiastical records contain detailed accounts of the entire circumstance, and, whatever may be said for the genuineness of the original relic, there can be no doubt about its having been destroyed. Nevertheless the priests of the Malayáwa produced another "Buddha's tooth," which they asserted was the genuine relic, explaining that a counterfeit had been foisted off upon the Portuguese by design. Unfortunately for this contention, the relic in the Temple of the Dalada is the most clumsy imitation of a human tooth imaginable. It is a piece of discolored ivory two inches long and a little less than an inch in diameter. Notwithstanding the palpable fraud imposed upon them, worshipers apparently accept the relic without question. In 1815 it fell into the hands of the British, and the greatest excitement prevailed whilst its fate remained uncertain, the change of dynasty being evidently a matter of much less importance to the Singhalese than the possible loss of what they regarded as a sort of national palladium. When the relic was restored to the priests, it was carried back to the shrine with the greatest pomp and ceremony.

The sanctuary devoted to the "tooth" is the innermost recess of the temple. It is a small chamber, to which not a ray of light penetrates. The hot and fetid air is laden with the stale odor of flowers. On a massive silver stand rests the bell-shaped depository. It consists of six graduated cases, the largest five feet tall, formed of silver gilt, and thickly inlaid with jewels. The others are similarly wrought, but "increasing in richness as they diminish in size." On the removal of the lowest of these shrines, which is about twelve inches high, a lotus flower of pure gold is disclosed, and upon it reposes the sacred relic. In front of the shrine is a table, upon which votaries deposit their offerings.

Gampola, a few miles due south of Kandy, was one of the ancient native capitals. For miles around, the hills are covered with plantations. A coach runs from Gampola to Nuwara Eliya along a winding mountain road which passes through Pussilawa, the "valley of flowers," and Ramboddie, whence the most striking views present themselves. "In the magnificent glen of Ramboddie we reach a barrier of mountains, seemingly impassable. Waterfalls on every hand come tumbling over precipices, and roaring through deep ravines mantled with palms and orchids, yellow gamboge trees, and white-flowered daturas. From this point, the road climbs the mountain gorge in terraces, cut in many places out of the rock, through a wild forest to a height of six thousand feet; and from the summit of the pass a view of Nuwara Eliya is obtained."

Nuwara Eliya is the Simla of Ceylon. The Governor has his residence here, and hither come European officials and merchants to escape the summer heat of Colombo, or Galle. The temperature seldom exceeds seventy degrees, and the air is fresh and bracing. The residents of the sanitarium evidently do all they can to make the place remind them of "home," and in this they are generously aided by Nature.

The villas are built after English models, and supplemented by such gardens as one might see in the country in England. Oaks and firs throw their shade over grassy lawns. The robin and the blackbird flit about amid English fruit trees. For a fitting setting there are green fields with hawthorn hedges.

The famous Adam's Peak is easily accessible from Nuwara Eliya. It is over seven thousand feet in height, but, although the best-known mountain in Ceylon, it is not the highest by several hundred feet. It is surmounted by a rocky cone, which is climbed with the aid of chains fastened to the rock. On the summit is a small temple, and hard by the Sripada, or holy footprint. This is a natural indentation in the rock, which has, with slight alteration, been made to assume the appearance of a human foot five feet long and about half as broad. By the Bráhmans this "footprint" is declared to have been made by Siva, while the Buddhists attribute it to Buddha. The Muhammadans also lay claim to it as the impress of Adam's foot. Adam, they declare, when exiled from Paradise, crossed the straits by the rocky ridge named after him, and took refuge in Ceylon. On this mountain he passed the intervening years before his reunion with Eve on Mount Arafath, near Mecca.

It is in the region between Adam's Peak and the ocean that the greatest quantities of precious stones have been found, and they are still sought in this district.

Ratnapura, the "City of Rubies," is the headquarters of the gemming industry. The whole country round about is dotted with the pits from which the stones are taken. Those most commonly found at present are sapphires, topazes and cat's-eyes. After digging for a certain distance down, the gem hunters come upon a peculiar clay, in which the sought-for stones are embedded. Every piece of this clay, as it is removed from the hole, is carefully broken up, sifted and washed. Although gems are found in large quantities, it is only rarely that a stone of any considerable value is unearthed. For the most part the find consists of fragments and of stones which are not marketable, by reason of a lack of color, or on account of the presence of flaws. Small particles of gems abound in the sands of the rivers, but they are valueless except as polishing material in lapidary's work.

Elephants are still to be found among the hills of Ceylon, but, as upon the continent, they are becoming scarce. In India proper, the animal is now to be met with only in the primeval forests of Coorg, Mysore and Travancore, and along the Terái, or submontane tract of the Himálayas. The chief source of supply at present is the irregular mass of forest-clad hills

Street Scene, Ceylon

which form the northeastern boundary of British India.

Unlike the African elephant, the Indian specimen does not inhabit the plains, nor even the mountain valleys, but frequents the higher ridges and lofty plateaus. There are two varieties of the Indian elephant—the gunda, or tusker, and the makna, which has no tusks. The elephant of Ceylon is generally tuskless and smaller than the animal found upon the mainland, which sometimes, though not often, attains a height of twelve feet.

The Government retains a monopoly of catching elephants in India, and for that purpose maintains a large corps of experienced natives under the superintendence of Europeans. This corps is termed the Kheda Department, at the head of which Mr. Sanderson made an enviable reputation in recent years. The animals are trapped by being driven in herds into large stockades. This is an operation requiring a great deal of skill and a thorough knowledge of the habits and characteristics of the beasts. The process of taming the captured elephants is often long and tedious in the case of unusually wild animals. It is effected with the aid of domesticated elephants, which have been trained for the purpose.

Elephants are chiefly used as beasts of burden, for transport, and in connection with heavy artillery. The best specimens are always in demand by native chiefs for purposes of parade. The elephant is protected by statute in India. A heavy fine or imprisonment may be imposed upon any one who injures, captures or kills one of the animals without a license.

Before the completion of the breakwater at Colombo, Galle was the principal port of Ceylon. It has but a small harbor, difficult of entrance in rough weather, and not altogether safe. The name of the city is derived from the word "galla," which in the vernacular signifies rock, but the Dutch settlers chose to associate it with the Latin *gallus*, a cock. On the façade of the old Government House, which dates from 1687, is carved a presentment of a cock in defiant attitude.

Galle hardly finds mention in the native chronicles before the middle of the thirteenth century. Batuta, who visited the place about 1347, refers to it as a small town. It rose rapidly in importance under the Portuguese, from whom it was wrested, after a hard struggle, by the Dutch. In the marriage treaty of the Infanta of Portugal with Charles the Second there is a curious clause, embodying an agreement on the part of the Portuguese to cede Galle to the British, in the event of Ceylon again becoming a possession of Portugal. In the neighborhood of Galle there are many ancient and curious Buddhist monasteries and temples. Buddhism appears to have retained more of its original purity here than in any other parts of Ceylon, and its influence over the people is greater and more beneficial than elsewhere.

The road to the east, along the seashore, passes

through a continuous succession of groves of the cocoa-nut palm. The shore is thickly populated by fisher-folk, their picturesque villages appearing at short intervals along the entire route. In the pursuit of their vocation the Singhalese fishermen use curiously constructed canoes, from twenty-five to thirty feet in length, less than two feet in beam, and about three feet in depth. The body of the boat is one piece, being nothing more nor less than the trunk of a palm scooped out. The most striking feature of the boat, however, is a peculiar balance-log, or outrigger, the same length as the canoe and similar to it in appearance, but solid. On this contrivance, which lies at right angles to the canoe, is carried a large sail hoisted on two bamboo poles. There is no distinction made as to bow or stern, and the steering is performed with a short paddle. The fishermen go twenty miles or more to sea in these strange crafts, and appear to handle them with perfect ease and safety.

Hambantotta, on the south coast, is a large town, and the official headquarters of a district. One of the two chief salt manufactories of Ceylon is here. This place and Puttalam supply the whole island with salt, which is a Government monopoly.

Not long since the steady inland march of sandhills threatened to submerge Hambantotta, and did, in fact, bury several streets and some considerable buildings, including the old post-office. Further encroachments of the sand have been checked by plantations of Palmyra palm, and by the cultivation of a grass of a peculiarly tenacious character.

About twenty miles to the northeast of Hambantotta is Tissamahárámá, the most ancient of the deserted capitals of Ceylon. The site had been entirely abandoned, except for occasional pilgrims, until the Government restored the tank, by which means several thousand acres were opened to cultivation. The population and the area under crops are now constantly increasing.

Ruins of great antiquity are thickly scattered through the dense jungle, and the place seems to present an unusually promising field for antiquarian research by means of excavation. There are several large dagobas, in a more or less ruinous condition. The largest, and probably one of the oldest, has been completely restored by the unassisted labors of the Buddhist population. It is over one hundred and fifty feet in height, and occupies a commanding position.

There are numerous remains of large buildings, creating the impression that an imposing city must have occupied the spot in olden times. The ruins of what is said to have been the royal residence, but which was more probably a many-storied monastery, like the Brazen Palace at Anuradhapura, consist of rows of huge monolithic columns, greatly exceeding in size any known to exist elsewhere in Ceylon.

Batticaloa is the capital of the Eastern Province.

The town has a remarkable situation upon an island in a salt-water lake, which extends for thirty miles along the line of the coast, and has a breadth of from two to five miles. This lake is separated from the sea by a broad belt of sand, intersected by one long, narrow channel. The intervening stretch of sandy land is thickly covered with groves of cocoanut palms, and crowded with Tamil and Moorish villages. Hence to the town a picturesque stone causeway runs across the lake.

Batticaloa Lake is famous as the habitat of that natural curiosity, the "singing fish." "On calm nights, especially about the time of the full moon, musical sounds are to be heard proceeding from the bottom of the lagoon. They resemble those which are produced by rubbing the rim of a glass vessel with a wet finger. The writer has never heard more than two distinct musical notes, one much higher than the other; but credible witnesses, such as Sir E. Tennent, assert that they have heard a multitude of sounds, 'each clear and distinct in itself, the sweetest treble mingling with the lowest bass.' The natives attribute the production of the sounds to the shell-fish *Caritheum palustre.* This may be doubtful; but it is unquestionable that they come from the bottom of the lagoon, and may be distinctly heard rising to the surface on all sides of a boat floating on the lake. If a pole be inserted in the water, and its upper end applied to the ear, much louder and stronger sounds are heard than without such aid."

The Great Tank of Kalawewa, situated almost in the centre of the island, is a good specimen of the several reservoirs which were constructed in various parts of Ceylon by different rulers. They were frequently works of unusual magnitude, and of inestimable benefit to the people. The splendid sheet of water at Kalawewa was formed by King Dhatu Sena about 400 A.D. He built a bund, or embankment, of masonry, six miles in extent and sixty feet high, which retains the waters of two rivers. The lake thus formed has a contour of nearly forty miles even at this time, when the spill only reaches a height of twenty-five feet. A great canal carries water from one of the sluices of this lake to Anuradhapura, a distance of fifty odd miles, and supplies more than a hundred village tanks on its way. The tank and its supplementary works were in a condition of ruinous disuse until restored by the Government in 1884–'87.

About ten miles to the east of Kalawewa are the extensive ruins of the ancient city of Pulastípura, buried, like those of Tissamahárámá, in dense forest. The city was founded by Prakrámá Bahu, the Third, and continued to be the capital of the Kandyan kings until the fourteenth century. Some of the remains here are in a good state of preservation, and present fine specimens of sculpture and carving.

In the main entrance to a huge Buddhist temple,

formed by two octagonal towers, stands a colossal image of Buddha, fifty feet in height. This statue is fashioned out of brick, covered with chunam, a kind of polished cement.

In front of a vihara, excavated from the rock, is an enormous sculpture, forty-five feet long, of Buddha, lying at full length upon his left side. This attitude is said to indicate the attainment of Nírvana; but it is much more reasonably accounted for on the supposition that the sculptor adapted his design to the shape and conditions of a rock already in position.

The famous ruins of Anuradhapura are by far the most interesting in the island. According to the "Great History" of Ceylon this city was the capital of the kingdom as early as four centuries before Christ, and attained its greatest magnificence at the commencement of the present era. When King Asoka sent his son Mahinda to introduce Buddhism to the people of Ceylon, King Tissa reigned at Anuradhapura. That monarch received the royal emissary with kindness, and ultimately adopted the new religion. He is said to have been presented with the collar-bone of Buddha, and to have erected the Thuparámá Dagoba as a receptacle for it. This, which must be almost, if not actually, the most ancient dagoba in Ceylon, is also one of the most elegant. It rises to a height of sixty-three feet, which is probably very much less than its original elevation, is bell-shaped in outline, and stands upon a platform fifty feet square, surrounded by one hundred and fifty monolithic pillars in a triple row.

There are countless dagobas at Anuradhapura, and they range from the enormous mass of the Abhayagiriya to objects of the same shape not more than two feet in height.

The largest dagoba, the Abhayagiriya, reaches a height of three hundred and thirty feet, but when its pinnacle was intact it stood at least seventy feet higher. Its diameter is nearly four hundred feet, and it rises from a paved platform covering eight acres of ground. Referring to the enormous quantity of brick used in the construction of this dagoba, Sir E. Tennent says that it would have been sufficient to build a city the size of Coventry, or to erect a wall ten feet high extending from London to Edinburgh. This dagoba was completed 87 B.C., but it is not so old as the Ruanwelli, which dates from 140 B.C.

About six miles to the east of the city, with which it was connected by a long, straight road, stands a precipitous rock one thousand feet high. Upon its summit was erected a large brick temple, the repository of a hair which grew from a mole between the eyebrows of Buddha. Rhys Davids writes: "It was upon this hill, the three peaks of which, each now surmounted by a dagoba, form so striking an object from the central trunk road which runs along its side, that the famous missionary Mahinda spent most of his after years. Here, on the precipitous western side of the hill, under a large mass of granite rock, at a spot completely shut out from the world and affording a magnificent view of the plains below, he had his study hollowed out, and steps cut in the rock, over which alone it could be reached. The great rock effectually protects the cave from the heat of the sun, in whose warm light the valley below lies basking; not a sound reaches it from the plain—now a far-reaching forest, then full of busy homesteads; there is only heard that hum of insects which never ceases, and the rustling of the leaves of the trees which cling to the sides of the precipice. I shall not easily forget the day when I first entered that lonely, cool and quiet chamber, so simple, and yet so beautiful, where more than two thousand years ago the great teacher of Ceylon had sat and thought and worked through long years of his peaceful and useful life. On that hill he afterwards died, and his ashes still rest under the dagoba, which is the principal object of the reverence and care of the few monks who still reside in the Mahintah Wihare."

Everywhere about Anuradhapura are to be seen the remains of ancient monasteries and bathing tanks, distinguishable from the reservoirs designed for irrigation by the lining of masonry or cement over their entire extent.

Not the least curious of the many remarkable antiquities at Anuradhapura is the sacred Bo tree. This venerable specimen is allowed the distinction of being the oldest tree in the world, and the parent of all other Bo trees upon the island. It is seriously asserted that the Bo tree of Anuradhapura is over two thousand years old. It is said to have grown from a branch of the famous Bo tree, or pípul, of Buddh Gáyá, which King Asoka sent to Ceylon about 245 B.C., and "from that time to this it has been watched over by a succession of guardians never interrupted."

Pilgrims come from the uttermost parts of the Buddhist countries to visit the sacred tree of Anuradhapura. It is now enclosed by a modern wall, and a flight of stone steps leads up to the terraced mound upon which it stands.

THE END.

GLOSSARY.

Abád. Populous; frequently compounded with a proper name to form the name of a city.

Adil Sháhi. A Musalmán dynasty which ruled at Bijápur for two hundred years, from 1489. It was an offshoot of the Bahmani line of sultáns.

Adináth. The first of the Jain arhats.

Afghán. The name applied generally to the people of Afghánistán, who include the Afgháns proper, a race of Semitic origin; the Patháns; the Ghilzais; and two tribes of Persian descent.

Afridi. A numerous and warlike Pathán tribe lying immediately upon the British border.

Ahmad Sháhi. The name of a branch of the Bahmani dynasty, which established itself in Berar at the close of the fifteenth century.

Allah. THE God. The Muhammadans have ninety-nine names for God.

Aranyaka. Derived from áranya, a forest, and applied to a treatise deemed to be so holy as to be fit only to be read in the solitude of a forest. The most important portion of the Aranyakas is that composed of the Upanishads.

Avatar. The sojourn upon earth of a god in the form of a man or animal. These incarnations are chiefly associated with Vishnu, who is said to have been avatar twenty-four times.

Bábu. A native clerk, book-keeper or manager. In a Bengal village the zamindár. The word is frequently used as an equivalent for "mister."

Bagh. A garden; particularly a pleasure garden, containing a pavilion or palace.

Bahádur. A warrior of distinction; an honorary title among the Mughals, and now frequently applied to native officials of high rank.

Bahmani. A Muhammadan dynasty which ruled in the Deccan from the middle of the fourteenth to the end of the fifteenth century.

Bái. A term applied respectfully to elderly ladies and to princesses below the highest rank.

Baluchi. An inhabitant of Baluchistán, or an emigrant from that country. Many of the latter or their descendants are settled in Sindh and Gujarát.

Banghy wallah. A banghy or bahangi is a bamboo with a cord at each end, designed to carry earthenware vessels or packages. Wallah signifies a fellow. Hence a banghy-wallah is a public carrier. A parcel is also termed a banghy.

Bangle. A bracelet.

Banyá. A trader; a shopkeeper; a money-lender. In Calcutta the native cashiers of European firms are styled banyás.

Baradari. A house of many doors; a summer residence in a garden; and often eventually the mausoleum of the owner.

Bazaar, or bázár. A market; a street composed of shops, or an aggregation of such streets; the shopkeepers' section of a city.

Begam. A Musalmán lady of rank.

Beni-Israel. The name of a small tribe abiding in the Konkan. They claim to be descended from a few men and women who came from a northern country and were shipwrecked on the Colaba coast in 1600. In physiognomy they resemble Arabian Jews. They use the Maráthí dialect, and dress in a mixture of Hindu and Musalmán costume. They practice circumcision, and use the Hebrew liturgy of the Sephardim. They engage in various occupations, but chiefly in agriculture and the manufacture of oil.

Bheestie or bhistí. A water carrier. He furnishes water for domestic use, and sprinkles the roads: in either case using a masak, or leather bag made of the entire skin of an animal.

Bráhmanas. Ritualistic precepts designed for the guidance of the Bráhmans, especially in conducting sacrificial ceremonies.

Bráhma Somáj. Literally, the Society of God. A theistical sect founded about one hundred years ago. The doctrine is based upon the Veda, large portions of which are rejected, and borrows something from other religious sources.

Budgerow. A heavy sailboat used upon large rivers. It is sometimes towed by the crew, and at others propelled with long sweeps. It contains cabins and a poop deck. The budgerow was much used for river travel before the extension of railroads.

Bulbul. A species of nightingale.

Bungah. A group of buildings arranged round a sacred tank; a palace.

Bungalow. A cottage of one story with thatched roof.

Caftan. A long-sleeved garment, fitting like a vest about the body and secured at the waist with a girdle. A long, loose open surtout is worn over it.

Caste. The many social divisions of the Hindus are so called. Caste is hereditary and generally coincident with occupation. Originally there were four great castes; the present number is incalculable. There are several hundred castes among the Bráhmans alone. A Hindu can never change the caste into which he is born, but he may become an outcast or pariah. He may not marry into any but his own caste, and he may not engage in the particular occupation of another caste.

Catamaran. A boat constructed on the principle of a raft and propelled by means of a sail or by oars. It is in use on the coasts of Madras and Ceylon.

Central India. A group of native states of which Gwalior and Indore are the principal.

Central Province. One of the eight divisions of British India. It was formed in 1861 from territory taken from the Northwest Provinces and Madras.

Chadah. A sheet; a shawl; a cloth; the toga-like garment of Hindu men and women.

Chaitya. Among Buddhists a place or object having sacred associations; a place of worship; a monument; a tombstone.

Chapáti. A thin, flat griddle-cake, made from flour and water without leaven.

Charpoy. The native Indian bed. It consists of a wooden frame set on legs; strong tape is stretched upon it to lie upon.

Chattri. A mausoleum; a monument in the form of an umbrella, that article being an insignia of royalty in the East.

Chauri. A fan or fly disperser made from a yak-tail, or of feathers.

Chohán. The name of a Rájput clan by whom Ajmír was founded at the beginning of the ninth century.

Choultrie. (A corruption of the Telugu word Cháwadi.) A public office; a rest-house for travelers; the pillared hall fronting the vimána of a pagoda.

Chout or chauth. A tax equal to one-fourth of the government revenue levied by the Maráthás upon certain princes as the price of immunity from pillage.

Chowkidar, or chawkidár. A policeman; a village watchman.

Chunam. A plaster made of quicklime and sand. The finest kind is very white and admits of a high polish. Chunam is largely used in building and decorative work.

Chupprassie or chaprási. A messenger. He wears a chaprá, or metal plate, bearing the name of the office to which he is attached, or that of his master.

Coolie. A laborer.

Dacoit. A member of an organised band of robbers.

Dacoity. Robbery committed by an organized gang. According to the Indian statutes, any robbery in which five or more persons jointly engage comes within the scope of the Dacoity Laws.

Dagoba. A dome-shaped Buddhist structure erected as the receptacle of relics or as a commemorative monument.

Dák-bungalow. A rest-house, or post-house, for travelers upon a stage route. Dák signifies post; dák-ghári, post-carriage; dák-ghar, post-office; dák-wallah, postman, etc.

Dák-ghári. See dák-bungalow.

Darbár. The court of a king, or rájá; a levee or audience; the persons composing or present at either of the former; sometimes applied to the building in which the court or levee is held.

Dargah. A Muhammadan shrine; the tomb of a saint.

Dassana. A system of philosophy.

Dharma. Right-living; law; the observance of morality, universal good will and duty; the obligation of justice in the magistrate, truth in the teacher, gentleness in the ruler, courage in the soldier, etc.

Dhotí. A cloth worn around the waist. It differs from the langauti, or loin-cloth, only in being allowed to fall to the knees.

Diwáni. Pertaining to a diwán, or court, as diwán-i-khás, a private court or chamber, as distinguished from diwán-i-ám, a hall of public reception.

Dravidian. Applied to several races of Southern India of Scythian-Turanian origin, who entered India at a very early date.

Duráni. An important tribe of Afgháns.

Eurasian. One of mixed European and Indian origin; sometimes spoken of as a half-caste.

Fákír. A religious mendicant. The fákírs are divided into a number of brotherhoods, which have various practices and customs.

Firmán. An edict; a mandate issuing from a potentate.

Gáekwár. The family name of one of the Maráthá chiefs who founded independent principalities, and since used as a distinctive title by the rulers of Baroda.

Gautama. The name of a once powerful clan in the lower Doáb. Buddha belonged to this tribe, which still has numerous representatives.

Ghát. A descent; steps approaching a river; a landing place; the place is generally used for bathing and often for cremations. Also a mountain pass; a range of mountains; specifically applied to the two principal mountain ranges of India.

Ghilzai. The most important, after the Duránis, of the Afghán tribes.

Ghorí. The name of a succession of dynasties whose representatives were of Afghán origin. Their name is derived from the city of Ghor.

Gopura. A building forming the gateway to a city or temple. In connection with the Buddhist pagodas of Southern India, the gopuras are pyramidal structures, through which entrance to the courtyard is gained.

Granth. A holy book; particularly the scriptures of the Sikhs. The Adi Granth, which was composed by the first four gurus, is the portion of the work most highly esteemed.

Guru. A religious teacher; an instructor in the Veda. Among the Sikhs the gurus were political chiefs as well as spiritual leaders.

Hadjí. One who has performed the haj, or pilgrimage to Mecca, which is enjoined upon every Muhammadan who has the means of making it.

Howdah. The seat placed upon the back of an elephant. It is constructed in a wide variety of styles, and may be designed to carry one or several persons.

Imambarah. The building in which the Muharram is celebrated, and the theatrical services held in commemoration of the deaths of Hásan and Husain.

Imáms. Muhammadan priests; specifically the twelve spiritual and temporal chiefs acknowledged by the Shiahs; the founder of the four schools of the Sunnis.

Jagheer or jagír. A district, village, or fort assigned to any person for the internal government and the enjoyment of the revenue in consideration of service to be rendered, generally of a military character.

John Company. A nickname of the East India Company.

Jungle. Forest; desert; wild country; a sparsely settled or uninhabited district.

Kaabah. A square building; the oratory in the mosque at Mecca, which is the chief objective of the haj.

Kachhwaha. A tribe of Rájputs; once the rulers of Gwalior and now of Jaipur.

Kafir. An unbeliever; all without the pale of Islám.

Kháki. Duck cloth dyed brown. It derives its name from the color. Kháki is largely used for the summer uniforms of the Indian troops.

Khilji. The name of the second of the Ghorí dynasties.

Khwábgah. A sleeping apartment in a palace.

Khwájah. A holy man; one of wealth or to be respected.

Kiblah. The point to which Muhammadans must look when they pray. The Kaabah at Mecca is the Kiblah.

Kos-minár. Pillars similar to mile-stones and serving the same purpose. The kos differs with locality, but is usually from one and a half to two miles.

Kotwali. Police station.

Kúkri, or Kúkuri. The national weapon of the Ghúrkas. It is a knife fashioned somewhat like a bill hook.

Kummerband, or Kamarband. A waist-cloth; a shawl or sash worn round the waist.

Kurán. The sacred book of the Muhammadans, who believe that it is the expression of divine revelation through the Prophet and some of his successors.

Kutab Sháhí. The name of a branch of the Bahmani dynasty.

Kylas, or Kailása. The heaven of Siva; the chief heaven. Swarga is the heaven of inferior gods.

Lama. The Tibetan name for a Buddhist priest.

Langauti. A loin cloth.

Lát. A pillar; a column; the ancient láts are generally inscribed.

Lingam or linga. The phallus or emblematic representation of Siva in his character of the supreme productive power. The symbol is a stone, whose form is designed to represent the blending of the male and female principles in creation. In miniature it is sometimes worn by followers of Siva.

Lodí. The name of an Afghán dynasty; the last of the series of Ghorí dynasties. The last of the Lodís (Ibrahim) was overthrown by Bábar.

Mahábhárata. A collection of epic poems by various authors. The work consists of upwards of 200,000 lines.

Mahál. A palace; a house; a seraglio; an apartment; a province; a district; an estate; a revenue division.

Mahárájá. Literally, great rájá. Formerly applied to rulers of exceptional power, but now used as a courtesy title in connection with every rájá. Also applied to the heads of certain religious orders.

Mahárání. The feminine form of Mahárájá.

Maháráshtra. Literally, the great kingdom. The territory of the Maráthás.

Mahout. The driver and keeper of an elephant. He sits on the neck of the beast, and controls it with the aid of an iron goad.

Maidán. A plain; an open space; particularly a large grassy tract maintained for public recreation or as a parade ground for troops.

Mandu. A temple; a house; a palace.

Mango-tree. *Mangifera Indica.* It grows to a height of forty feet, with dense foliage, and bears a delicious egg-shaped fruit, three or four inches long.

Mantapa, or Mandapa. A porch; particularly one of the porches of a vimána. The choultrie or colonnade is sometimes styled a mantapa.

Mantras. Prayer and praise in prose and metre, generally addressed to certain manifestations of Nature in a deified sense. Mantras are of three classes: those of the Rig-Veda, being metrical and designed for public recitation; those of the Yajur-Veda, which are prose, for use in sacrificial ceremonies; those of the Sáma-Veda, which are metrical chants, used in Soma worship. Every Hindu is taught a particular mantra by the family guru, and private devotions consist in the repetition of mantras. The word mantra is commonly used in the sense of a charm or incantation.

Masjid. A mosque. The jamá masjid is the principal mosque in a city.

Masúla. The surf boat used on the Madras coast. The planks of which it is formed are sewn together, so as to give to the action of the water.

Mhut or math. The cell or hut of an ascetic.

Minár or minaret. The balconied tower of a mosque, from which the muezzin chants the azán, or call to prayer: "God is great! I bear witness there is no God but one God! I bear witness that Muhammad is his prophet! Come to prayer! Come to salvation! Prayer is better than sleep! God is great! There is no God but one God!" The minaret is generally a portion of the building, but when detached, as in the case of the Kutab Minár, it is more correctly termed a minár.

Mofussil. The country; the provinces as distinct from a capital; the outlying district as distinct from the station or town.

Mosque. A Muhammadan place of worship. The plan of a mosque

is rectangular, and includes an open court, with cloisters, a tank for ablutions, and several minarets, besides the domed building designed for prayer and worship.

Muharram. The first month of the Musalmán year. The great Shiah mourning for the death of Husain, the third imám, is held on the first ten days of the month. The streets are paraded, and theatrical representations of the tragic fate of Husain are given. The Sunnis ridicule the ceremonies and those who take part in them, with the frequent result of creating riots.

Múllah. The spiritual and temporal head of certain Muhammadan communities; a Musalmán of exceptional wisdom and learning; an officer of the mosque who leads in prayer, and acts as sexton and janitor, and sometimes calls the azán; a teacher; a mystic: a title of honor and respect similar to the ancient Jewish term *rabbi*.

Musallah. The prayer-carpet of the Muhammadan.

Musalmán. A Muhammadan; a Muslim.

Musnud. A cushion; a seat; hence a throne.

Naubat Khánah. The chamber in which the band plays. It is generally over the gate of a palace.

Nautch. Dancing; acting. A nautch is usually a combination of dancing and pantomime, to the accompaniment of music.

Nautch-girl. The common name of several classes of women whose profession is to dance, either in temples or at private entertainments.

Nawáb. A viceroy or provincial governor under the Mughal Empire. The nawábs were often virtually, and sometimes actually, independent. The word has been corrupted into nabob.

Nazír. An overseer; an officer charged with the ordering of a ceremony or the execution of a decree.

Nirvána. Extinction; liberation from the burden of future existences. Nirvána is attained by the Buddhist when he becomes perfectly holy, immune to mental and physical action, and when the effects of all his past acts and thoughts have ceased.

Nizám. An administrator; a viceroy. The title of the rulers of Haidarábád.

Omráh. Synonymous with amír. A Muhammadan military chief; a nobleman.

Pachísi-board. A square of cloth somewhat similar to a chess-board. The game of pachísi resembles backgammon, cowries, or shells, being used for dice.

Paddy. Rice in the husk, whether growing or cut.

Pádsháh. A king.

Pagoda. The name applied to temples in Southern India, and more especially to Buddhist temples. For description see Vol. I, p. 210.

Palki or palanquin. A long, box-like conveyance, in which the traveler reclines at full length. It has a projecting pole at each end, by means of which it is carried upon the shoulders of coolies.

Paraiyan or pariah. One who is of no caste. The paraiyan are very numerous. They are employed in all sorts of menial and degrading occupations. Natives of caste are defiled by the touch of a pariah, and the latter is obliged to live apart. The term pariah is applied generally to the ownerless village dog who acts as a scavenger.

Pathán. In India the name is applied indiscriminately to all natives of Afghánistán, and to their descendants; but in Afghánistán the word Pathán is used to designate only the Pashtú-speaking tribes, and so excludes the Afgháns proper and the Ghilzais.

Pergunnah or parganá. A district; a province.

Peshwá. Prime minister of the Maráthá kingdom. In time the office and title became hereditary, and the sovereign power passed into the hands of the Peshwás.

Pettah. A suburb of a city, or a village adjoining a town.

Pír. A Muhammadan saint.

Povindah. Traveling merchants of Afghánistán, who are a combination of trader and soldier. They belong mainly to the Ghilzai tribe.

Pundit or pandit. A learned man.

Punkah-wallah. A man who is employed to work a punkah, which is a large fan formed of a canvas-covered frame with a weighted cloth attached to it. The punkah is hung from the ceiling and swung back and forth by means of a cord which passes through the wall and is worked from the passage, or veranda.

Puránic. Pertaining to the Puránas, a series of volumes containing the genealogies of the Hindu deities.

Purdah. A curtain; a screen; especially applied to such a contrivance for excluding women from the public view.

Ráj. The territory of a rájá.

Rájá. A king, a prince. At the present day the title is applied with little discrimination to any Hindu ruler or extensive land-owner.

Rájput. Literally, the son of a king. The common name of many tribes claiming descent from the traditional Solar race of the Rámáyána, or the Lunar race of the Mahábhárata. They composed the warrior class (Kshattriyas) of the ancient Hindu political division. It is believed by some authorities that the Rájputs are of Scythian descent, and that they preceded the Aryans in India. They differ greatly from other Hindus in their use of flesh, alcoholic liquors and drugs; in the practice of primogeniture, and in the prohibition of marriage between members of the same clan.

Rámá. The hero of the Rámáyána, who is deified in the modern poem of that name by Tulsi Dás. Rámá is said to have been Vishnu in his seventh avatar.

Rámáyána. The older of the two great Sanskrit epics. It was probably composed about 500 B.C. A modern Rámáyána, written by Tulsi Dás in the sixteenth century, is very popular with the masses.

Ráná. Synonymous with rájá. The title of the chief of Udaipur and of some rájás of Central India.

Rání. The feminine form of rájá.

Ráo. A chief; a prince.

Rath. A chariot; the vehicle of a god; the car in which the image of a deity is borne; in the south of India, a temple hewn from a single rock or boulder.

Ráyat. A peasant; an agricultural laborer.

Rishi. A holy man; an ascetic. Originally one to whom divine truths had been supernaturally revealed.

Roza. A garden; a Muhammadan tomb, which is very often a summer house converted into a mausoleum after its owner's death.

Rupee. A silver coin; the unit of the standard of value in India. Nominally worth two shillings, it has depreciated until its present exchange value is about one shilling and fourpence. Large sums of Indian money are expressed in "tens of rupees," the sign Rx being employed.

Sakya Muni. The saint of the family of Sakya, to which Buddha belonged.

Salaam, or salám. An interjection signifying respect or good will; a form of salutation in general use throughout India, usually accompanied by an obeisance.

Samadh. The mausoleum of one who has been cremated; the ceremony of burning. The word has several other widely differing applications.

Sáree or sári. The outer garment of the Hindu woman, consisting of a long piece of cloth or silk draped round the head and body, and falling below the knees.

Satí. Literally, a faithful wife. A woman who burns herself with the corpse of her husband; the act of so burning; the ceremony attending the act. See the chapter upon Satí in Volume I.

Sayid. The designation of the descendants of Ali, the son-in-law of Muhammad.

Sepoy. A native Indian soldier.

Serai, or Caravanserai. A public rest-house for travelers. It is usually a large walled enclosure with a central courtyard, in which animals are tethered, and surrounding store-rooms and sleeping apartments.

Sheik, or shaikh. A descendant of Abbas, the uncle of the Prophet, or a descendant of one of the first two caliphs.

Shiah. A follower of Ali, the son-in-law of Muhammad; the name of a great division of the Muhammadans. The Shiahs hold that Ali was the rightful head of Islám after Muhammad, and they do not acknowledge the caliphs.

Shigram. A carriage; the shigram of Bombay is not unlike a large oblong box on wheels. In the country it is a heavy carriage, with a removable roof, and is drawn by horses or bullocks.

Shikári. A hunter; applied to sportsmen as well as to professional hunters.

Shráds. Prayers and certain ceremonies performed on behalf of the dead.

Singh. A lion; a common adjunct to Rájput and Sikh names.

Sitar. A string instrument somewhat like a guitar.

Sivala. A temple dedicated to Siva; a small shrine, containing a linga.

Soma. The moon, goddess of planets, plants, sacrifices and penances. The moon-plant, *asclepias acida*, was the subject of an ancient worship, with regard to which the Sáma-Veda appears to have been especially arranged.

Sowár or sawár. A horseman; a cavalryman; a mounted policeman; an orderly.

Stupa. See Tope.

Súdra. The name of the lowest of the four original social divisions of the Hindus. During modern times several of the Súdra castes have risen to respectable positions in Hindu society.

Sunni. A follower of the Sunnah or traditional law; a great division of the Muhammadans, as opposed to the Shiahs. The Sunnis dispute the right of Ali to the succession, and uphold the caliphs Abubakr, Omar and Usmán.

Sutra. A thread; a string of rules, or precepts for conduct. One of the three pitakas of the Buddhists.

Tank. This word in Anglo-Indian phraseology generally refers to a large reservoir or lake. A tank is commonly several acres in extent.

Tarbosh. The thimble-shaped cloth cap, with tassel pendent from the crown; sometimes called a fez.

Thag. A member of an organization of murderers, whose ramifications extended all over India at one time.

Thagí. The practices of a class of professional murderers and robbers. See the chapter upon the subject in Volume I.

Thákur. A Rájput; a feudal chief.

Tirthankar. Among the Jains, an arhat, or one who has reached an exceptionally advanced stage of saintliness. There were twenty-four Jain tirthankars.

Tom-tom. A sort of kettle drum.

Tonga. A low, two-wheeled springless cart, drawn by ponies and designed for use over rough roads.

Tope, or Stupa. A mound constructed over Buddhist relics, or as a monument.

Trisula. The trident of Siva.

Tulwar. A sword.

Turk or Turkí. A native of Turkístán. The word is frequently used in India as a synonym for Mughal, or even Musalmán.

Upanishad. Mystical or esoteric doctrine. The Upanishads are held to be the part of the Vedas designed for a select few, who are capable of comprehending the true doctrine, while the Mantras and Bráhmanas were for the mass, whose religious conceptions are limited to invocation and ceremony.

Vaisya. The third of the four original Hindu castes. They founded the ancient Gupta dynasty.

Varna. Literally, color. Hence the word was used by the early Aryans to distinguish themselves from the darker aborigines, and so came to signify caste.

Veda. The Hindu scriptures, consisting of four parts, viz.: Rig-Veda, Sáma-Veda, Yajur-Veda, Atharwa-Veda. The work. the oldest portions of which probably date back beyond 2000 B.C., originally consisted of but three parts, corresponding to the three classes of priests employed in the sacrifices, the Rig being for the Hotri priests, the Yajur for the Adhwaryu, and the Sáma for the Udgátri. The Atharwa-Veda, which is a later addition, was not designed for use in sacrificial performances, but teaches expiatory, preservative, or imprecatory rites. Each of the original vedas consists of metrical prayers and praise, sacrificial, ritual and philosophical treatises. See Mantra, Sutra, Bráhmana, Aranyaka, Upanishad.

Vihara. A Buddhist monastery; a pleasure garden; a place where

Buddhist teachers walked and discoursed. The rock-hewn viharas are often nothing more than a range of small cells, with perhaps a hall adjoining.

Vimána. The central point of a pagoda containing the shrine.

Yádu-wallah. One who practices magic; a juggler; a fortune-teller.

Yogí. An ascetic; one who practices the Yoga philosophy, which prescribes the practice of holding the body rigid while concentrating the mind on one thought.

Yuva-rájá. Vice-rájá; regent.

Zamindár. A landholder. Under the Mughals the zamindárs were responsible for the collection of the revenues on behalf of the government. In the Punjab, the ráyats are termed zamindárs.

Zenána. The women of a family; the apartments occupied by the women.

INDEX.